Transforming Relationships Through Participatory Justice

LAW COMMISSION OF CANADA
COMMISSION DU DROIT DU CANADA

Ce document est également disponible en français : *La transformation des rapports humains par la justice participative.*
ISBN : 0-662-89974-1
Catalogue : JL2-22/2003F

This Report is also available online at www.lcc.gc.ca.

To order a copy of the Report, contact:

Law Commission of Canada
222 Queen Street, Suite 1100
Ottawa ON K1A 0H8
Telephone: (613) 946-8980
Facsimile: (613) 946-8988
E-mail: info@lcc.gc.ca

The Law Commission of Canada in partnership with the National Film Board of Canada has produced a DVD to accompany this Report: *Community Mediation: Two Real-Life Experiences* (Catalogue: NFB 153C03303106).

Cover illustration by Sophie Beaulieu.

Canada

ISBN: 0-662-35152-5
Catalogue: JL2-22/2003E

The Honourable Martin Cauchon
Minister of Justice
Justice Building
Wellington Street
Ottawa, Ontario
K1A 0H8

Dear Minister:

In accordance with section 5(1)(c) of the *Law Commission of Canada Act*, we are pleased to submit the Report of the Law Commission of Canada on the promises and challenges of participatory justice in Canada.

Yours sincerely,

Nathalie Des Rosiers,
President

Roderick J. Wood,
Commissioner

Bernard Colas,
Commissioner

Mark L. Stevenson,
Commissioner

Table of Contents

Preface

In the last few decades, new ways of resolving conflicts have been developed beside the formal adversarial model that characterizes our courts. At times it is a program of mediation and counselling for families on the verge of separation, at other times it is a judge's invitation to parties to resolve their cases with the help of a mediator, an Aboriginal sentencing circle, a restorative justice initiative to curb violence in the neighbourhood, or a mediation service for customers and businesses on the Internet. Often these forms of conflict resolution are developed because of perceived deficiencies in the traditional court system, which is seen as too long, too costly, too complex, too punitive, inaccessible or unresponsive to communities' concerns. These initiatives respond to the weaknesses of the adversarial model used in our tribunals by giving parties and often communities the ability to participate in designing the solution to the conflict. *Transforming Relationships Through Participatory Justice* is about the promises and the challenges of such participatory justice.

This Report is addressed not only to governments, but also to a broader audience. The Law Commission of Canada hopes that the Report will

- help Canadians learn more about processes of participatory justice;

- enable Canadians to better judge the alternatives that exist within the justice system so that they choose the conflict resolution method that suits them best;

- encourage Canadians to reflect on issues of conflict resolution for our society;

- support Canadians who want to participate in conflict resolution within a judicial system;

- celebrate the many initiatives that have been developed throughout Canada;

- prompt self-reflection among the people who are currently engaged in different participatory justice initiatives in order to strengthen the many good programs that exist throughout Canada; and

- guide governments and civil society in their support, financial and otherwise, of participatory justice programs throughout Canada.

The Commission is happy to have partnered with the National Film Board of Canada in its Citizen Project by making available as part of this report a DVD, *Community Mediation: Two Real-Life Experiences.* This DVD is intended to educate mediators and the general public about mediation and participatory justice and to encourage reflection about the issues involved.

The way in which citizens resolve their conflicts must reflect their values. This Report articulates some of the values that support the development of participatory justice. It also makes recommendations to the many actors involved in participatory justice: to the people who design participatory justice projects, to the citizens who wish to participate in them and to governments who support such initiatives. How we resolve conflicts defines who we are as a society. It must be part of an ongoing search for harmonious and respectful social relationships founded on principles of justice.

The Law Commission of Canada welcomes your comments and ideas.

Acknowledgments

The Law Commission of Canada acknowledges the contributions of many people. In preparing this Report, it has benefited from the counsel and advice of numerous Canadians. Citizens active in restorative justice and in mediation programs, both advocates and critics, and many community groups involved in justice initiatives have participated in a variety of conferences, workshops, or discussion forums organized or supported by the Commission over the last three years. This Report could not have been written without their input.

Over the years, many members of the Advisory Council of the Law Commission have been involved in discussions of restorative justice and the Commission has been enriched by their wise comments. Thank you to Wendy Armstrong, Jacques Auger, Darin Barney, Lorraine Berzins, Céline Bureau, Dave Cassels, Dan Christmas, June Callwood, Bradley Crawford, Ervan Cronk, Janet Dench, Margaret Denike, Irène d'Entremont, Priscilla De Villiers, Wilma Derksen, Emerson Douyon, Leena Evic-Twerdin, Dave Farthing, Gerry Ferguson, Jean-Pierre Gariépy, Vinh Ha, Mavis Henry, Bernice Hollett, Andrée Lajoie, Alcide Leblanc, Wade MacLauchlan, Hans Mohr, Michael Morrison, Irma Murdock, Katherine Peterson, Alan Reynolds, Morris Rosenberg, Jennifer Stoddard and Mary-Ellen Turpel-Lafond.

The work of many scholars has inspired this Report: Jennifer Llewellyn and Robert Howse, Gerry Ferguson, Joan Ryan, Brian Caillou, Wendy Stewart, Audrey Huntley and Fay Blaney. The Commission benefited from the work undertaken in the context of its partnership with the Social Sciences and Humanities Research Council (Relationships in Transition 2000): Augustine Brannigan, Erin Gibbs Van Brunschot, John A. Baker, Julie Macfarlane, Paule Halley, Rebecca Hagey, Lucie Lamarche, Francine Tougas, Georges Legault and Lucie Lalonde.

Many commentators were asked to review different drafts, comment on our work or provide us with information. We wish to thank Kent Roach, Jamie Scott, Robert Cormier, Justice Louise Otis, David Daubney, Peter Bruer, Wilma Derksen, Mylène Jaccoud, Serge Charbonneau,

Jane Miller-Ashton and Johanne Vallée for their time and conscientious review of the work.

This Report is accompanied by a DVD, *Community Mediation: Two Real-Life Experiences*, produced by the National Film Board of Canada. Our partnership with the National Film Board has been very rewarding and we thank Stéphane Drolet, Yves Bisaillon, Jack Horwitz, David Boisclair and Christian Madagawa. Our thanks as well to the producer of the brochure accompanying this Report, Gaston St-Jean, and to the translators and production team.

Our Virtual Scholar in Residence for the year 2002–2003, Dr. Julie Macfarlane, is the primary author of this report. We owe her an enormous debt of gratitude.

The Commissioners want to thank in particular the director of research, Dr. Dennis Cooley, for his leadership in carrying this project forward. Dr. Cooley wrote the initial discussion paper *From Restorative Justice to Transformative Justice*, coordinated the production of the video, *Communities and the Challenge of Conflict: New Perspectives on Restorative Justice*, orchestrated the consultations and engagement strategies surrounding this project; and finalized the report—all while fulfilling his responsibilities as research director. We want to thank him very much for his dedication.

Other members of the team from the Commission to be thanked include: Maryse St-Pierre and Jocelyne Geoffroy (administrative support), Lise Traversy and Stéphane Bachand (communications) and Lorraine Pelot, Karen Jensen and Steven Bittle (research). Our co-op research students, Drew Mildon and Jennifer Schmidt, also contributed to finalizing the report. Thanks go as well to the Executive Director of the Commission, Bruno Bonneville, for supervising the production of the report.

Our past president, Roderick A. Macdonald and past Commissioners Alan Buchanan, Gwen Boniface and Stephen Owen all contributed to the early stages of this project. We acknowledge their contribution.

The final product is a joint effort of the staff and Commissioners of the Law Commission of Canada.

Executive Summary

Wherever there are people, the possibility of conflict exists. One of the ways we deal with conflict is through the justice system. But, over the past several decades, some Canadians have become dissatisfied with how the formal justice system responds to conflict. Conflicts are framed in legal language, rather than in terms of how individuals experience them; remedies often do not provide adequate redress for those who have been harmed; and the process is frequently time-consuming, costly and confusing.

Frustration with an adversarial justice system has spurred the rise of alternatives such as victim–offender mediation, sentencing circles, community mediation and judge-led settlement conferencing. These alternatives are usually grouped under two broad categories: restorative justice and consensus-based justice. **Restorative justice** refers to a process for resolving crime and conflicts, one that focuses on redressing the harm to the victims, holding offenders accountable for their actions and engaging the community in a conflict resolution process. **Consensus-based justice** refers to innovative methods of resolving mostly non-criminal conflicts. Because the participation of the parties in the resolution of the dispute is an essential part of both restorative and consensus-based justice, they can both be considered forms of **participatory justice**.

Over the past three years, the Law Commission of Canada has consulted with Canadians about meaningful methods of resolving conflicts. The Commission's consultations revealed that Canadians want choices for resolving their conflicts, and that many want to actively participate in the conflict resolution process. The Commission believes that participatory justice—with its emphasis on the reconstruction of relationships through dialogue and on outcomes developed and agreed to by the disputants themselves— responds to this need. The challenge, as the Commission sees it, is for governments and civic institutions to find ways to support participatory justice without limiting its innovative potential.

As such, this report has several objectives:

- to clarify the underlying values and principles of both restorative justice and consensus-based justice by drawing from the literature, research and experiences that these innovations have generated;

- to challenge thinking about the classification and division of disputes for the purposes of fair process and just resolution, in particular the distinction between criminal and civil disputes;

- to identify the remarkably similar concerns and critiques that have been expressed about restorative and consensus-based justice;

- to identify best practices in participatory justice across Canada;

- to address policy questions and explore the changes necessary to make restorative and consensus-based justice processes part of the mainstream of dispute resolution practice in Canada, without losing their creative elements; and

- to make recommendations that enhance the capacity of the justice system to provide meaningful results for Canadians and to develop a culture of participatory justice in Canada.

The Current Experience of Participatory Justice

Participatory justice in criminal law: restorative justice

The failure of the punitive system to lower crime rates or contribute to greater public safety, and the disillusionment of victims and their families with the criminal justice system, are some of the factors behind the rise of restorative justice in Canada. Another important influence has been the emergence of the community justice movement, which seeks a return to local decision-making and community-building independent of the formal justice system. Restorative justice in Aboriginal communities, in many cases based on traditional healing and spiritual practices, has grown in response to an overwhelming need for emotional and spiritual healing, as well as out of the movement to assert community control over government functions.

Many of the early restorative justice processes were developed without a specific legislative framework. However, within the past several years, a series of court decisions, legislative initiatives and policy statements have sought to provide parameters for the growth and development of restorative justice processes.

The more common forms of restorative justice in use in Canada are:

- *Victim–offender mediation (VOM) and victim–offender reconciliation programs (VORPs).* Among the earliest models of restorative justice, VOM and VORPs bring the offender and the victim voluntarily together in the presence of a trained mediator, either before sentencing or sometimes many years after incarceration. Most of these models complement the formal justice system: regardless of the outcome, the offender may receive a formal conviction, a criminal record and a traditional punishment.

- *Community and family group conferencing.* A co-ordinator invites the family and friends of both the victim and the offender to participate in a discussion to explore appropriate ways to address the offending behaviour and desired outcomes for the family or community. The focus is usually somewhat broader than that of VOM and VORPs, since it involves an evaluation of the impact of the offence on a wider group. The group develops a plan for monitoring the future behaviour of the offender and sets out any reparative elements deemed necessary.

- *Sentencing circles.* Operating in many Aboriginal communities in Canada, sentencing circles allow victims, offenders, community elders, other community members and court officials to discuss the consequences of a conflict and to explore ways of resolving it. Some sentencing circles operate within the formal justice system as an alternative to the conventional sentencing process. Sentencing circles are sometimes also used for cases that are diverted from the justice system.

- *Community boards or panels.* Made up of volunteers from the community, who formally meet with offenders and victims to facilitate a discussion of appropriate outcomes, community boards or panels are used either as a pre-charge diversion from the formal system or as an alternative means to determine an appropriate sentence after a guilty plea has been entered.

- *Other participatory processes.* Restorative justice principles have influenced the development of many school-based programs, including peer mediation training and anger management education. Work also takes place in prisons with incarcerated offenders, preparing them for reintegration into their communities.

The Commission believes that most restorative justice initiatives share the following objectives and values.

Restorative justice objectives	Restorative justice values
• The delineation and denunciation of unacceptable behaviour • Support for victims • The reform of individual offenders via active responsibility-taking • Community order and peace • The identification of restorative, forward-looking outcomes	• Participation • Respect for all participants • Community empowerment • Commitment to agreed outcomes • Flexibility and responsiveness of process and outcomes

Participatory justice in a non-criminal context: consensus-based justice

Whether in commercial litigation, bankruptcy, landlord–tenant disputes, administrative law, family law or other areas of non-criminal law, the growth of consensus-based justice processes in Canada over the past two decades has been remarkable. Consensus-based justice shares many similarities with restorative justice, including the conditions that led to the development of alternatives to the formal justice system.

As with restorative justice, a factor in the rise of consensus-based justice is the gap between the needs of disputants and what the formal justice system offers them. Parties who have access to commercial arbitration for resolving disputes concerning online transactions, for example, seek outcomes to business conflicts that recognize the conventions of business practice, that are developed by adjudicators familiar with these conventions and the impacts of conflicts on commercial operations, and that can be implemented without unnecessary delay or cost. Similarly, more couples are bypassing lawyers or court procedures to formalize their separation, whether for financial reasons or simply because they are dissatisfied with the animosity divorce proceedings frequently generate.

The cost of legal fees and the investment of time required to bring a civil action to trial are significant factors in the rise of consensus-based justice initiatives. There has also been growing awareness of the other costs of a more adversarial process: lower productivity and workplace morale, for example, or weakened mental health and family stability.

Statutory provisions to incorporate mediation into the resolution of civil disputes are common, both at the federal and provincial levels, particularly in personal information protection acts, human rights codes, statutes related to land disputes, family law acts and labour dispute legislation. Several organizations offer mediation and arbitration services, such as the American Arbitration Association, the International Chamber of Commerce, the Canadian Commercial Arbitration Centre, and the Commercial Arbitration and Mediation Center for the Americas. Professional associations offering mediation accreditation, such as the ADR Institute of Canada and Family

Mediation Canada, have sprung up at both the national and provincial levels over the last few years.

Forms of consensus-based justice operating in Canada include the following:

- *Community mediation.* Most community mediation programs are attached to a community centre, where services are provided by some funded staff and by trained volunteer mediators.

- *Court-connected mediation.* In the civil justice system a case can be referred to a mandated mediation process.

- *Judge-led settlement conferencing.* Rules of court are allowing more opportunities for judges to play a proactive role in moving the parties toward settlement. (This is also known as judicial dispute resolution or JDR.)

- *Collaborative family lawyering.* This involves a contractual commitment between a lawyer and client to resolve differences amiably and not to resort to litigation to resolve the client's problem.

The Commission believes that most consensus-based processes share the following objectives and values.

Consensus-based justice objectives	Consensus-based justice values
• Clarification of the wrong and an appraisal of its impact	• Participation
• Distribution and assumption of responsibility	• Respect for all participants
• Relationship transformation	• Fair treatment
• Moving forward	• Respect for agreed outcomes
	• Flexibility of process and outcomes

Restorative Justice and Consensus-based Justice: Common Elements, Critiques and Concerns

Common elements

There are three key areas in which the vision of restorative justice and that of consensus-based justice overlap: in their conception of harm, their conception of justice and their focus on relationships.

Restorative justice and consensus-based justice see harm as occurring first and foremost to an individual—as a breach of a relationship—and secondarily as having implications for the whole community. Harm is not necessarily inherent in the act itself or an automatic consequence of a breach of rules, but arises from the circumstances of the act and its impact on others as individuals and community members. This view is in contrast to the focus of criminal law, where an act is assumed to cause harm simply if it violates the *Criminal Code*, while its impact on a particular individual has historically been considered somewhat irrelevant.

Both restorative justice and consensus-based justice traditions conceive of justice as multidimensional. Both approaches reject the idea that a just outcome must only be consistent with pre-existing rules. Instead, the presumption goes the other way—that in almost every case the solution is integrative, rather than winner takes all.

While prosecution and litigation often assume that there will not and cannot be any kind of future relationship between the parties, restorative justice and consensus-based justice are open to the potential for future relationships of many kinds.

Critiques and concerns

The introduction of informal and unregulated dispute resolution processes has been subject to sustained criticism by those concerned about the protection of vulnerable parties. The fear is that private, unregulated processes may privilege more powerful parties in ways that—at least in theory—formal, public processes do not. A related critique is that delegating the power to develop solutions to communities, even to the parties themselves, assumes that these are healthy communities or people whose decision-making will be fair and balanced.

A quite different concern—and sometimes criticism—of restorative and consensus-based justice practices is that their original innovative vision could be corrupted by assimilation into institutional and bureaucratic structures.

The Future of Participatory Justice

A solution for all conflicts?

Are some conflicts unsuitable for a restorative or consensus-based justice approach?

Research has not yet established which types of cases are most likely to benefit from participatory processes. However, from its study of Canadian restorative and consensus-based justice, the Commission concludes that these participatory processes are most suitable for disputes in which each party participates voluntarily and has sufficient capacity to engage fully in a process of dialogue and negotiation. Perhaps most important, the process must reflect local conditions and individual circumstances, for example face-to-face dialogue may not always be appropriate, and there may be a need to constrain or monitor the outcomes of community decision-making to prevent intolerance and vigilantism from surfacing.

That said, the Commission also believes that, with sufficient safeguards in place, participatory processes may be appropriate for all types of conflict—monetary, biparty or multiparty, private or public, criminal or civil—across a broad spectrum, and for all types of communities, urban and rural, Aboriginal and non-Aboriginal.

What should participatory processes look like?

There is some tension between setting out even general principles for the design of participatory processes and meeting the needs of those participating in them. The Commission believes that some general principles for the design of participatory processes can be drawn from a survey of the most promising restorative justice and consensus-based justice initiatives. These principles are:

1. *Early intervention.* The earlier that non-threatening, constructive, participatory interventions can be made, the more likely the conflict may quickly de-escalate.

2. *Accessibility.* If participatory processes are to be used by community members and justice system officials, it is critical to design them to be easily accessible, user-friendly and not overly bureaucratic.

3. *Voluntariness.* That participants make informed choices about participating in restorative justice or consensus-based justice initiatives is fundamental to success. Mandatory participation should be considered only under specific and limited conditions.

4. *Careful preparation.* Notwithstanding the principle of voluntariness, careful attention should be paid to disputant relationships that suggest fear or intimidation. As well, all participants should have adequate time to prepare for the process.

5. *Opportunities for face-to-face dialogue.* Face-to-face dialogue should be offered as one of a range of strategies that parties may use to resolve conflicts.

6. *Advocacy and support.* Participatory processes should welcome those who want to provide support to the parties, while making clear that control of the process rests with the disputants.

7. *Confidentiality.* The assurance of confidentiality and of the legal inadmissibility of what is said are often critical to the efficacy of participatory processes.

8. *Fairness.* Generally, the parties themselves should make the decisions about what is "fair." However, this does not remove the need to monitor whether a decision to accept an outcome is truly voluntary, as well as the need to monitor the quality and legality of the outcomes of participatory processes.

9. *Relevant and realistic outcomes.* Agreements reached in participatory processes must reflect available resources (e.g., drug rehabilitation programs, income to pay agreed-upon compensation). Where possible, compliance with agreements, and their durability, should be monitored so that problems can be identified quickly.

10. *Efficiency.* Although it is important that costs not be measured solely in monetary terms, participatory processes that place increased long-term costs on either disputants or the state are unlikely to be accepted.

11. *Systemic impact.* By moving decision-making into the hands of individual disputants and their communities, participatory processes have the potential to alter society's habitual responses to conflict and conflict resolution. Participatory processes create the capacity for the disputants to learn new ways of responding to their conflicts.

12. *Flexibility and responsiveness.* The assumption of self-determination that lies at the heart of participatory processes means that parties can and must be trusted to make decisions about the process, such as who should be present, how long the meeting should last, what will be discussed, and what types of solutions or outcomes should be considered.

A role for government?

There have been many positive outcomes from participatory justice initiatives in Canada, and strong support for such initiatives from a variety of quarters. Civil mediation programs have demonstrated significant savings of cost and time for individual litigants, and restorative justice processes consistently report high rates of agreement. Federal and provincial governments have shown strong support for restorative justice, and academic and community interest in participatory justice has increased markedly over the past few years. Even those who raise concerns about restorative justice processes in Aboriginal communities do not reject their use; instead, they press for more information to be provided to vulnerable participants, for a strong emphasis on the dynamics of family violence and for the development of broader antiviolence initiatives.

Yet, despite demonstrated benefits and increasing interest, participatory processes remain secondary—marginalized, even—alternatives to the dominant justice model. These initiatives may simply cease to grow and flourish without some government role in legitimizing and promoting them. But some point to a danger that dependence on government structure and resources will undermine the ability of communities to make good decisions for themselves and their members.

Recommendations

Over the course of its consultations, the Commission has heard from groups and individuals involved in participatory justice processes. These consultations have led the Commission to propose a number of specific recommendations for governments, legal professionals and community groups.

The Commission believes that it is appropriate for all levels of government and community agencies to invest in the development of new programs and in the enhancement of those already existing in light of an integrated approach to disputes, whether criminal or civil.

To support services and programs that can offer communities participatory processes for resolving all types of conflict, and to promote participatory processes that offer benefits to individuals and communities, governments should adopt a proactive role and facilitate the development of participatory conflict resolution initiatives. Specifically, the Commission recommends that

- governments develop meaningful partnerships with existing participatory justice research centres and centres of excellence, and local communities that have an interest in participatory justice;

- governments encourage research centres to work in partnership with communities to develop best practices in participatory justice;

- legal aid plans ensure that counsel preparation for, and participation in, extrajudicial conflict resolution processes is paid at the same rate as in conventional litigation or trial work;

- the Canadian Institute for the Administration of Justice and the National Judicial Institute strengthen judicial education in alternative conflict resolution processes to ensure that such training is available to all judges;

- law societies make the provision of continuing education in alternative conflict resolution a priority, encourage their members to undertake such training and review their codes of professional conduct to ensure that the role of the lawyer as an advocate in restorative or consensus-based justice processes is adequately anticipated;

- universities and colleges, and law schools in particular, continue to expand the quality of teaching in alternative dispute resolution offered to law students; and

- businesses and voluntary organizations review their policies to ensure that employees' participation in participatory processes is considered in the same light as court attendance and that they continue to develop participatory justice projects to resolve conflicts within their organizations.

Part I — Introduction and Overview

Chapter 1   Introduction

Conflict, and our response to it, is an enduring feature of our lives. We encounter conflict in our families, at work, at school and in most other aspects of our lives. Conflict causes pain and loss. It damages people and property, sometimes irreparably. Conflict has the potential to destroy relationships between people. But conflict can also have positive effects. Conflict can define boundaries, both in a physical sense and in a social sense. It can establish limits to what is and is not acceptable behaviour. On an individual level, conflict provides an opportunity for growth and moral development. We may learn from our mistakes. We may learn to develop an appreciative understanding of the interests and concerns of others. At the community level, conflict provides an opportunity to discuss the values that underpin rules and regulations, to examine their assumptions, and to test their validity against opposing claims.

There are many strategies for resolving conflicts. Some of these strategies are healthy, others are not. We often ignore neighbours who play their music too loudly. We may tolerate offensive behaviour because the process for making a complaint is too difficult. We may negotiate with clients who will not abide by a contract. We may avoid locations that are perceived as dangerous. As consumers we often accept the fact that we receive inferior products or service rather than complain. And, occasionally, we use the justice system— both the criminal law, and the civil and administrative remedies—to resolve some of our conflicts.

Over the past several decades, some Canadians have become dissatisfied with how the formal justice system operates. As we will explore further in this Report, tribunals are frequently seen as unresponsive to the needs of people in conflict; conflicts are framed in legal language, rather than in terms of how individuals experience them; remedies often do not provide adequate redress for those who have been harmed; and the process is frequently time-consuming, costly and confusing. The frustrations with conventional dispute-processing—including excessive formalism, processing delays, and limited efficacy in resolving problems—that have stimulated the growth of the restorative justice movement are similarly reflected in consensus-based justice initiatives, both inside and outside the formal justice system. Restorative justice initiatives directed at criminal matters may have lessons to teach non-criminal programs, and vice versa.

The dominance of the adversarial framework in Canadian law is an expression of our commitment to principled and just outcomes. While these commitments continue to be central to our understanding of a just society, they are also increasingly seen as insufficiently flexible to respond to diverse social relationships in a changing socio-demographic context. Adjudication can destroy personal and social relationships. Its commitment to formal equality can appear naïve in light of economic and other disparities among Canadians and its focus on the protection of individual rights may neglect the impact of conflict on collective coexistence and on particular communities. Finally, the adjudicative system has a limited range of outcomes: probation, fines and incarceration in the criminal justice system, and monetary compensation in the civil justice system. Often, these outcomes fail to address the needs and desires of the parties involved in the conflict.

The questions the Commission seeks to answer in this Report are simple: Can we do better? Is it possible to imagine a way to frame and to respond to conflicts that provides more satisfactory outcomes while safeguarding principles of justice? How do we safeguard the justice values of the adjudicative model without limiting our capacity to resolve conflict in a way that is more meaningful to those involved in disputes? There is a case to be made both for change and for caution.

1.1 RESTORATIVE JUSTICE, CONSENSUS-BASED JUSTICE AND PARTICIPATION

Restorative justice refers to a process for resolving crime and conflict that focuses on redressing the harm to the victims, on holding offenders accountable for their actions and on engaging the community in the conflict resolution process. For victims, restorative justice may be an opportunity to restore a sense of control over their lives by expressing their anger, getting answers to questions they may have about the incident and re-establishing order and predictability in their lives. For offenders, restorative justice involves accepting responsibility for their actions by repairing the harm they have caused. It also means addressing the issues that contribute to their propensity to engage in harmful behaviour. This may require dealing with anger or drug and alcohol dependency. For the community, restoration involves denouncing wrongful behaviour and reaffirming community standards. Restoration also includes ways of reintegrating offenders into the community. While there are many different visions of restorative justice in Canada and abroad, a common element of restorative justice processes is that the victim, the offender and the community have some control over the process.

Consensus-based justice refers to innovative methods of resolving mostly non-criminal conflicts. Much as with restorative justice in the criminal justice system, there have emerged new ways of thinking about civil conflicts such as breaches of contract, marital disputes and environmental disagreements. These new ways of responding to conflict place the parties to it at the centre of the resolution process. The goal of processes such as collaborative lawyering, mediation and conciliation is to provide non-adversarial ways for parties to resolve disputes. Much as in the case of restorative justice processes, the thrust of consensus-based justice programs is to allow parties to a dispute to control how their dispute is resolved.

Restorative justice processes, both community based and court based, emphasize relationship-building, reconciliation and the development of agreement driven outcomes between victim and offender. These transformative processes are responses to frustrations with an adversarial justice system. Broadly similar goals are reflected

> ## "My need is to dialogue with him—hold him to account.": A Victim's Story
>
> "I'll need to meet with him face to face. I have dozens of questions that were never touched on in the justice process. I need to ask him 'Why?' and 'Why me?' And I need to be open to his humanity, his pain, to see if we can find some new freedom for us both ... I'd like to ask him 'What was all your pain about, and why was it that your rage was turned out on others?' 'Just relax,' he said, 'and you'll survive.' Well someone didn't survive—my twins lost their lives. I want to see how he responds to the news of the loss of my babies. I want him to have to deal with my pain and his responsibility for the consequences. It may sound funny, but I don't hate him. Maintaining anger for the rest of my life will just eat away at me. My need is to dialogue with him—hold him to account."
>
> As reported in David Gustafson, "Victim–Offender Mediation and Reconciliation: Towards a Justice Which Heals," address to the 3rd International Prison Chaplains' Association Conference, Aylmer, Quebec, 18–23 August 1995, at 13–14.

in the development of innovative non-criminal programs. Program goals cover a spectrum from negotiation (emphasizing therapeutic and systemic benefits from the development of peaceful consensus-building paradigms) to pure efficiency models (quicker disposition of civil disputes). Among others, examples of these civil programs include a judge-led conciliation in the Quebec Court of Appeal;[1] Ontario's Mandatory Mediation Program;[2] Saskatchewan's Mediation Orientation Program;[3] Alberta's Queen's Bench Mediation Program;[4] judge-led settlement conferences;[5] workplace conflict resolution systems and other in-house dispute management programs in the private, not-for-profit and government sectors;[6] peer mediation programs in schools;[7] and a network of community mediation centres (in Ontario, British Columbia and Quebec) that offer mediation for disputants in landlord–tenant conflicts, consumer disputes, and so on.[8] These and similar innovations will be described throughout this Report as consensus-based justice models.

Restorative justice in the criminal justice system and consensus-based justice in the civil and administrative justice system are ways of thinking about conflict that place those who are touched by conflict (victims and offenders, plaintiffs and defendants, claimants and respondents, and members of the community) at the centre of the process. Restorative justice in the criminal law and consensus-based justice in the civil and administrative law are connected. They are attempts to rethink how conflicts are named and framed, rethink our assumptions about who is properly a party to a dispute, and rethink how we ought to respond to conflicts. These processes represent a departure from our adversarial criminal and civil justice systems. Just as the principles of restorative justice challenge our entrenched assumptions about how to respond to criminal behaviour,[9] consensus-based justice rejects a conventional right/wrong analysis of conflict, preferring a more creative approach to accommodating differing needs and interests and the development of integrative solutions.

There are conceptual and practical differences between restorative justice used to respond to the aftermath of criminal offences and consensus-based justice used to resolve non-criminal disputes. In later chapters of this Report, we explore some of these differences. There is, however, a fundamental feature that is common to both approaches. Both restorative justice and consensus-based justice seek transformation through the participation of the parties involved in the conflict. Conflict causes pain and suffering, but it also provides an opportunity for change and growth. Both restorative justice and consensus-based justice attempt to capitalize on the transformative potential of conflict, to use conflict as a springboard for moving toward a more just society. Participation is the key to the transformation process. Parties to a conflict ought to be actively involved in finding resolutions to it. In this report, therefore, we refer generically to restorative justice and consensus-based justice as **participatory processes**.

A Note on Nomenclature

For the purposes of this Report, the expressions **restorative justice** and **consensus-based justice** will be used to describe dispute resolution processes that explicitly or implicitly[10] focus on encouraging the parties to actively participate in the resolution of the dispute. We will use the expression **participatory processes** to refer generically to both restorative justice and consensus-based justice.

Not all alternative dispute resolution programs ought to be described as consensus-based justice,[11] nor should all non-custodial sentences be described as restorative. In fact, there is a lively debate about what both of these terms mean for conflict resolution processes. For the purposes of this Report, adopting a particular nomenclature to identify a definition or orthodoxy seems less helpful than looking for those underlying principles that may enhance our existing dispute resolution systems.

"A restorative justice way of thinking can influence the way any alternative conflict resolution program operates— whether the program is dealing with a dispute over money or property, the misbehaviour of a young person which falls short of being reported to police, a parent/child relationship which draws the attention of Child Welfare, or adult criminal behaviour."

Provincial Association Against Family Violence, *Making It Safe: Women, Restorative Justice and Alternative Dispute Resolution* (St John's, Nfld. and Lab.: Provincial Association Against Family Violence, 2000) at 7.

1.2 OBJECTIVES AND THE CHALLENGES OF THIS REPORT

This Report evaluates the extent to which participatory justice values and practical initiatives have taken root in Canadian justice systems. The growing interest in participatory justice offers an excellent opportunity to assess the impact of pressure for change within both the criminal justice system and the civil justice system. How influential has the restorative justice movement been, not only in the criminal context, but also in the growth of civil justice initiatives such as court-connected mediation and judge-led settlement conferences? How do restorative justice and consensus-based justice relate to conflict resolution outside a formal legal arena such as peer mediation in schools and community mediation programs?

By emphasizing the reconstruction of relationships through dialogue and the consensual outcomes developed by the disputants themselves, the Commission believes that both restorative justice models and consensus-based justice models offer a valuable alternative to the conventional adversarial paradigm of dispute resolution.[12]

The first objective of this Report is to clarify the underlying values and principles of both restorative justice and consensus-based justice by drawing from the literature, research and experiences that these innovations have generated. The purpose here is not to create an orthodoxy of doctrine in either case. Rather, the objective is to explore the origins of each of these social movements in order to better understand their meaning in action and how this is driven by core beliefs about the nature of conflict and by our desire to change the way conflict is handled in our communities. Chapter 2 describes the conditions that appear to have stimulated the development of participatory alternatives to traditional dispute management. Chapter 3 explores the core objectives and values of each participatory alternative. The goal in these first chapters is to identify the origins, the distinctiveness and the potential of each approach.

Our present thinking is constrained by equating of restorative justice practices with criminal matters and equating consensus-based justice approaches with civil non-criminal matters. A second objective of this Report is to challenge thinking about this classification and division of disputes for the purposes of fair process and just resolution, in particular the distinction made between criminal and civil disputes. This is more than simply a procedural question. Integrating best principles and practices from restorative justice and consensus-based justice models challenges us to think deeply about the character of conflicts themselves as they are manifested and presently understood in the criminal and civil contexts. In the first half of Chapter 4, we offer some common themes and elements that link restorative and consensus-based justice processes.

A third objective of this Report is to identify the concerns and the critiques that have been expressed, often in similar form, about restorative and consensus-based justice approaches. The second half of Chapter 4 addresses these concerns and critiques, alerting us to the risks and exploring ways in which these risks might be managed. This is a reoccurring theme throughout the Report. One of the risks associated with the increased use of restorative and consensus-based justice processes is the potential for vulnerable groups that might otherwise seek the protection of formal rights-based justice processes to be disempowered in an informal process. It is critical to the development of any alternative that it be fully responsive to the power relationship between disputants and between disputants and the wider community or the state.

The fourth objective of this Report is to identify best practices across Canada. Chapter 6 offers some principles for the design of participatory justice systems, drawing on the most promising outcomes seen in current restorative and consensus-based justice initiatives.

The fifth objective of this Report is to address policy questions and explore the changes necessary to make restorative and consensus-based justice processes part of the mainstream of dispute resolution practice in Canada without undermining their creative elements. The opening section of Chapter 7 reviews some examples of best practices in a range of applications, including criminal, civil, administrative, family and extralegal conflicts. Chapter 7 also considers the role of the state in community-based justice initiatives. Community participation is key to both restorative justice and consensus-based justice initiatives, and many proponents regard government as threatening their work. At the same time, as long as the traditional justice system operates as the hub of formal dispute processing, community justice initiatives must develop structural and political relationships with the criminal and civil justice systems.

The final objective of this Report is to make recommendations that enhance the capacity of the justice system to provide meaningful results for Canadians and to develop a culture of participatory justice in Canada. Chapter 8 gives a number of recommendations for governments, justice officials, lawyers, social service agencies and members of the community who have an interest in participatory justice. Our recommendations are about how governments, justice officials, community groups, and other agencies and individuals working in conflict resolution can develop a culture of participatory justice.

Report Objectives

- To clarify the underlying values and principles of both the restorative justice and the consensus-based justice perspectives

- To challenge the conventional wisdom about how we think about and categorize disputes

- To alert us to the risks of restorative and consensus-based justice practices and how these risks might be managed

- To highlight best practices and their implications for the design of fair, safe and effective alternatives to adjudication

- To explore the changes necessary to advance restorative and consensus-based justice processes and practices, in particular the role of government in promoting alternatives to traditional dispute processing

- To make recommendations to develop a culture of participatory justice in Canada that would promote the development of restorative and consensus-based justice processes

---

The task set for this Report involves many inherent tensions. The promise held out by new approaches to dispute resolution is that they are participatory. Both restorative justice and consensus-based justice focus on relationships. It is important to evaluate alternative programs to ensure that our expanding experience enables us to enhance both the process and the outcomes of conflict resolution. This means identifying best practices and articulating the underlying values and principles of conflict resolution in order to anchor restorative and consensus-based dispute resolution. We must also begin to clarify the role of government in enabling and legitimizing such programs. However, the institutionalization of change carries many risks. There is a danger that "packaging" the potential of an interactive and dynamic process might diminish its radical and transformative power and lead to new orthodoxies as inflexible and unresponsive to context as those of the existing system. There is pressure to create neat definitions and models of practice. This pressure denies the spirit of alternatives that seek to respect diversity and to challenge assumptions of homogeneity in both the processes and the outcomes of disputes.

1.3 ORGANIZATION OF THE REPORT

The rest of this Report consists of Part 2 and Part 3. Part 2 synthesizes what we know from existing research about the meaning and significance of participatory justice principles for our existing dispute resolution processes. This part of the Report also explores innovative conflict management methods developed to respond to criminal and non-criminal matters. It examines the following questions:

- To what types of needs—needs that are not met by the existing legal system—are initiatives in restorative justice and consensus-based justice appropriate responses?

- How do restorative justice and consensus-based justice challenge us to reconceptualize conventional dispute resolution processes and concepts, including concepts of justice, causation, harm and culpability, participation, equality and accountability?

- What critiques and opposition have been encountered by current initiatives in restorative justice and consensus-based justice, and how might these be addressed?

- Are there themes and principles common to both restorative and consensus-based justice approaches? How might these themes help us understand the conflict resolution process in general?

Part 3 addresses the policy implications of participatory justice for existing dispute resolution processes in both criminal and non-criminal disputes. These questions will help guide policy development.

- How does the experience of participatory justice processes contribute to our understanding of best practices in dispute resolution?

- What results have been achieved by current initiatives, both inside and outside the formal justice system?

- What distinctions between conflict types (criminal acts and civil wrongs) and conflict circumstances (conflict within Aboriginal and non-Aboriginal communities, or between more or less powerful parties) are significant in considering the suitability of a relationship-focused approach to conflict resolution?

- What have we learned about best practices in designing restorative and consensus-based justice processes and, in particular, how can these processes become more responsive to various needs in the community?

- What is the appropriate relationship between communities and government in developing and operating restorative and consensus-based justice programs? How should policymakers support community programs to achieve good outcomes within an accountable and democratic social structure?

Part 3 concludes by suggesting a roadmap for how we can move toward a culture of participatory justice. It provides a number of specific recommendations to governments and other actors and agencies. These recommendations are based on extensive consultations with Canadians and on research conducted by the Commission over the past few years.

1   This program is described by Justice Louise Otis in a recent edition of the *World Arbitration and Mediation Report.* See The Honourable Justice L. Otis, "The Conciliation Service of the Quebec Court of Appeal" (2000) 11:3 *World Arbitration and Mediation Report* at 80.

2   Rule 24.1 Ontario Rules of Civil Procedure, O. Reg. 194/90, known as the Ontario Mandatory Mediation Program.

3   *Queen's Bench (Mediation) Amendment Act,* S.S. 1994, c. 20.

4   Mediation Rules of the Provincial Court, Civil Division for Alberta, Alta. Reg. 971/97.

5   See, for example, W. Brazil, "Hosting Settlement Conferences: Effectiveness in the Judicial Role" (1987) 3 *Ohio State Journal on Dispute Resolution* 1; and in Canada see, for example, Rule 77 Ontario Rules of Civil Procedure, O. Reg. 194/90.

6   See, for example, the review of non-unionized workplaces by M.L. Coates, G.T. Furlong and B.M. Downie, *Conflict Management and Dispute Resolution Systems in Canadian Non-unionized Organizations* (Kingston: Industrial Relations Centre, Queen's University, 1997).

7   An extensive literature has been developed on peer mediation in schools. See, for example, R.J. Bodine and D.K. Crawford, *The Handbook of Conflict Resolution: A Guide to Building Quality Programs in Schools* (San Francisco: Jossey-Bass, 1998); and in the university context, W. Waters, *Mediation in the Campus Community* (San Francisco: Jossey-Bass, 2000).

8   For example, Community Justice Initiatives of Kitchener/Waterloo, St. Stephen's Community House Conflict Resolution Services, and Downsview Conflict Resolution Services.

9   Law Commission of Canada, *From Restorative Justice to Transformative Justice* (Ottawa: Law Commission of Canada, July 1999) at 15.

10 For an argument that the attachment of dispute resolution labels should be a matter of actual practice rather than abstract theory, see C. McEwen, "Toward a Program-based ADR Research Agenda" (1999) 15:4 *Negotiation Journal* 325.

11 A somewhat contestable term of art, largely due to Bush and Folger's celebrated book, *The Promise of Mediation: Responding to Conflict Through Empowerment and Recognition* (San Francisco: Jossey-Bass, 1994), which marked the beginning of efforts to delineate and separate a transformative, as opposed to problem-solving, approach in mediation.

12 British Columbia's policy framework, *A Restorative Justice Framework*, makes this connection explicit. (Victoria: Ministry of the Attorney-General, 1999).

Part II — The Current Experience of Participatory Justice

Chapter 2   Participatory Justice in Criminal Law: Restorative Justice

What is restorative justice? Is restorative justice a philosophy? An intellectual tradition? A way of life? Or is restorative justice a process? A program? Or a specific initiative with identifiable interventions and measurable outcomes? Most people would recognize that restorative justice is a different way of thinking about crime and conflict, but just what makes it different?

There are many ways of thinking about restorative justice, and each offers a different insight into how conflict is understood and resolved. Some proponents focus on restorative justice as a program or a specific type of intervention, such as victim–offender mediation or sentencing circles. Other proponents place a greater emphasis on the outcome of restorative justice processes. They focus on restorative justice as a way of healing victims, offenders and the community.

The starting point for the Commission is that restorative justice is a process that brings victims, wrongdoers and the community together to collectively repair harm while satisfying each participant's conception of justice. This Report adopts this process-centred conception of restorative justice.

The adversarial process is **event based**. The key driver for the adversarial criminal justice system is the event that caused a conflict: how the event is defined and shaped goes a long way in determining how the conflict is resolved. The criminal justice process revolves around establishing that the act occurred and that the accused is or is not guilty. Either an accused can plead guilty to committing the act, or the case can go to court where evidence is presented to prove or disprove that the accused is criminally responsible.

> "[Restorative justice is] a way of dealing with victims and offenders by focusing on the settlement of conflicts arising from crime and resolving the underlying problems which cause it. It is also, more widely, a way of dealing with crime generally in a rational problem solving way. Central to restorative justice is recognition of the community, rather than criminal justice agencies, as the prime site of crime control."
>
> Ministry of Justice of New Zealand, "Restorative Justice: A Discussion Paper." Ministry of Justice of New Zealand, 1996, at 1, online: <http://www.justice.govt.nz/pubs/reports/1996/restorative/chapter2.html>

Restorative justice is **relationship based.** Restorative justice processes focus on helping the victim to come to terms with the aftermath of the crime, holding the offender accountable for the crime and its consequences and, where appropriate, re-establishing their relationship in the community.

Restorative justice processes embody a set of values, which point toward a process, or set of processes, for addressing how individuals are affected by conflict. Restorative justice processes attempt to facilitate the personal growth and recovery of both the victim and the offender and, where warranted, to transform their relationship and restore some basis of understanding and common purpose. Restorative justice principles emphasize respectful and inclusive processes that exemplify many of the values of procedural justice (sometimes described as "justice as process").[1] The orientation of restorative justice favours consensual outcomes over imposed ones. Therefore a set of process values—for example, personal voice, dialogue, respect for other participants and respect for outcomes—flow directly from restorative justice principles. There is also an important relationship between the types of processes implied and promoted by restorative justice principles and the desired or anticipated outcomes of restorative processes.[2]

While there is a healthy debate regarding the question "What is restorative justice?"[3] the Commission believes it is possible to distil five underlying objectives and five underlying values common to most restorative justice processes. In this chapter, we review some of the

Restorative justice objectives	Restorative justice values
• Denounce unacceptable behaviour	• Participation
• Support victims	• Respect for all participants
• Reform individual offenders via active responsibility-taking	• Community empowerment
• Restore community order and peace	• Commitment to agreed outcomes
• Identify restorative, forward-looking outcomes	• Flexibility and responsiveness of process and outcomes

factors that led to the development of restorative justice. We then sketch out some of its core objectives and process values. Finally, we provide an overview of restorative justice processes currently in use in Canada and elsewhere.

2.1   THE CONTEXT

The principles of restorative justice have deep roots in both Western and non-Western traditions. Some argue that a move toward a restorative model of justice is perhaps best understood as a return to the roots of justice. While the roots of restorative justice can be traced back to antiquity, in its modern form restorative justice emerged in the 1970s.[4] This section will review the rise of restorative justice in Canada.

2.1.1   The failure of the punitive system

Over the past two decades, many have argued that the adversarial model has not helped lower the crime rate nor contributed to greater public safety; until recently, crime rates and incarceration rates continued to rise.[5]

The limitations of the justice system are particularly acute for Aboriginal people.[6] Aboriginal people are significantly over-represented in the prison system. In 2000–01, Aboriginal people accounted for 19 percent of provincial and territorial sentenced admissions to custody and 17 percent of federal sentenced admissions to custody, but constituted only 2 percent of the adult Canadian population, according to 1996 census counts. The over-representation of Aboriginal people in the prison system is particularly evident in western and northern Canada. In the Yukon, Aboriginal people represented 72 percent of sentenced admissions to prison but only 17 percent of the adult population; in Manitoba, they represented 64 percent of sentenced admissions to prison but only 9 percent of the adult population; in Saskatchewan, they represented 76 percent of sentenced admissions to prison but only 8 percent of the adult population; and in Alberta, they represented 39 percent of sentenced admissions to prison but only 4 percent of the adult population.[7] These data suggest that a punitive penal model has had limited, if any, impact on rates of crime and re-offending, particularly among Aboriginal people.

High crime rates and high rates of incarceration lead many to question the functioning of the justice system.[8] During the 1970s and 1980s many countries adopted the "just deserts" model of punishment.[9] "Just deserts" is premised on the belief that offenders ought to be punished in direct proportion to the wrong they have committed.[10] Under this model, proportional punishment is seen as a measure of true justice. The relative severity of sentences must be closely linked to the nature of the offence and tempered by the principle of parsimony—the principle that the least restrictive sanction necessary to achieve defined social purposes should be imposed. The concept of "just deserts" is couched in moral terms; indeed, it is understood as "an integral part of everyday moral judgment."[11]

Unlike other countries, Canada did not adopt the "just deserts" model. A parliamentary committee headed by David Daubney, then a member of Parliament, was convened to address the recommendations of the Sentencing Commission's report. Daubney's committee recommended that Parliament explore alternatives to imprisonment, including the use of restorative justice.

> "[I]t is now generally recognized that imprisonment has not been effective in rehabilitating or reforming offenders, has not been a strong deterrent and has achieved only temporary public protection and uneven retribution, as the lengths of prison sentences handed down vary for the same type of crime … [A]lternatives to imprisonment and intermediate sanctions … are increasingly viewed as necessary developments."
>
> *Taking Responsibility* (Standing Committee on Justice and Solicitor General, 1988) at 75.

The failure of the punitive model has led others to explore an approach to crime and punishment that reconceptualizes the nature of harm done by an offender and the impact of punishment on individuals and communities. The motivation to look beyond the punitive model takes a variety of forms, many of which have contributed to the restorative justice movement. These include philosophical and pragmatic concerns, as well as the promotion of concerns, such as victims' rights.

2.1.2   Victims' movements

The disillusionment of victims and their families with the criminal justice system has been a highly significant factor in the growth of restorative justice initiatives. The past twenty years have seen a significant growth in the number of lobby organizations representing the interests of the victims of crime. These organizations are variously described as victims' rights, or victim advocacy groups and victim

> "[I]n the legal process, victims represent footnotes to the crime."
>
> Howard Zehr, *Changing Lenses: A New Focus for Crime and Justice* (Waterloo: Harold Press, 1990) at 31.

support programs. These groups have highlighted the alienation of victims in a prosecutorial system in which the state stands in the shoes of victims and effectively excludes them from the process. The victim is not a party to the criminal prosecution of the accused, but only a witness to the crime.

Victims are largely left out of the court process, except in their role as witnesses. It is assumed that the interests of the state and those of the victim are the same. Most victims need a public affirmation that what occurred to them was wrong and the criminal justice system is capable of responding to that need. However, many victims also want answers to questions, questions that the criminal courts are not structured to answer such as "Why did this happen to me?" and "Will I be compensated for my damaged property?" Victims' rights organizations have also expressed concerns about procedural issues. They feel that they have been excluded from the process and have lobbied for greater control over, and input into, decisions that are made regarding how cases are processed through the system. Finally, victims lack important information about what happens to offenders as they progress through the correctional system.

So removed are victims from the process used to address the harms they have suffered that for some offences, such as those involving

> "Victims are confused, fearful, and angry. They want to know why this happened, and why it happened to them. They feel insecure and do not know who to trust or rely on for support, understanding, and help. Not only do they suffer physically, emotionally, and financially from their victimization, but they then face, often for the first time in their lives, the confusing complexity of the criminal justice system and all of its at times conflicting elements."
>
> Standing Committee on Justice and Human Rights, "Victims' Rights—A Voice, Not a Veto." Report 14 (Ottawa: Standing Committee on Justice and Human Rights, 1998) at chapter 1, online:
>
> <http://www.parl.gc.ca/InfoComDoc/ 3...URI/Studies/Reports/jurirp14-e.htm>.

personal relationships in which charges are sometimes difficult to bring, the consent of the victim is dispensed with altogether. While originally intended to empower victims, mandatory or presumptive charging in domestic assaults has been resisted by some women's groups, who argue that this policy does little to erode or confront the belief structure that supports male violence against women and may even heighten the risks (physical, emotional, and economic) that these women face in their domestic situations. The promise of safety and of long-term transformation, which requires the redistribution of power between men and women in domestic relationships, has not been realized.[12]

Many victims' organizations can be characterized as support focused.[13] These groups emphasize the need for the criminal justice system to be sensitive and responsive to the needs of victims; these groups concentrate much of their effort on raising the consciousness of the public at large and of justice system officials in particular, about the ways in which the present system excludes and even re-

> "As victims we know the power of truth to hold the offender accountable. We know we have the right to feel angry and to give the person who has hurt us a piece of our mind ... We need to remember that justice isn't only about giving a stolen five-dollar bill back to the person from whom it was stolen. It is about mending the broken relationship and restoring trust. Violent crime is about hurting someone physically, spiritually, and emotionally. Crime steals from us our safety, our dignity and our trust. Therefore to really do justice, it is more than simply establishing who did the crime and compensating the victim; it is about restoring the safety, dignity and trust. A New Zealander, Judge James Rota, a descendant of the indigenous people from Mauit said it best. 'Justice must elevate the human spirit or it isn't justice.'"
>
> Wilma L. Derksen, *Confronting the Horror: The Aftermath of Violence* (Winnipeg: Amity Publishers, 2002) at 103.

victimizes and further traumatizes the victims of crime.[14] Some of these groups also criticize the fact that pre-existing stereotypes and social structures often result in victim-blaming, for example the mistreatment of women who are the victims of sexual assault.[15] Some victim support groups actively support restorative justice processes that give victims a voice in the process of resolving the conflict. Victims' groups also offer advice, counselling and other practical assistance to victims and their families.

The alienation of victims from the criminal justice system is well documented. But what do victims need? Many researchers emphasize the significance of victims regaining a sense of control in their lives, which may include the resolution (and not necessarily the restoration or reconciliation) of their relationship with the person who has harmed them. The traumatic impact of crime often includes a sense of powerlessness and vulnerability, and this can both demoralize and paralyse. Being swept along in a justice process that can be confusing, intimidating and impersonal—and sometimes even unsafe—only heightens this sense of loss of personal autonomy and control. Victims need a strong statement and clear acknowledgment that they have a right to protection and that the behaviour that damaged them was wrong.[16] Howard Zehr describes this as "the moral statement implied in the recognition that the act was wrong."[17] Zehr also makes the point, as do others, that victims frequently need answers to their questions—Why did this happen? Why did he do this to me?—that the criminal trial process may or may not provide. "[A]nswers restore an essential sense of order."[18] This type of information can help victims develop a framework for making sense of their experience, both on a cognitive level and on an emotional level.

In response to victims' rights movements, some efforts have been made in Canada in the past decade to refocus the justice system on the unmet needs of the victims of crime.[19] One example is the introduction of victim impact statements into the sentencing process.[20] Victim impact statements may be read by the victim into the court record. This requires special permission from the judge. When they are read in court, victim impact statements are not subject to cross-examination, nor are they made under oath.

In Manitoba, victims of crime now have the right to:

- Be informed about the status of an investigation

- Know the name of any person charged or arrested in connection with the crime

- Be informed about any decision not to lay a charge and the reasons for the decision

- Be consulted on the use of pre-charge alternative measures being considered

- Know the charges against the accused

- Give their opinion to the Crown attorney about whether an accused should be placed in custody or subject to conditions if released

- Be informed about the status of the prosecution

- Be consulted about the prosecution of the case

- Be informed about the use of victim impact statements and pre-sentence reports

- Be informed about how to apply for restitution

- Have an interpreter while testifying

- Know the date, time and place of court proceedings and the sentence given

- Have information about court security measures and facilities

- Access court records

- Ask for a separate waiting area

- Take time off work, without pay, to testify, to present a victim impact statement, or to observe sentencing

- Know if the accused is in custody and where

- Be informed about release dates, temporary absences or other dates if the accused is in custody

- Know the terms and conditions of supervision orders

- Make suggestions about a person's release on bail or temporary absence

Provinces have also introduced legislation to enlarge the recognition given to victims of crime. For example, in 1986, Manitoba enacted legislation specifically directed to protecting the rights of victims.[21] Recently, Manitoba introduced a newer *Victims' Bill of Rights*,[22] which provided victims with a host of new rights.

Other provinces have similar legislation.[23] In Ontario, a *Victims' Bill of Rights* describes a series of measures intended to enhance the role played by the victim in the criminal justice process, including the right of a sexual assault victim to be interviewed by a person of the same gender and the right to be informed of the release of a person convicted of an offence against them.[24] Ontario and Manitoba have each established an Office for the Victims of Crime, which provides counselling and other assistance to victims. All provinces have initiated services for victims. Some programs provide victims of crime with compensation, long- and short-term counselling services, and assistance with preparing victim impact statements. Quebec has set up an extensive network of Centres d'aide aux victimes d'actes criminels throughout the province that provide a full range of victims' services, including compensation.[25] The services of the New Brunswick Victim Services Program include direct support in crisis situations, referrals to psychologists working in trauma, support for victims throughout the criminal justice process, and liaison with police and other community agencies providing victim services. Parallel programs include a Victim Impact Statement program and short-term counselling and compensation for victims of crime programs.[26] However, in many jurisdictions, only victims of serious crimes—where a death or sexual assault has occurred—are provided services and even these services are limited.

2.1.3   The emergence of a community justice movement

Another significant factor in the evolution of restorative justice initiatives has been the development of a social movement that seeks a return to local decision-making and community-building, independent of the formal justice system. Advocates of community justice have argued that no amount of system reform could eliminate the effects of institutionalization and bureaucratization, which treat all individuals as formally equal, thereby failing to recognize the reality of diversity and power differences.[27] Conflict is often seen by the state as a negative force, something to be controlled and eliminated, thereby taking away the opportunity to discuss conflicting values, which are often at the root of conflicts.[28] In contrast, community-based justice initiatives can encourage the peaceful expression of conflict, build respect for diversity, and promote responsibility-taking by the community.[29]

Another important theme in community justice projects is an attachment to social justice issues, such as tolerance and inclusiveness, environmental care and stewardship, and fair working environments.[30]

An early Canadian community justice initiative is Community Justice Initiatives of Kitchener/Waterloo, established in 1978. Like many community dispute resolution programs, this type of initiative offers intervention and facilitation for both criminal and civil disputes—also for matters in which no legal steps have been taken.[31] Many of the values of community-based justice are especially significant for faith communities, which have often been at the forefront of initiatives in community justice.[32] In Canada, the Mennonite community has been played an enormous role in furthering the development of restorative justice, as has the Church Council on Justice and Corrections.

People who are not members of a faith also have the opportunity to give meaning to their experiences of conflict through participation in community justice. Neighbourhood justice centres have often originated in very large urban environments, which are often characterized as culturally individualist.[33] The Regroupement des organismes de justice alternative du Québec (ROJAQ) is a provincial non-profit organization that promotes community participation in the administration of justice. Similarly, the Conflict Resolution Co-Op of Prince Edward Island, the Conflict Resolution Network in Kitchener/Waterloo, and the Native Counselling Services of Alberta bring together individuals interested in conflict resolution in their respective communities.

Participation in community panels and boards and other informal dispute resolution processes represents an important effort to build community identity in these settings and perhaps offers an important alternative to "amusing ourselves to death"[34] in isolation from our neighbours and neighbourhood issues.

> "The value of a Community Circle extends beyond its impact upon victims and offenders. The most important value of the Circle lies in its impact upon the community. In allowing community members to assume ownership for resolving their own issues, a Circle restores a sense of collective responsibility—of being a community."
>
> B. Stuart, "Key Differences: Courts and Community Circles" 11 *Justice Professional* (1998) at 94.

One further characteristic of the community justice movement is important to note. This is a focus on the lessons of experience, or "what works."[35] Disillusionment with the formal criminal justice system has led to a willingness to innovate and experiment in an effort to do things better. This is reflected in the history of neighbourhood justice centres, the continuing development of new programs and processes (such as healing circles and group conferencing), a strong commitment to seeing results in action, and a growing interest in program evaluation that is faithful to the consensus-based goals of community restorative justice.[36] While individual advocates and community justice activists are undoubtedly influenced by theoretical work on the values and principles of restorative justice, community models are primarily grounded in practical experience.

The desire to opt out of the formal justice system and establish an alternative has provoked fierce debate among community justice activists. Some of them argue that the community movement needs connections with justice officials—courts, judges, and police—to gain legitimacy and, for practical purposes, to obtain referrals. Others see any relationship with the formal justice system as weakening the values of grassroots justice and the commitment to peaceful consensus-seeking rather than to the application of legal rules and principles.

2.1.4 Aboriginal community justice

The roots of restorative justice are particularly strong in Canadian Aboriginal communities. Aboriginal leaders have developed initiatives in response to an overwhelming need for emotional and spiritual healing in their communities. Moreover, in many Aboriginal communities, restorative justice initiatives are a part of a larger movement to assert control over governance functions.

"Restorative justice programs in Aboriginal communities have a broader mandate and set of goals and expectations than similar programs in non-Aboriginal communities. For Aboriginal communities, the development of restorative justice programs is part of a reclaiming of the process of social control and order maintenance—a process that was explicitly taken away from Aboriginal communities during the period of colonization. In this way, the development of restorative justice programs by Aboriginal communities is very much a part of decolonization of reasserting the importance, vitality and significance of Aboriginal community control over Aboriginal people."

Jonathan Rudin, "Pushing Back-A Response to the Drive for the Standardization of Restorative Justice Programs in Canada," paper presented at the 6th International Conference on Restorative Justice, Simon Fraser University, Vancouver, B.C., June 2003.

In many cases, traditional healing and spiritual practices have been taken up as restorative justice measures, so justice practices have come to reinforce and extend the influences of those traditions in the communities.[37] The "circle" is symbolic and, in some cases, sacred. It is used extensively across many Aboriginal communities as a form of social control and governance. A crime against an individual has an impact on the whole community because everyone is connected through relationships and through belief and value systems based on connections with land, animals and spirits. In some communities, a crime committed by an individual must be repaired by the extended family or clan, and amends must be made to all other families or clans. Specific rituals exist to fulfil these reconciliatory and compensatory obligations. The unwillingness to break an offender's connections to the community is exemplified in the statement of the Hollow Water researchers: "The People of Hollow Water do not believe in incarceration ... The difference in Hollow Water is that offenders face their responsibilities with the love, respect, and support which the Anishnabe people believe are due to all creatures." [38]

The Tsuu T'ina Provincial Court in Alberta is an Aboriginal court. It has mostly Aboriginal personnel, including an Aboriginal judge, an Aboriginal crown prosecutor; many of the clerks of the court and administrative staff are Tsuu T'ina Band members. Native court workers assist the court by providing non-legal advice and assistance to the accused. The peacemaker coordinator attends court each day the provincial court is in session and a peacemaker or elder may attend as well. Some Aboriginal lawyers attend on occasion to provide legal services and there are tribal police in attendance inside and outside the courtroom.

A variety of alternative measures are possible at the Tsuu T'ina court. Perhaps the most significant alternative measure used by this court is the peacemaker's process. This process serves as an alternative to the court system and helps resolve issues by employing such dispute resolution mechanisms as healing circles, family group conferencing, and sentencing circles. The intent of the Tsuu T'ina peacemakers' process is to resolve disputes, avoid the courts, get to the underlying causes of the actions, restore community relationships and bring back a sense of harmony to the community.[39]

In Nunavut, justice programs have been shaped by the legislature's commitment to the traditional Inuit knowledge and understanding of the world, a policy direction called Inuit Qaujimajatuqangit.[40]

> "An Inuit Elder, Emile Imaruittuq, described the methodology he had learned from his father for dealing with offenders:
>
> 'We had a system in place that did not damage a person emotionally. We would deal with a wrong-doer with sincerity and without hurting the person; we would rectify most behavioural problems. Only if there were repeat offences, were severity and intensity necessary during counselling. You have to look at someone's face. You have to show a person that they are loved and that people care for them.'"
>
> F. Laugrand, J. Oosten and W. Rasing, *Tirigusuusiit, Piqujait and Maligait: Inuit Perspectives on Traditional Law* (Iqaluit: Nunavut Arctic College and the Pairijait Tigummivik Society, 1999) at 51.

Inuit Qaujimajatuqangit includes unwritten traditional knowledge, as well as family and political structures, learning and social development schemes, and even the understanding of local weather patterns. The underlying justice principles being sought under this framework are alternatives, healing and community involvement. To meet these ends, the Nunavut Department of Justice has set up community justice committees throughout the territory and incorporated the advice and efforts of elders into the sentencing process. The traditional role of elders is reflected in modern restorative justice practices.

Through these community justice committees a Land Program has been implemented that delivers one month of traditional life skills on the land to youth offenders between 15 and 32 years of age. Inuit adults and elders teach the participants traditional skills, knowledge and values unique to the Inuit culture and environment. The learning activities include hunting and fishing; attending healing sessions; learning about firearms safety, the environment, tool-making and the practical uses of natural resources harvested from the land and sea; hearing stories about the past; and learning to speak Inuktitut. The Land Program is founded on the belief that learning more about traditional life skills, knowledge and values, will help participants develop cultural self-esteem, form healthy relationships with other community members, and learn the basic values that will help them make better choices in their lives. Similar programs have been made available to youth at risk through the Department of Justice Canada's National Strategy on Community Safety and Crime Prevention.

We would be ignoring important cultural differences if we were to suggest that restorative justice fits into a worldview that is shared by all Aboriginal communities.[41] The Aboriginal Healing Foundation notes that clear and generic healing principles and processes have not evolved "because of the necessity for communities to develop their own models and processes which are closely linked with their own cultures, resources and needs."[42] It may also be unwise to accept restorative justice processes as distinctly Aboriginal.[43] Finally, the Aboriginal Women's Action Network (AWAN) notes that the rush to implement restorative justice processes in some Aboriginal communities may place victims in danger of re-victimization, particularly for victims of violent or sexual assaults.[44]

2.2 THE POLICY FRAMEWORK

Section 2.2 provides a brief overview of the policy framework for the development of restorative justice processes. It is important to recognize, however, that many of the early restorative justice processes were developed without a specific legislative framework. Within the past several years, there have been a series of court decisions, legislative initiatives and policy statements that have sought to provide parameters for the growth and development of restorative justice processes. This section reviews some of these initiatives.

2.2.1 Restorative justice and the *Criminal Code*

The sentencing principles set out in the *Criminal Code* provide legislative support for the implementation of restorative justice processes.[45] Although the Code says that sentences ought to be proportional to the harm caused by the act, the principle of proportionality is balanced by another provision that states that an offender should not be deprived of liberty if less restrictive sanctions may be appropriate in the circumstances. Moreover, recent amendments[46] introduced, for the first time, a provision that explicitly refers to alternatives to incarceration—which might include sanctions agreed to through restorative processes—to be considered when a court imposes a sentence. This provision also emphasizes the need to give special consideration to alternatives in the case of Aboriginal offenders.

In addition, imposing conditional sentences[47] is also an option in a restorative process. Considerable case law has been generated regarding the appropriate conditions for imposing a conditional sentence. The Supreme Court of Canada makes it clear that a conditional sentence is "generally ... more effective than incarceration at achieving the restorative objectives of rehabilitation, reparations and promotion of a sense of responsibility in the offender"[48,49] and that "restorative sentencing goals do not usually correlate with the use of prison as a sanction."[50] Moreover, the Supreme Court points out that a conditional sentence, properly imposed, can meet the goals of both denunciation and deterrence.[51] There continues to be much controversy in our society regarding the availability of conditional sentences for certain serious crimes.[52]

2.2.2 Aboriginal people and the application of sentencing principles

The *Criminal Code* states that "all available sanctions other than imprisonment that are reasonable in the circumstances should be considered for all offenders, with particular attention to the circumstances of Aboriginal offenders."[53] This provision is widely regarded as a response to the high level of incarceration among Aboriginal people. It reflects some formal recognition of the need to develop culturally appropriate outcomes for behaviours within Aboriginal communities. It also reflects efforts to return some types of decision-making to Aboriginal communities, including determining the consequences of criminal behaviour. During the 1990s, Aboriginal sentencing (or healing) circles were developed in several Aboriginal communities, often with the support of local judges.[54] These initiatives have achieved some success in retaining offenders within their communities and developing rehabilitative processes for them, often including traditional Aboriginal practices such as sweat lodges or retreats to places of reflection. As one Aboriginal scholar and judge has put it, "Healing is an Aboriginal justice principle which is slowly being merged into Canadian criminal law through the practice of circle sentencing and community-based diversion programs."[55]

The Supreme Court of Canada has recognized the necessity of responding to the over-representation of Aboriginal people in Canadian penal institutions. The Supreme Court has stated that "the excessive imprisonment of Aboriginal people is only the tip of the iceberg insofar as the estrangement of the Aboriginal people from Canadian justice is concerned."[56] According to the Supreme Court, a sentencing court ought to consider other sentencing options, even if a term of incarceration would normally be appropriate.

2.2.3   The *Youth Criminal Justice Act*, 2002

The *Youth Criminal Justice Act* (YCJA) formalizes some of the informal strategies advocated under the previous youth legislation and used by police. These include warnings and cautions, referrals to community programs and other measures taken outside the formal court process. The YCJA confers statutory recognition on these types of informal interventions and provides a detailed set of principles for their application. Extra-judicial measures include warnings and referrals to community programs for less serious offences, as well as formal reparation orders and community service for more serious cases. In the latter case, the offender must first accept responsibility for the offence in order to access extra-judicial measures.

The YCJA contains an important declaration of principles that sets out the objectives behind the implementation of this new regime. These objectives are to ensure a rehabilitative focus in responses to youth crime; to maintain a separation between the adult and youth systems; and to reinforce respect for community and individual values, and for interests that are affected by criminal behaviour. Many of these principles are contained in the earlier *Young Offenders Act*, but the new legislation "appears to reflect a shift away from considerations such as society's denunciation of offending behaviour, and the short-term protection of the public from offenders, that tend to favour custodial dispositions for young offenders."[57]

2.2.4   UN Declaration of "Basic Principles on the Use of Restorative Justice Programmes in Criminal Matters"

The United Nations Commission on Crime Prevention and Criminal Justice developed a draft resolution, "Basic Principles on the Use of Restorative Justice Programmes in Criminal Matters."[58] Canada has taken a leading role in sponsoring this resolution and hosted a major meeting of international experts in October 2001 to draft a set of basic principles for further consideration by this Commission. The "Basic Principles on the Use of Restorative Justice Programmes in Criminal Matters" lends strong international support to the concept of restorative processes and outcomes at "all stages" of the criminal justice process. The principles of the Declaration emphasize party self-determination and voluntariness and refer to the need for procedural safeguards, including the availability of legal advice and full provision of information to participants in advance of any restorative process.[59]

Most significantly, perhaps, the Declaration calls for national governments to take steps—through consultation between criminal justice authorities and program administrators— to develop guidelines and standards for the operation of restorative justice processes. These standards may require the imprimatur of legislative authority. As one commentator on the Declaration expresses it, "If restorative justice is to become a legitimate legal alternative in the international setting, this Declaration is a promising first step."[60]

The Declaration provides a clear acknowledgment that states should develop national policy for the development of restorative justice initiatives that assume a proactive role for government. How the Government of Canada may take such steps toward the "mainstreaming" of fair, effective and safe restorative justice processes is taken up in Chapter 7.

2.2.5 Department of Justice Canada's values and principles of restorative justice in criminal matters

Following the release of the United Nations declaration, the Department of Justice Canada launched a round of consultations to develop a statement of values and principles of restorative justice in criminal matters and guidelines for restorative justice programs that could be used in Canada. The values and principles document establishes eleven basic principles and procedural safeguards for the use of restorative justice, and a set of program guidelines. The values and principles and the program guidelines were the subject of extensive consultation undertaken in conjunction with the Conflict Resolution Network. Results of this consultation are posted on the network's website.[61]

Basic Principles and Procedural Safeguards for the Use of Restorative Justice

1. Participation of a victim and offender in a restorative justice process should be based on their free, voluntary and informed consent. Each party should receive a clear explanation of what the process might involve and the possible consequences of their decision to participate. Consent to participate may be withdrawn at any stage.

2. The victim and offender must accept as true the essential facts of the offence, and the offender must accept responsibility for the offence.

3. The facts must provide sufficient evidence to proceed with a charge, and the prosecution of the offence must not be barred at law.

4. The offender has the right to seek legal advice before and at all stages of the process.

5. Referrals to a restorative process can occur at all stages of the criminal justice system from pre-charge diversion through to post-sentencing and post-release from custody in appropriate cases, and taking into account relevant prosecution policies.

6. Referrals to and conduct of a restorative process must take account of the safety and security of the parties and any power imbalances between victim and offender with respect to either person's age, maturity, gender, intellectual capacity, position in the community or other factors. In particular, implied or explicit threats to the safety of either party, and whether there is a continuing relationship between the parties, must be of paramount concern.

7. All discussions within the restorative process, other than those conducted in public, must remain confidential, unless agreed to the contrary by the victim and offender, and may not be used in any subsequent legal process.

8. The admission of responsibility by the offender for the offence is an essential part of the restorative process, and cannot be used as evidence against the offender in any subsequent legal process.

9. All agreements must be made voluntarily and must contain only reasonable, proportionate and clear terms.

10. The failure to reach or to complete a restorative agreement must not be used in any subsequent criminal proceedings to justify a more severe sentence than would otherwise have been imposed on the offender.

11. A restorative justice program should be evaluated regularly to ensure that it continues to operate on sound principles and to meet its stated goals.

2.3   RESTORATIVE JUSTICE PROCESSES

It is within this context that restorative justice processes emerged in Canada. In this section, we review some of the more common forms of restorative justice in use in Canada. Each of these short descriptions will address three critical design issues for restorative justice processes: the convening and format of the intervention, the timing of the intervention, and the relationship between the restorative justice initiative and the formal criminal justice system.

2.3.1 Victim–offender mediation

Victim–offender mediation (VOM) and victim–offender reconciliation programs (VORPs) are among the earliest models of contemporary restorative justice processes. In VOM and VORPs the offender and the victim are voluntarily brought together—either before sentence or sometimes many years after sentence and incarceration—in the presence of a trained mediator.[62] In Kitchener, Mark Yantzi and Dave Worth asked a judge to permit them to try a different approach in dealing with two young offenders arrested for vandalism. The approach was to allow the victims and the offenders to take a key role in deciding the most appropriate method of responding to the harm done by the conflict. A satisfactory resolution—direct reparations—was reached, and the first Canadian VORP was born. Since then, the scope of mediation practices has grown considerably, with VORPs emerging across North America in the 1980s, often initiated by faith communities attempting to facilitate some type of face-to-face engagement between minor offenders and the victims of their crimes. In their earliest days, VORPs were staffed wholly or almost wholly by community volunteers and operated quite independently of the formal justice system. Formal systems for the diversion of cases into VORPs gradually developed during the late 1980s.

VOM and VORPs usually rely heavily on a volunteer base, and they are now generally located within the criminal court. Many VOM programs are formally sponsored by probation or youth justice departments, which make referrals of individual cases. Some programs work closely with Crown prosecutors to select cases appropriate for referral to mediation.[63] Sometimes a local criminal court judge will recommend that a matter be referred to mediation.[64]

In common with other restorative justice initiatives, referral into mediation can take place at any of four points in the processing of a criminal event: police entry point (that is, pre-charge); Crown entry point (that is, post-charge but pre-trial); court entry point (generally at the sentencing stage); and corrections entry point (following incarceration and before release).[65,66]

Intervention at any of these four points requires a close working relationship with the formal justice system. These schemes can function as a form of diversion from the formal justice system and they are often built into existing alternative measures programs that are operated by community agencies in cooperation with justice officials.[67] In some programs, when a referral takes place pre-charge, an offender may not receive a criminal record since there is no formal finding of guilt by a criminal court.[68] Where mediation takes place before sentencing and the matter has not been formally diverted to an alternative measures program, the outcome of a VOM usually goes back to the Crown and the trial judge for consideration.

Fraser Region Community Justice Initiatives Association

The Fraser Region Community Justice Initiatives Association has been running conflict resolution programs for more than 20 years. First conceived by the Langley Mennonite Fellowship, the Association has grown into a multi-program organization, operating within settings that include the criminal justice system, educational institutions, businesses and community centres. The Association provides training in mediation through a framework that involves materials development and a practicum-based curriculum. Current programs also include the Victim–Offender Reconciliation Program, the Victim–Offender Mediation Program, and the Educating for Peacebuilding initiative. Both programs involve direct contact between the parties to create understanding and initiate the healing process. Through the Educating for Peacebuilding initiative, the Association has developed a relationship with Langley School District 35 to help foster a climate that promotes restorative justice principles and values.

For more information visit <http://www.cjibc.org/>.

In another example, the Collaborative Justice Project characterizes its work as facilitating "the human repair work that is not addressed by the legal process. Where this repair work results in a resolution agreement developed by all parties, the agreement is submitted to the court for consideration at the time of sentencing."[69] In addition, rather than operating as an alternative to punishment, some restorative justice processes operate after sentencing, with the express purpose of providing an opportunity for a victim and offender to meet to exchange information.[70]

Restorative Resolutions

Restorative Resolutions is operated in Winnipeg by the John Howard Society of Manitoba in conjunction with Manitoba Justice and other stakeholders. The program was initiated in 1993 as a restorative justice demonstration project. Organizers included periodic evaluations in the development of the program structure. Restorative Resolutions was undertaken with a firm commitment to finding community-based alternatives to incarceration. Referrals are invited from a wide variety of sources, including Community and Youth Corrections, Crown and defence attorneys, judges, family members and community agencies. A framework for acceptance into the program was created with criteria based on Crown sentencing recommendations, offender motivation, and a requisite guilty plea. Accepted offenders must agree to a jointly developed community action plan that incorporates victim options, recommendations to the court and ongoing supervision. The most recent outcomes report (November 2002) cites 1,039 referrals to the program since its inception.

For more information about Restorative Resolutions, visit the John Howard Society of Manitoba website: <http://www.johnhoward.mb.ca/>.

2.3.2 Community and family group conferencing

Originating in family group conferencing, which was developed and applied to youth justice processes in New Zealand,[71] conferencing

Calgary Community Conferencing

Calgary Community Conferencing (CCC) began as a part-time initiative of Calgary's Youth Probation Services in 1998. The following year, a collaborative, community-based approach was developed and extended to include the participation of Calgary Family Services, the Calgary Board of Education, Calgary Police Services, the John Howard Society and the Mennonite Central Committee. CCC brings together youth and their family or supporters, and anyone affected by the young person's wrongful acts. High-impact incidents are referred to the program from Calgary Youth Court or from schools where a student is in danger of suspension or expulsion. Preparatory meetings are held with every individual affected and together they develop and implement an agreement. CCC stresses community involvement in the justice process, facilitation of youth-initiated agreements, and effective preparation of all participants in the justice process.

The number of youth referred to CCC has steadily increased over the four years of the program. In 2001–02, CCC worked with more than 150 youth and their families and victims. Halfway through 2002–03, CCC had worked with 140 youth.

For more information visit:
<http://www.calgarycommunityconferencing.com/>.

models are now widely used in restorative justice initiatives. A coordinator will invite the family and friends of both the victim and the offender to participate in a discussion to explore appropriate ways to address the offending behaviour and desired outcomes for the family or the community. The focus of conferencing processes may, therefore, be somewhat broader than that of VOM since conferencing processes evaluate the impact of offender's behaviour not just on the primary victim, but on others as well. Those involved will then develop a plan for monitoring the offender's future behaviour and set out any reparative elements deemed necessary. Conferences are seen as an effective means of ensuring follow-through on agreed outcomes because of the larger number of individuals who are asked to commit to the rehabilitation plan.[72] This is in marked contrast to traditional criminal procedure in which community input into sentencing is rarely, if ever, available.[73]

2.3.3 Sentencing circles

Sentencing circles operate in many Aboriginal communities in Canada. Sentencing circles allow victims, offenders, community elders, other community members and court officials to discuss the consequences of a conflict and explore ways of resolving it. Restitution for damages and reintegration of the wrongdoer into the community are high priorities. Community members play an active role in assisting the victim and the wrongdoer with the healing process. Some of these circles—for instance, the Circle Sentencing model developed in the Yukon by Judge Barry Stuart[74]—operate within the formal justice system as an alternative to the conventional sentencing process, and include justice professionals (police, probation officers, defence counsel, Crown counsel and judges). The plan developed by the circle may be adopted by the judge either in the circle (if the judge sits in on circles) or in a subsequent court hearing. As with the outcomes of court-connected VOM, in cases not formally diverted, the plan formulated by the circle is not binding on the court, although it is generally taken very seriously.[75]

Circles are also sometimes used if cases are diverted from the justice system into alternative-measures programs (usually reserved for first-time youth offenders). Where diversion programs are hosted by community agencies, the agency itself—and principally the members of the circle or panel—will take primary responsibility for monitoring the alternative measures, with or without oversight by justice officials. Other circles are simply a gathering of those most concerned about the offender and the victim, and any other community members with an interest in the process.

Aboriginal Legal Services of Toronto's Community Council Program

"The Community Council is a project that allows the Aboriginal community of Toronto to take a measure of control over the manner that the criminal justice system deals with Aboriginal offenders.

If the Crown consents to the diversion, the offender is approached and asked if they wish to go before the Council. Since the Council cannot decide guilt or innocence, the accused person must first admit that they are responsible, to some degree, for their charge(s). Before the individual decides whether they wish to go before the Council, they are required to consult with defence/duty counsel. Counsel will also stress to individuals that if they feel they are not guilty of the offence then they should try for an acquittal in court. If the accused person agrees to go before the Council, the charge(s) against him or her are stayed or withdrawn by the Crown Attorney.

The Council will reach its decision by consensus and only the individuals involved with the offence themselves discuss their cases with the Council. Where the offence involves a victim, every effort is made to encourage victim participation in the hearing.

The role of the Community Council is to begin the healing process necessary to reintegrate the individual into the community. In deciding how best to accomplish this healing, the Council will make a decision requiring the individual to do certain things. Any option, except jail, is available to them in making this decision. Some options include counselling, restitution, community service, treatment suggestions or a combination of the above.

(continued)

> The concept of the Community Council is not new. This is the way justice was delivered in Aboriginal communities in Central and Eastern Canada for centuries before the arrival of Europeans to North America. It is also the way that disputes continue to be informally resolved in many reserve communities across the country. The idea behind the Community Council Program is that the Aboriginal community best know how to reach Aboriginal offenders. We know that the dominant justice system does nothing but provide a revolving door from the street to the jail and back again for most Aboriginal accused."
>
> Excerpt from the Aboriginal Legal Services of Toronto's website:
> <http://www.Aboriginallegal.ca/council.php>.

2.3.4 Community boards or panels

Community panels are made up of volunteers drawn from the community who meet formally with offenders and victims to facilitate a discussion of appropriate outcomes. Again, panel hearings can be conceived either as a pre-charge diversion from the formal system or as an alternative means to determine an appropriate sentence after a guilty plea has been entered. The use of community panels is presently more developed in the United States than in Canada,[76] and data on their activities are limited. One of the first panels in Canada was developed in Whitehorse, Yukon Territory.

Following a discussion (or "hearing"), the panel and the offender make a contract stipulating what the offender will do during a probationary period. There is an emphasis on reparation and responsibility-taking by the individual offender. The probation contract is generally supervised by members of the panel, but in the event of breaches[77] the offender will be referred back to the court for sentencing. In the United States, state corrections departments have sponsored a number of the leading programs that take referrals directly from criminal court judges.[78]

The Whitehorse Youth Justice Panel

"The Whitehorse Youth Justice Panel, Yukon, Canada is a post-charge inter-agency screening program for young offenders. The first of its kind in Canada, the Youth Justice Panel was implemented in March 2001. The Youth Justice Panel goals are to increase referrals to extra judicial measures; reduce court-processing time; reduce length of stay in remand; reduce custody committals; build partnerships; and enhance family and community capacity to repair harm. These goals embody restorative principles of the *Youth Criminal Justice Act* (2003), including victim, family and community participation; diversion and reduced custody; reparation of harm; offender accountability and rehabilitation."

Charles R. Stuart and Jennifer Eakins, "The Whitehorse Youth Justice Panel: an Evaluation," paper presented at the 6th International Conference on Restorative Justice, Simon Fraser University, Vancouver, B.C., June 2003.

2.3.5   Other participatory processes

Besides VOM and community circles and panels, a range of other restorative justice practices has evolved, and innovative processes continue to emerge. For example, restorative justice principles have influenced the development of many school-based programs, including peer mediation training and anger management education.[79] In addition, circle processes have been used to address school-based conflicts.[80] Churches in Canada are also exploring restorative justice applications. The United Church of Canada, for example, has developed a restorative approach to conflict resolution and has trained volunteer conflict resolution facilitators (CRF) nationally who use restorative approaches such as circle processes and mediation to deal with disputes in local church congregations.

Restorative justice processes also take place in prisons with incarcerated offenders, preparing them for reintegration into their communities.[81] For example, the Correctional Service of Canada (CSC) has shown a strong commitment to the principles of restorative justice by establishing a Restorative Justice and Dispute Resolution Branch that works with internal and external partners. Successful restorative opportunities have been created through victim-offender mediation of serious crime, surrogate programs, peacemaking circles and other initiatives. At several penitentiaries, inmates, community members and staff have collaborated to create Restorative Justice Coalitions that have advanced educational initiatives. At Grande Cache Institution, a research-based pilot Restorative Justice Living Unit has been established where restorative justice principles have been integrated into operational routine. Working with local Aboriginal communities, the CSC has incorporated many restorative justice principles in Healing Lodges across the country and in working to develop and implement inclusive measures intended to safely and successfully reintegrate Aboriginal offenders. In addition, many of CSC's Citizens Advisory Committees have demonstrated an active interest in restorative justice. Working with the Mennonite Church, CSC funded the development of the successfully researched Circles of Support and Accountability, a program in which small groups of volunteers form a support circle with a high-risk sex offender. CSC has also taken steps to enhance interaction with victims as part of its ongoing commitment to inclusive processes. CSC recently completed an international literature review summarizing correctional restorative justice developments.[82]

2.4 OBJECTIVES OF RESTORATIVE JUSTICE

The diverse origins of restorative justice initiatives, as well as the wide range of practice models, makes developing shared objectives and values for restorative justice processes a challenging task. It is, however, possible to distil from these practices a set of objectives and values that animate most restorative justice processes.

The discussion that follows describes five key objectives for restorative justice processes that seem to be shared among programs and proponents of restorative justice. These objectives are:

- Denouncing unacceptable behaviour;

- Supporting victims;

- Reforming individual offenders through active responsibility-taking;

- Restoring community order and peace; and

- Identifying restorative, forward-looking outcomes.

2.4.1 Denouncing unacceptable behaviour

Restorative justice processes do not take a value-free approach to anti-social behaviour. Denunciation of certain behaviours is an objective of restorative justice, just as it is in the formal retributive model.[83] However, the process of arriving at a denunciation is quite different from that used by the adversarial criminal justice system, and the measure of what is unacceptable is examined in a broad context.

Restorative justice attempts to deliver "deliberative justice" that is not circumscribed by legal definitions.[84] Restorative justice processes aim to identify the locus of responsibility and assess the impact of the harm caused by the behaviour in question, rather than meeting pre-existing criteria of harm. Restorative justice is a flexible response to the circumstances of the behaviour. Because each case is considered individually, the parameters of unacceptable behaviour may change from case to case. In this way, the nature of the wrong and that of its consequences are flexible. Nonetheless, the commitment of restorative justice to identifying unacceptable behaviours and to acting to minimize their impact and reduce potential repeat offending means that restorative justice processes go beyond dealing with particular incidents and cases of law-breaking and harm, and offer a general social mechanism for the reinforcement of standards of appropriate behaviours.[85]

Of course, the assessment of behaviours as inappropriate and unacceptable does not take place in a vacuum. Participants in restorative justice processes are undoubtedly affected by their knowledge and experience of the existing criminal law, their degree of proximity to the offender and the behaviour, and the prevailing social climate in relation to crime and recidivism. There are also entrenched assumptions—although these are now being challenged in a few restorative justice processes[86]—about the appropriateness of restorative justice for serious crime. These assumptions reflect wider external values about punishment and imprisonment. What behaviour should be declared off-limits and where the lines on punishable or culpable behaviour should be drawn may vary widely between restorative justice advocates. At the same time, just what denunciation should look like and amount to will also vary widely.[87]

This pluralism gives rise to concerns about delegating the authority to denounce and forgive certain types of conduct to restorative justice processes, which may function inside or outside the formal justice system. The development of standards for acceptable and unacceptable behaviour can be a vehicle for progressive and community development, as well as for the intolerance and even tyranny of homogeneous groups. This is a particular concern if there are already entrenched inequalities of power and privilege within the community.[88]

2.4.2   Support for victims

A central theme in restorative justice initiatives has been to give a voice to the victims of crime in the dispute resolution process. We have already discussed the disenfranchisement and alienation of victims from the criminal justice process. As that discussion recognizes, motivations for placing the needs of victims centre stage in criminal justice processes vary widely.[89] Most victims' groups challenge the assumption that the state can and should stand in the shoes of victims. Instead, victims' groups are looking to the state for "a much greater appreciation of the legitimacy of the participation by victims in the disposition of the crimes they have experienced."[90]

The focus on the offender in the state prosecutorial model means that the expertise of justice professionals is oriented toward offenders, not victims. Restorative justice processes reconceptualize the victim as the focal point in the conflict resolution process. As a consequence, the victim's role is central to restorative justice processes—victims are provided a voice, an opportunity to ask questions and a process in which to confront their fears.[91] Further, by participating in decision-making, victims can exercise some power regarding outcomes.

"In victim–offender mediation, the needs of the victim and the degree to which the victim desires retribution or recompense may be more influential on the outcome of the process than either the category of offence or the culpability of the offender."

John Belgrave, "Restorative Justice: A Discussion Paper," Secretary for Justice, Ministry of Justice, New Zealand, 1996, online: <www.justice.govt.nz/pubs/reports/1996/restorative/Default.htm> at 2.5.1.

When they participate, victims are generally satisfied with restorative justice processes. Most evaluation studies report a high rate of victim satisfaction with these processes. Mark Umbreit, director of the Center for Restorative Justice and Peacemaking at the University of Minnesota, has conducted a number of thorough program evaluations. In one of these, Professor Umbreit and his colleagues in the Minneapolis and Saint Paul Victim–Offender Reconciliation Program found that 84 percent of victims interviewed indicated that it was helpful to them to meet with the offender, and some reported reduced fears about re-victimization.[92]

A recent study by Justice Canada found that restorative justice programs, when used in appropriate cases, are effective methods of improving satisfaction for both victims and offenders, increasing offender compliance with restitution and decreasing recidivism when compared with more traditional criminal justice measures.[93] Wemmers and Canuto[94] reviewed the literature on victims' experiences with restorative justice. Their review showed that most victims who participated in a restorative justice program were satisfied with their experiences and that they benefited from the process, particularly through meetings with the offender. Victims participate in restorative justice programs to seek reparation, help the offender, confront the offender with the consequences of the crime, and ask questions, such as why the offence was committed. Victims decline to participate in restorative justice programs for a variety of reasons: they do not think it is worth the effort; they fear the offender; they are too angry with the offender; or they disbelieve the offender's sincerity.

The Results of a Meta-analysis

"We are currently in a period of substantial change; but, as the results of this meta-analysis indicate, we are moving in a positive direction. The addition of restorative justice programs has enhanced victim satisfaction in a process that was, by its very nature, rather unsatisfactory. Moreover, this response to criminal behaviour has a strong impact by encouraging more offenders to take responsibility for their actions and repair through restitution some of the harm they have caused. And while the gains made in recidivism are not as strong as 'appropriate correctional treatment', restorative justice does appear to reduce recidivism for those who choose to participate. Finally, offenders in restorative justice programs report moderate increases in satisfaction compared to offenders in the traditional system."

J. Latimer, C. Dowden and D. Muise,
The Effectiveness of Restorative Justice Practices: A Meta-analysis
(Ottawa: Department of Justice, 2001) at 23.

Umbreit and colleagues have published the results of evaluation studies of four American VOM programs,[95] four Canadian programs[96] and two VOMs located in the United Kingdom.[97] Each study included a control group. In each case participation in mediation was voluntary (about 40 percent of those referred to mediation took up the opportunity), and in all but a small number of the cases in the United Kingdom, dialogue between victim and offender was face-to-face in the presence of a third party. The group recording the lowest victim satisfaction with the outcome of the mediation (74 percent) was the one that participated in shuttle mediation rather than in face-to-face discussions. In the United States, 90 percent of the victims declared themselves satisfied with the mediation outcome, and 89 percent did so in Canada.[98] In the four Canadian programs, 79 percent of the victims did not fear being re-victimized.

> "In terms of victims specifically, there appears to be overall satisfaction (89 percent) [with the Collaborative Justice Project] due mainly to the fact that someone in the system attended to their needs, they had an active role in the criminal justice process, and there was an attempt to repair the harm that they experienced. However, it is important to note that only 58 percent of cases resulted in a victim–offender meeting, suggesting that a face-to-face meeting is not necessarily needed to meet the victims' needs."
>
> T. A. Rugge and R. B. Cormier (Department of the Solicitor General of Canada), "Restorative Justice in Cases of Serious Crimes: An Evaluation," paper presented at the 6th International Conference on Restorative Justice, Simon Fraser University, Vancouver, B.C., June 2003.

While generally promising, victim satisfaction data have some limitations. First, it is important to distinguish between victims of minor crimes and those of serious crimes. Are satisfaction rates as high for victims of serious crimes as they are for those of minor crimes? Second, high satisfaction scores may be a result of self-selection. For example, it is possible that victims who participated in a restorative justice process had a positive attitude toward mediation prior to participating in the process. Third, it is necessary to examine the relationship between victim satisfaction and demographic variables such as age, gender, race and ethnic origin. Finally, evaluations must examine why some victims refuse to participate in restorative justice processes.[99]

Preliminary evaluation data on victim satisfaction are promising, but this is only part of the story. Victims' personal accounts are perhaps more revealing of the ways in which restorative justice processes can meet the needs of victims in the aftermath of crime. Many personal accounts testify to the power of the processes to facilitate healing and closure for victims.[100]

Another practical dimension of victims' needs that appears to be met by restorative justice initiatives is follow-through with agreed reparations and restitution. Like civil mediation, restorative processes claim a higher rate of individual compliance with outcomes that are consensually agreed to than orders imposed by a court. Umbreit reports that victims who participate in court-administered VOM programs receive reparation in 81 percent of cases, compared with 54 percent who did not participate in mediation.[101] Marshall and Merry also report on a number of American studies that show higher rates of compliance as a result, they suggest, of the positive attitudes developed between the parties in the process of face-to-face dialogue.[102] Further, and perhaps more importantly, victims may receive an apology as a result of a participatory process—apologies are not generally available to them in the adversarial process.[103]

> "If cases are mediated, there is no question about short-term success: most victims and offenders are satisfied with the process and outcomes, an agreement is reached in practically all cases, and the vast majority of restorative plans are completed by offenders. This is true for earlier as well as more recent studies, both juvenile and adult programmes, and in U.S. and international evaluations. Satisfaction, agreement, and completion rates typically vary between 75 and 100 per cent."
>
> L. Kurki, "Evaluating Restorative Justice Practices," in A. Von Hirsch, J.V. Roberts, A. Bottoms, K. Roach and M. Schiff (eds.), *Restorative Justice and Criminal Justice: Competing or Reconcilable Paradigms* (Oxford: Hart Publishing, 2003) at 295.

Nonetheless, significant concerns persist about the capacity of restorative justice to place victims at the centre of the process of resolution, especially initiatives operating within the formal criminal justice system and including justice officials. Can restorative justice really be victim oriented? It is not clear that given the opportunity, victims would jump at the chance to engage in face-to-face dialogue with an offender. A number of programs report low rates of take-up by victims invited to participate in either mediation or group conferencing.[104] Some victims reject the idea of meeting and talking with the offender altogether; others agree to communicate by proxy (such as through written statements or shuttle mediation). A further concern is that some victims may be pressured-by their families, communities or perhaps program advocates-to participate in restorative processes in which they feel uncomfortable or even intimidated.

Aboriginal women in particular have voiced fears that women who have experienced sexual or physical abuse may feel pressured to participate in community circles, despite feeling unsafe. A 1996 evaluation of the Hollow Water First Nations Holistic Circle Healing (CHCH) process reported that victims were generally supportive of the program but less so than offenders; many victims felt pressure from the community to process their complaint (at that time the Hollow Water program was dealing primarily with sexual abuse cases) in the circle, rather than in criminal court; and generally felt unsupported by the community.[105] A report prepared for the Law Commission by AWAN highlighted a paradox that some Aboriginal women are confronted with. While many Aboriginal women recognize the debilitating effects that the adversarial justice system has on Aboriginal communities and want to support alternative ways of resolving conflict, they question whether their concerns and their interests can be met in their communities as they currently exist.

More broadly, restorative justice processes must include specific protection for vulnerable populations. For example, a significant number of individuals who get caught up in the criminal justice system have mental health problems, which may impair their ability to make an informed decision to enter into a restorative justice program. Where the mental health of a victim or an offender is an issue, mental health professionals should participate in intake procedures to ensure that the victim is fully aware of the implications of any decision they make. Special care should be taken to ensure that they have the cognitive capacity to meaningfully participate in the process. Once the restorative justice process commences, a mental health professional should be available to provide services when required.

"It was evident in many of the accounts that women felt they had less power in their communities than men and that the system was designed to privilege and benefit males. The power imbalances within these communities are usually complex and bureaucratic. Band councils were often cited as reflecting the ways of the colonizer, with men holding power in the communities. Focus group participants expressed tremendous concern with the diversion of cases of violence against women and children because they felt that the majority of support goes to offenders along with a prevalence of victim-blaming mentalities. A lack of concern for the safety needs of women and children, particularly in isolated communities was also cited as a major concern in processes such as 'Victim–Offender Mediation'. In such situations, women must confront her abuser. This could have grave implications, in terms of psychological and physical safety, if the offender were to remain in the community."

W. Stewart, A. Huntley and F. Blaney, "The Implications of Restorative Justice for Aboriginal Women and Children Survivors of Violence: A Comparative Overview of Five Communities in British Columbia," research report prepared for the Law Commission of Canada, July 2001.

Seniors are another potentially vulnerable segment of the population. A study conducted for the Commission examined how the justice system responds to the financial exploitation of the elderly.[106] The authors analyzed the adequacy of the various components of Canadian law in this regard (provisions of the Criminal Code, common law, Quebec civil law, and special legislation applicable to the elderly). They concluded that Canadian law is currently adequate to combat the various forms of elder abuse, including financial exploitation. The difficulty, however, is the application of the law. Many individuals who are exploited are reluctant to ask the police to intervene in what is perceived as a family matter. For example, some elderly victims do not want to take legal action against their children, while others who have been abused and financially exploited tend to feel guilt and shame about what has happened to them, particularly if the abuser is a relative.[107]

Case Example: A Healing Approach to Elder Abuse and Mistreatment

"Mrs. Smith (pseudonym) is an 89-year-old widow who lived alone. The assistance of private and public funded services, plus her family, made it possible for her to live in her own home. One day, she disclosed [to her personal support worker] that her son had taken $40,000.00 from her bank account. Mrs. Smith was given information about various community resources including calling the police and reporting the theft. She refused these options. She said that her son was a good man [and] probably needed the money more than [she]. Furthermore, she needed him to buy her groceries, to run errands, to take her to church each Sunday. The relationship with her son and his family was more important to her than the $40,000.00."

A. Groh, "Restorative Justice: A Healing Approach to Elder Abuse."
Kitchener: Community Care Access Centre of Waterloo Region,
at 2. Online: <http://www.sfu.ca/cfrj/fulltext/groh.pdf>.

2.4.3 The reform of individual offenders through active responsibility-taking

Retribution as a sentencing philosophy has evolved into a moral choice for its advocates, regardless of its instrumental value in reducing recidivism. The retributive model understands responsibility-taking as essentially passive.[108] The offender receives a punishment for engaging in prohibited conduct. It is an acknowledgment of responsibility for past actions, with no sense of taking responsibility for the consequences of the behaviour.[109] Moreover, it is imposed on the offender by the state, instead of being assumed or actively embraced by the offender.

Restitution succeeds where retributive theories fail in relating the punishment to the circumstances of the actual offender and victim and focusing on forward-looking behaviour—both making amends and dealing with other consequences of the offence. Restorative justice processes have a component of restitution attached to them. In their focus on the individual offender and victim, restitution and restorative justice share many objectives and values. What distinguishes restorative justice from restitution is its enlarged lens, which includes the wider community surrounding the individual offender and victim. Whether using VOM or larger group processes—such as circles, community panels or group conferencing—restorative justice has the central objective of encouraging offenders to take responsibility for their actions. Confronted with victims in a mediation setting, offenders are asked to recognize and take responsibility for the impact of their actions. Offenders are asked to take responsibility for their behaviour, not so much in relation to the state as in relation to the individual victims and the communities in which they live.[110] Circles and group conferences enable other community members to be included in responsibility-taking indirectly (for example, by encouraging offenders to take authentic responsibility for the impact of their actions) and perhaps also directly (by sharing in the sense of vulnerability that crime creates for a community).

A circle setting also facilitates the development of group norms and group identity, challenging offenders to take responsibility for the impact of their behaviour, rather than allowing them to hide behind the technical language and rules of the courtroom. The circle includes offenders, making them a part of the group rather than outsiders. Restorative justice processes appear to reduce the likelihood that offenders can simply avoid the human consequences of their actions by pleading guilty or by not testifying. Instead, restorative justice "uses passive responsibility to create a forum in which active responsibility can be fostered."[111]

Certain restorative justice advocates go further in searching for a means of encouraging personal cognitive and emotional change in the offender. Some writers distinguish making amends or feeling sorry from feeling ashamed and taking responsibility.[112,113] The key is that shaming must be "re-integrative"—that is, accepting an offender's acknowledgment of wrong and ensuring that he or she has supporters present during discussion of the impact of his or her behaviour.

> "Shame will become complicated, chronic, more likely to descend into rage if it is not fully confronted. If there is nagging shame under the surface, it is no permanent solution to lash out at others with anger that blames them."
>
> J. Braithwaite, "Restorative Justice: Assessing Optimistic and Pessimistic Accounts" 25 *Crime and Justice* (1999) 1 at 43.

Restorative justice moves beyond assessing legal guilt to determining responsibility for a conflict. Determining responsibility means addressing the immediate context of the event—Did the individual commit the act? But it also means placing the act within a broader context—What were the relationships between the victim, the offender and the community? What are some of the underlying factors that may have been associated with the conflict?

The adversarial criminal justice system equates the attribution of responsibility to a conviction, and conviction is a win–lose proposition: the accused is either guilty or not guilty. Most restorative justice processes allow for a much more nuanced approach to responsibility. In many conflicts, including those that result in criminal charges, the accused may be guilty of the criminal charge and may be fully or partially responsible for the conflict. This is a key difference between restorative justice processes and the adversarial system. In many situations, the accused is both legally guilty and fully responsible for the crime—for example, a typical case of robbery, break and enter, or drunk driving resulting in death. In other situations, the accused may be legally guilty of the crime, but the question of responsibility is less clear-cut.

2.4.4 Community order and peace

Restorative justice aims to increase the effectiveness of our response to crime in terms of community order and peace. Functionally, this means both reducing levels of individual recidivism and, more widely, preventing crime. But an effective response to crime also has a broader and deeper meaning for restorative justice advocates and for actively engaging the community in the dispute resolution process.[114] Restorative justice advocates argue that peace and order can be achieved by expanding community control and narrowing state control over the justice system. While there are fears that restorative justice may expand the state's social control—"net widening"[115]—many argue that the devolution of dispute resolution processes is a way of building stronger, healthier communities.[116]

Traditionally, the jury has been the primary method of involving the community in the justice system.[117] Restorative justice processes suggest a departure from this traditional way of incorporating the community. Juries and community members in a restorative justice process perform many of the same functions. Both examine the facts of the case, both add a layer of accountability, both act as the conscience of the community, and both are a buffer against oppressive and unjust law. The two differ, however, in at least two significant ways. First, juries are supposed to be impartial. Impartiality is a cornerstone of the Canadian justice system. The justice system values decision-making by independent individuals. Juries operate under the assumption that individuals with nothing to lose and nothing to gain from the outcome of the case will make a reasoned decision. Indeed, citizens can be disqualified from participating on a jury if they have any personal connection to the case or if they possess knowledge that may prejudice the decision-making process. Detachment fosters impartiality, and impartiality encourages rational decision-making. Unlike juries, community representatives in restorative justice processes are not impartial.

Second, whereas juries represent communities in the abstract, community representation in restorative justice processes is concrete. The families of the victim and offender, the people who live in the area, those who know the conflicting parties, and those who have a vested interest in the outcome of the case participate directly in the proceedings. Unlike the value of juries, the value of community participants in a restorative justice process resides in the possibility of leveraging their relationship with the offender to bring about a meaningful resolution to the incident. Restorative justice advocates suggest that this expanded role for communities is empowering. It allows communities to actively participate in decisions that have a direct bearing on their lives. The expanded role of communities does, however, suggest a shift away from a formal, detached and rational style of decision-making to one that is much more informal, involved and emotional.

Restorative justice offers the possibility of harnessing the power of individuals to create the social capital required to build strong communities. **Social capital** refers to the elements of social organization, such as networks, norms and social trust, that foster coordination and cooperation for mutual benefit.[118] Social capital helps create interconnections between community members and networks of civic engagement. The interconnectedness of community members often encourages trust, discourages political and economic opportunism, and facilitates collaboration for a common goal.

Participating in a restorative justice program helps build relationships between members of a community. Restorative justice processes bring these individuals into a safe place where differences can be discussed and conflicts can be resolved. Sentencing circles, community justice forums, VOM sessions and other forms of restorative justice offer the possibility of bringing together individuals from a variety of backgrounds who may not normally enter into meaningful relationships with one another. In the context of a sentencing circle or a community forum, these individuals are asked to interact with one another, speak openly and listen to the contribution of others. This increases the density of the web of relationships among community members.

Communities, however, are complex. Communities can be highly stratified by race, gender, class or age. Communities can be inclusive, but they can also impose membership conditions that are highly exclusionary and unjust. Many women's groups, including Aboriginal women's groups, have cautioned about the danger of accepting "the community" as an unqualified social good. There are real concerns that

> "To rebuild a democracy ... we need to do more than motivate people to participate in circles that address problems of living that directly affect their personal relationships. The extra step to democratic citizenship is taken when the citizen moves from participating in a restorative justice conference to being active in some way in the social movement for restorative justice."
>
> J. Braithwaite, "Democracy, Community and Problem Solving," paper presented at the Building Strong Partnerships for Restorative Practices Conference, 5–7 August, 1999, Burlington, Vermont.

> "Restorative Justice envisions the community taking significant responsibility for conducting programs. The creation of new positions of authority creates concern about the participation of diverse community members and how their views are included. The dynamics of communities involve relationships of power—the existence of dominant groups based on age, religion, colour, ability/disability, gender, race, socio-economic status, ethnicity, and sexual orientation; those that lead and those that are led. We cannot assume communities are healthy or safe, or are concerned with creating an equitable status for all their residents. Safeguards must be developed to prevent possible misuse of power created by the alternative programs."
>
> Provincial Association Against Family Violence, *Making It Safe: Women, Restorative Justice and Alternative Dispute Resolution* (St John's, Nfld. and Lab.: Provincial Association Against Family Violence, July 2000) at 12.

restorative justice will reproduce many of the inequalities of the current adversarial process.

AWAN conducted focus groups with women in rural Aboriginal communities in British Columbia.[119] It reported that violence in some rural Aboriginal communities in British Columbia was so pervasive that it had become normalized. Moreover, when women spoke out against violence their voices were silenced. The normalization of violence was accompanied by a lack of social supports and antiviolence programs for the community. AWAN reported that even where social services were available, Aboriginal women often faced discrimination—the police and other social service agencies did not always respond to their calls for help. Finally, the interconnectedness of the lives of community members, particularly those who deliver programs and services, made it especially difficult to maintain confidentiality.

"In Wha Ti, for example, the community sought to establish a justice committee with members who were 'reliable'. This meant that no person who is abusing alcohol, drugs or persons [is] eligible. These criteria proved virtually impossible to meet and so community discussions centred on who had 'recovered' and were now good models and on an acceptance that negative experiences in the past could inform people about appropriate behaviour for the future. This has implications for the restorative justice system as now practiced in many areas, since community members on restorative justice committees are vetted for any criminal record and presumed unable to contribute if they have served time. The flip side of that is that people who have had trouble with the law may have developed the wisdom learned from their experience and may indeed be in a position to counsel people on how to avoid similar problems."

J. Ryan and B. Calliou, "Aboriginal Restorative Justice Alternatives: Two Case Studies", (Ottawa: Law Commission of Canada, 2002), at 5-6.

There is always a danger that restorative justice processes may produce "counterfeit communities." Restorative justice is part of a larger movement, in which governments are entering into partnerships with communities. These new partnerships raise a number of issues regarding the relationship between governments and communities. Partnerships are voluntary arrangements between two or more individuals or organizations that agree to work cooperatively toward a common goal. Successful partnerships extend further than consultation. Successful partnerships are those in which there is a recognition that all parties may not come to the table with equal power and in which steps are taken to ensure that even the least powerful members of the partnership are given equal standing. Partnerships must involve a willingness on the part of government to share power and decision-making with the community. But community members must also be encouraged to assume control of the decision-making process.

A restorative justice program in which experts act on victims and offenders or otherwise exert control over the process is not a partnership, regardless of how much information these experts share with their "clients."

> "The shift from meaningless consultation and sometimes vacuous engagement—usually a snapshot of public opinion captured at a particular moment in time—to genuinely deliberative and interactive citizen engagement will require a fundamental change ... True citizen engagement involves dialogue and listening, the expression and exchange of views, group and individual deliberation, reflection and learning."
>
> S. Torjman, "Strategies for a Caring Society," paper presented at the Conference on Investing in the Whole Community: Strategies for a Caring Society, Toronto, On., 15–16 October 1998, at 10.

Restorative justice principles see conflict within communities as an opportunity for dialogue and change—as a means to better understand the dimensions of peaceful order in a truly inclusive way.[120] The community must take responsibility for high levels of both control and support if peace and order are to be established and maintained, resisting the slide to taking a punitive approach (characterized by high control and low support) or to becoming overly permissive (characterized by low control and high support).[121]

It is implicit that the shape that "peace and order" takes when a community conceptualizes and designs it for itself reflects the community's unique needs and fears. It will be a reflection of what troubles that community, its diversity, and to some extent, its strongest and most persuasive voices. Assessments of what will bring peace and order to the community are made by community members themselves, rather than by justice professionals, who may otherwise "steal" conflicts away from the community and apply the system's definition of peace and order.[122]

> The achievement of community peace and order in the restorative vision thus shifts power away from professionals and toward citizens. In this way, restorative justice enriches democracy. Kay Pranis—one of the leading program developers in the United States—describes restorative justice processes as a classic embodiment of "grassroots democracy." In the face of concerns that community empowerment could result in communities as tyrannical and intolerant as the state itself, the aspiration is that the form of peace and order that emerges will be less about solidarity and more about hospitability and more about inclusivity than exclusivity.
>
> K. Pranis, "Restorative Justice, Social Justice and the Empowerment of Marginalised Populations," in G. Bazemore and M. Schiff (eds.), *Restorative Community Justice: Repairing Harm and Restoring Communities* (Cincinnati, OH: Anderson Publishing, 2001) 287 at 299.

2.4.5 Identifying restorative, forward-looking outcomes

A broadly shared objective for restorative justice processes is the use of constructive, contextually appropriate, and forward-looking outcomes or restorative resolutions. Instead of basing sentencing on predetermined rules with a strong retributive flavour, restorative justice processes strive for outcomes that satisfy a wide group of stakeholders (of whom the Crown is just one). Fair punishment should also have a forward-looking component, for example, apology and reparation by the offender, community service of some sort and, when warranted, a term of incarceration.

When determining an appropriate outcome, those involved in a restorative justice process reflect on the needs of victims, offenders and members of the community. Restorative justice processes do not rule out a term of incarceration as one component of a restorative resolution to a conflict, but they generally are resistant to using incarceration as a reflex reaction to a crime. For example, incarceration may not be the most appropriate punishment if it deprives a family of the principal breadwinner or deprives a community of a person who can contribute positively.

There is also a preventive aspect to forward-looking outcomes.[123] "Prevention" includes the prevention of further interpersonal harm and, if possible, the neutralization of the social harms caused by continuing power imbalances. The objectives of restorative processes are met if the processes are responsive to these types of practical, forward-looking criteria, rather than being overwhelmed by conventional assumptions about the intrinsic moral value of punishment.

The notion of looking forward is key to understanding restorative justice as it affects not only society, but also what transpires between victim and offender. The possibility of a face-to-face discussion between a victim and an offender presupposes that there is a relatedness (not relationship) that will continue to exist between them and that dialogue may help to calm fears and may bring closure. The theme of forgiveness runs through much restorative justice writing, and some programs—although not all—see this as their highest goal. For some faith communities, the willingness to forgive is an important spiritual value. However, it would be inaccurate to characterize forgiveness as an essential objective of restorative justice processes.[124]

While religious values can inspire and motivate forgiveness, these are not a prerequisite.[125] Forgiveness as a coping strategy has many emotional and rational benefits for those who are not motivated by faith but simply want to better survive life's storms. Some values associated with coping with harm in this way include emotional venting, the humanization of the offender and a re-appraisal of the costs of not forgiving and the benefits of doing so.[126]

The Objectives of Restorative Justice

The Commission believes there are five objectives that restorative justice processes ought to strive for:

- Delineating and denunciating unacceptable behaviour;

- Supporting victims;

- Reforming individual offenders through active responsibility-taking;

- Restoring community order and peace; and

- Identifying restorative, forward-looking outcomes.

2.5   CORE PROCESS VALUES FOR RESTORATIVE JUSTICE

Section 2.5 develops the five objectives just described into key process values for restorative justice undertakings. What types of processes and practices best result in achieving the objectives of restorative justice?

2.5.1   Participation

A key process value of restorative justice is to engage victims and offenders in resolving a conflict. Restorative justice objectives can only be met if victims and offenders are permitted to participate in the conflict resolution process. Participation offers several advantages: having a voice in the conflict resolution process, being listened to, and having control over how a conflict is resolved. Participation in the conflict resolution process increases one's sense of fair treatment. Each of these elements is discussed below.

Experience suggests that the expression of an individual voice in a determinative process has value in itself regardless of the impact on eventual outcomes.[127] Writing about mediation processes, some authors [128] argue that the self-expression that empowers the speaker by giving voice to his or her concerns and goals is itself a legitimate objective for the process of dialogue, regardless of whether an agreed, or a "good" outcome results.

The Commission's consultations and research has shown that victims and offenders experience a strong need to articulate thoughts and express feelings about the crime in question.[129] A meeting format that enables a face-to-face exchange of information and perspectives is often key to the premise of restorative justice that "truth" is established through personal experience and interaction. Among other things, discussion can challenge assumptions about the other side's motivations and rationale, fill in gaps or explode theories about the meaning of one another's acts, and challenge stereotyping of motives and behaviours.[130]

Face-to-face dialogue encourages a number of positive outcomes that are important to restorative justice while mitigating the potential for some anticipated negative consequences.[131] Positive outcomes include achieving individual empowerment (through giving voice to fears and hopes); being listened to; developing a process in which, perhaps regardless of outcome, each party feels fairly treated; and gaining some control over a process, rather than being swept along by an unfamiliar procedure.[132]

> "There is nothing in traditional criminal justice procedure that offers to match a successful personal meeting of this kind in destroying delinquent self-images or the assumption that everyone is 'against them' and will be rejecting (the experience most offenders had always anticipated)."
>
> T. Marshall and S. Merry, *Crime and Accountability: Victim/Offender Mediation in Practice* (London: Home Office HMSO, 1990).

Face-to-face dialogue between a victim and an offender may be the purest expression of restorative justice principles in action. Face-to-face dialogue is not, however, the only way in which victims and offenders can participate in the resolution of a conflict. Some victims and offenders may not want to participate in a dialogue. Others may prefer to engage in a video exchange. For example, in the Collaborative Justice Project in Ottawa, only about 40 percent of cases that go through their restorative justice process result in a face-to-face meeting between a victim and an offender. It is vitally important to provide individuals with a range of options. In the end, face-to-face dialogues are one tool that can be used in a restorative process intended to help victims and offenders come to terms with a conflict.

"We contacted the victim and, although somewhat sceptical, he agreed to meet. The victim is a young immigrant who was deeply impacted by the robbery. At this point in the process, he wanted nothing from the accused. He did, however, want to convey to the accused how this had affected him, i.e., his increased fear, his growing bias against teenagers and what the loss of his immigration card would have meant to him.

We relayed this information to [the offender] who seemed to gain a fuller comprehension of the issues the victim was dealing with. He offered to write a letter of apology to the victim.

The victim was open to receiving a letter. He seemed to be somewhat surprised at the level of sincerity expressed in the letter. The victim began to share more of what this experience had meant to him and admitted that he had missed work the week following the robbery due to his fear. As a result he lost wages amounting to $800.00."

Case story from the Collaborative Justice Project, Ottawa, available on the Church Council on Justice and Corrections website: <http://www.ccjc.ca/news/casestories.cfm>.

A parallel element to having a voice is being listened to.[133] Being listened to is strongly associated with validation and the acknowledgment of one's losses or suffering. Acknowledgment and validation are strongly advocated by a growing number of mediation practitioners and scholars who propose what is sometimes described as a communication frame for negotiation and dialogue (as contrasted with the settlement frame, which focuses on the delineation of the technical and factual issues to resolve the presenting dispute).[134] "The need to be heard is often as important as the need to resolve the problem."[135]

For some disputants, control over process is exemplified by being able to tell their own story in their own words. Control over process may also extend to developing suitable process norms; for example, participants can be invited to propose their own basic rules of courtesy and civility for a circle setting or a VOM. Restorative justice processes characteristically impose on participants a set of threshold ground rules that recognize the importance of respect and civility (other particular ground rules may be added by the participants themselves). Perhaps most important of all for restorative practices, however, is the idea that in meeting in this way the participants are taking back control over their conflict from a state model that de-personalized their experience.[136] One strategy used by many practitioners working in the restorative justice area is to conduct preparatory sessions with both offenders and victims, either separately or together. This can assist the parties by clarifying how the process will work, what their role in it will be, what expectations they will face, what will make the process constructive, and so on.[137]

The importance of face-to-face dialogue in giving voice to both offender and victim, as well as others affected by the behaviours, highlights the need for a skilful third party, whether acting as a circle moderator, mediator, panel chair or in some other position. It is important that the third party ensure that these values are maintained throughout the dialogue, for example by requiring respectful listening and shared talking time. However, the third party must not "take" the opportunity for conciliation, or at least better understanding, from the parties by over-structuring and controlling the dialogue.[138]

2.5.2 Respect for all participants

Respectful behaviour toward all participants in a circle, a mediation or other restorative justice forum is a necessary corollary of the principle of face-to-face dialogue. However, it is not an inevitable consequence and, in the often emotionally charged environment of victim–offender interaction, it is worth stating explicitly as a key process value for restorative justice. Respectful treatment is a procedural value and need not be identical to structural equality of the parties, something which might be difficult to achieve in a criminal justice context. The offender will usually have already accepted responsibility for the wrongful conduct, and the victim will already have been seen as the wronged person, thereby establishing a structural inequality from the outset. While circles and other restorative processes cannot provide structural or psychological equality, they must be explicit and proactive in their commitment to respectful treatment of all participants, including offenders. Significant in achieving this goal is the effort of restorative justice practices to place the problem, and not the person, at the centre of the process. The offender often cares deeply what the victim thinks about them.[139] The opportunity for face-to-face dialogue can reduce or alleviate the tendency to demonize the offender and enables the beginnings of mutual respect.

2.5.3 Community empowerment

Another key process value for restorative justice is the participation of the community, whether delineated by family ties, membership in a geographically defined group (for example, neighbourhood or residents of an Aboriginal community, etc.), or some other connection to the victim or offender or affected community. The concept of community involvement has provoked some scepticism, especially outside more closely knit communities such as Aboriginal groups or smaller rural communities. Questions that are raised include: Who decides who should participate in a circle or other restorative justice process? Is participation by invitation only—the practice with family group conferencing[140]—or can anyone sit in the circle to discuss fair outcomes when an offender has admitted a charge? The victim may feel that the circle is stacked with friends and supporters of the offender.[141] Who speaks for the wider community in the circle, and with what legitimacy and what mandate? Are there key persons of influence (and sometimes expertise) in communities whose participation is critical, such as elders, respected older students within a school community, youth workers or probation officers, or even the local magistrate?

If decisions about participation in the circle or other restorative justice process are made unwisely, other key process values risk being compromised: for example, the value of ensuring that the offender and the victim find their voice in face-to-face dialogue and the values of respecting all participants and any agreed outcomes. To better understand the significance of participation as a process value in restorative justice, it is important to link it to the notion of empowerment. This means that the participants in the process see the problem not just as something that affects their lives now, but as something that may continue to affect their community and see that the problem requires the attention of more than just the two formal parties-the Crown and the offender-or even these two parties and the victim. Community empowerment assumes that antisocial behaviours and criminal events are not entirely private affairs.[142] It also assumes that even though the state has made a decision to prosecute the accused, the community still has a role in the conflict resolution process.

If this ideal notion of community empowerment is not to descend into community tyranny and vigilantism, it is critical that when community members discuss accountability for antisocial or criminal behaviour, they do more than look for an individual to blame. Instead, participation must be based on a genuine recognition that the wider group-the neighbourhood, the school or the extended family circle-has a role to play in the restorative process. This includes working with the offender to enable them to take personal responsibility by "harnessing sources of social control within families, schools and neighbours as well as among public institutions."[143]

2.5.4 Commitment to agreed outcomes

Restorative justice practices vary widely in the degree to which they rely on formal enforcement and compliance monitoring. In some programs, any breach of the terms of a restorative resolution may result in referral back to a trial judge for formal sentencing. In other situations, including some types of community service and some Aboriginal circles, there is less formal monitoring and greater reliance on the integrity and honour of the offender. Just as respect for participants in restorative justice processes is not the same as equality of the participants, a commitment to agreed outcomes is not the same as an entirely voluntary acceptance of outcomes: for the offender, there may be significant incentive to avoid a custodial term, and for the victim, there may be an incentive to avoid the trauma of testifying at a trial. However, data collected from restorative justice processes suggest that voluntary compliance rates are high.[144]

2.5.5 Flexibility and responsiveness of process and outcomes

This fifth and final process represents an important tenet of the restorative justice movement. A tension arises between, on the one hand, the goal of providing respectful and respected processes for a dialogue that reflects individual and community needs and, on the other hand, the need for structure and control. The very nature of restorative justice processes and their emphasis on informality rejects the one-size-fits-all approach of the traditional adjudicative model. Moreover, some of the concerns about the potential for the tyranny of community are only properly addressed if communities are self-conscious about their assumptions of good or fair process and ensure that they can be responsive to both cultural diversity and individual needs. An author writes of the need to provide "openings" and "hospitality," rather than imposing an orthodoxy of structure on restorative justice processes.[145] But there is also pressure for protocols and the emergence of claimed orthodoxies in restorative justice, just as in other areas of innovation. To resist this temptation to recreate a rigid and unresponsive process or set of processes, the restorative justice movement must continuously reaffirm the importance of process flexibility and creativity.

The same issues arise in relation to outcomes. The commitment of restorative justice to consensual and context-sensitive outcomes as the end result of facilitated dialogue processes does not mean that there is no recognition of relevant rules and principles, experience in past cases, and so on; it means simply that this is also a part of, and not all of, the context in which an outcome is fashioned by these participants. Again, there is pressure to produce outcomes that can be matched to identifiable standards and do not go soft on offenders, pressure that needs to be resisted if restorative justice is to remain committed to its core goals and values.

> "Placing victims' needs first requires that programs be flexible. Different victims will have different needs. Rather than trying to impose a single ideology of what victim-offender mediation should be like, programs should strive for flexibility in response to victims' wishes. Programs should offer a variety of services, such as indirect mediation, the exchange of videos or letters, and the offer of a meeting with the offender."
>
> J. Wemmers and M. Canuto, "Victims' Experiences with, Expectations and Perceptions of Restorative Justice: A Critical Review of the Literature." (Ottawa: Policy Centre for Victims Issues, Department of Justice, Canada, 2001) at iii.

Core Process Values for Restorative Justice

- Participation

- Fair treatment

- Respect for all participants

- Community empowerment

- Commitment to agreed outcomes

- Flexibility of process and outcomes

2.6 SUMMARY: RESTORATIVE JUSTICE — A FOCUS ON PROCESS

Restorative justice has been described as way of thinking about conflict resolution. Restorative justice processes embody a set of values that set them apart from the traditional justice system. Restorative justice is a process for resolving disputes that places victims, offenders and members of the community at the centre of the conflict resolution process.

Some writers have pointed out that the sheer variety and diversity of definitions of restorative justice—from principles to process, to outcomes and back again—means that in a sense there is something for everyone in the promises held out by restorative justice. Those who are dissatisfied with the ability of the existing criminal justice system to change behaviours and protect both individuals (especially individual victims) and communities see restorative justice as a means of confronting and dealing with the harm caused by criminal acts. Those who reject the "just deserts" model of punishment—which sees punishment as an inherently moral response, justifiable in the face of harm—regard restorative justice as a more human and humane approach to managing antisocial behaviours. Yet others see restorative justice as a means for the community to take back from the state the control of justice systems and outcomes.

It may be inherent in the enterprise of restorative justice that any single innovation or initiative must be sufficiently fluid and dynamic to respond to highly varied needs.[146] In general, the need for the protective intervention of the state in conflicts seems much less obvious than it might once have been. Indeed, some communities are questioning whether they might accomplish as much or more than the current criminal system by introducing processes that include community members, as well as justice officials, and consensus agreement on appropriate outcomes.

---

[1] See, for example, J. Thibaut, L. Walker, S. LaTour and S. Houlden, "Procedural Justice as Fairness" (1974) 26 *Stanford Law Review* 1271; and J. Thibaut and L. Walker, *Procedural Justice: A Psychological Analysis* (New York: Erlbaum, 1975).

2   For example, the United Nations, in articulating and adopting its "Basic Principles for the Use of Restorative Justice Programs in Criminal Matters", describes "restorative outcomes," as agreements reached "as a result of restorative process"; further, "Restorative outcomes include responses and programs such as reparation, restitution and community service." See "Basic Principles for the Use of Restorative Justice Programmes in Criminal Matters," at III(3) and see the further discussion of the United Nations principles of restorative justice available online: <http://www.restorativejustice.ca/National Consultation/BasicPrinciplesBody.htm.

3   For a review of the debate see R.B. Cormier, "Restorative Justice: Directions and Principles—Developments in Canada" (prepared for delivery at the Technical Assistance Workshop of the Programme Network of Institutes, 11th Session of the Commission on Crime Prevention and Criminal Justice, Vienna, 16–25 April 2002.

4   One of the first references to "restorative justice" is linked to Albert Eglash who used the term in his 1977 article "Beyond Restitution: Creative Restitution". See A. Eglash, "Beyond Restitution: Creative Restitution" in J. Hudson and B. Galaway, eds., *Restitution in Criminal Justice* (Lexington: Lexington Books, 1975) at 91.

5   For a review of Canadian crime statistics, see Canadian Centre for Justice Statistics, Canadian Crime Statistics (Ottawa: Statistics Canada, 2001); D. Garland, *The Culture of Control: Crime and Social Order in Contemporary Society* (Chicago: University of Chicago Press, 2001).

6   For a review of Aboriginal over-representation in the criminal justice system, see Canadian Welfare Council, *Indians and the Law: A Survey Prepared for The Honourable A. Laing* (Ottawa: Canadian Welfare Council, August 1967) 42; Albert Task Force, *Justice On Trial: The Report of the Task Force on the Criminal Justice System and Its Impact on the Indian and Métis People of Alberta* (Edmonton: Government of Alberta, 1990); Manitoba, *Report of the Aboriginal Justice Inquiry of Manitoba*, Volume 1: *The Justice System and Aboriginal People* (Winnipeg: Queen's Printer, 1991); Indian Justice Review Committee (Canada), *Report of the Saskatchewan Indian Justice Review Committee* (Regina: The Committee, 1992); C. LaPrairie, *Examining Aboriginal Corrections in Canada* (Ottawa: Ministry of the Solicitor General, 1996); Canada, Royal Commission on Aboriginal Peoples, *Bridging the Cultural Divide: A Report on Aboriginal People and Criminal Justice in Canada* (Ottawa: Supply and Services Canada, 1996); and M. Jackson, "Locking Up Natives in Canada" (1988–89) 23:1 *University of British Columbia Law Review* 216.

7   Canadian Centre for Justice Statistics, *Adult Correctional Services in Canada*, 2000/01 (Ottawa: Statistics Canada, 2002).

8   D. Garland, *The Culture of Control: Crime and Social Order in Contemporary Society* (Chicago: University of Chicago Press, 2001); D. Cayley, *Expanding Prison, The Crisis in Crime and Punishment and the Search for Alternatives* (Toronto: Pilgrim Press, 1999); and N. Christie, "Conflicts as Property" (1977) 17:1 *British Journal of Criminology* 1.

9   A. Von Hirsch, *Doing Justice: The Choice of Punishments: Report of The Committee for the Study of Incarceration* (New York: Hill and Wang, 1976); and A. Von Hirsh, *Past or Future Crimes: Deservedness and Dangerousness in the Sentencing of Criminals* (New Brunswick: Rutgers University Press, 1985).

10 Canadian Sentencing Commission, *Sentencing Reform – A Canadian Approach: Report Of The Canadian Sentencing Commission* (Ottawa: Canadian Sentencing Commission, 1987) at 143–144.

11 A. Von Hirsch, "Penal Theories" in M. Tonry, ed., *The Handbook of Crime and Punishment* (Oxford: Oxford University Press, 1998) at 666. In the 1980s, the Canadian Sentencing Commission studied the criminal sentencing process in Canada. The Sentencing Commission recommended that Parliament adopt "just deserts" as the paramount consideration governing the determination of a sentence; it proposed a two-pronged reform strategy. First, a legislative statement of sentencing principles was to be made. Then a rigid system of guidelines would be imposed—offences would be ranked according to severity, and each offence would have a presumptive sentence. The proposals represented an attempt to create a system of sentencing based on proportionality, where the most important factor in sentencing would be the gravity of the offence, rather than the offender's past convictions. Past convictions would be only one factor among many to be taken into account in determining the sentence within the presumptive range or in deciding whether to depart from the presumptive sentence. Canadian Sentencing Commission, *Sentencing Reform – A Canadian Approach: Report Of The Canadian Sentencing Commission* (Ottawa: Canadian Sentencing Commission, 1987).

12 D. Martin and J. Mosher, "Unkept Promises: Experiences of Immigrant Women with the Neo-criminalisation of Wife Abuse" (1995) 8 *Canadian Journal of Women and the Law* 3. Martin and Mosher argue that alternatives should focus on talking with victim and offender to ensure safety and to clearly reinforce the wrongfulness of abusive behaviour.

13 Other victims' organizations have instead chosen to lobby for harsher punishments, longer sentences and reductions in parole. H. Strang, "The Crime

Victim Movement" in H. Strang and J. Braithwaite, eds., *Restorative Justice and Civil Society* (New York: Cambridge University Press, 2001) at 72.

14 See the discussion in T.F. Marshall, *Restorative Justice: An Overview* (London: Home Office, 1998) at 24–25.

15 See the discussion of victim-blaming in J. Braithwaite and D. Roche, "Responsibility and Restorative Justice" in G. Bazemore and M. Schiff, eds., *Restorative Community Justice: Repairing Harm and Transforming Communities* (Cincinnati: Anderson Publishing Co., 2001) at 74. Braithwaite and Roche also point out that since victim-blaming is a reflection of existing social beliefs, this tendency is equally likely to occur in restorative justice processes.

16 See, generally, D. Van Ness and H. Strong, *Restoring Justice* (Cincinnati: Anderson Publishing, 1997).

17 H. Zehr, *Changing Lenses: A New Focus for Crime and Justice* (Waterloo: Harold Press, 1990) at 28.

18 M. Achilles and H. Zehr, "Restorative Justice for Crime Victims: The Promise and the Challenge" in G. Bazemore and M. Schiff, eds., *Restorative Community Justice: Repairing Harm and Transforming Communities* (Cincinnati: Anderson Publishing Co., 2001) at 89; and generally, H. Zehr, *supra* note 17, chapter 1.

19 For an exhaustive review of the rise of the victims' movement in Canada and policy responses to this movement, see K. Roach, *Due Process and Victims' Rights: The New Law and Politics of Criminal Justice* (Toronto: University of Toronto Press, 1999).

20 Section 722 of the Canadian *Criminal Code*. Provincial legislation also establishes procedures for the submission of such statements (see below). Parole boards are also empowered to ask for victim impact statements when considering a request for the reduction of a term of ineligibility for parole; see *Criminal Code* s. 645.63(1)(d). See generally, The Honourable Justice C. Hill, "Expanding Victims' Rights" in A.D. Gold, ed., *Alan D. Gold's Collection of Criminal Law Articles* online: <http://www.quicklaw.com> (Quicklaw: GOLA [database], 1999).

21 *Justice for Victims of Crime Act*, S.M. 1986–7 c. 28.

22 *Victims' Bill of Rights*, C.C.S.M. 1998 c. V-55.

23 *Victims of Crime Act*, R.S.B.C. 1996, c. 478.

24 *Victims' Bill of Rights*, S.O. 1995 c. 6 at s. 2(vi) and (xiii).

25 For more information, see online:<http://www.justice.gouv.qc.ca/english/ publications/generale/rec-ress-a.htm#rights> (date accessed: 17 September 2003).

26 For more information about the New Brunswick program, see online: <http://www.gnb.ca/0276/corrections/vicser_e.asp> (date accessed: 17 September 2003).

27 For a classic exposition of the arguments for a rejection of the state system and the development of community-based justice, see R. Shonholtz, "Neighborhood Justice Systems" (1984) 5 *Mediation Quarterly* 3.

28 L. Nader, "Controlling Processes in the Practice of Law: Hierarchy and Pacification in the Movement to Reform Dispute Ideology" (1993) 9:1 *Ohio State Journal on Dispute Resolution* 1.

29 For example, N. Christie has written about this tendency of the formal criminal justice system to attempt to "explain conflicts away" and, in particular, to ignore their relationship to socio-economic and class structures. Christie, *supra* note 8 at 5.

30 K. Pranis recognizes this tension when she writes that "[c]ommunity justice seeks equal consideration for the well-being and wholeness of all community members … [W]ell-being requires *being able to meet one's own needs without harm to others and being able to exercise control in one's life*" (italics added). K. Pranis, "Restorative Justice, Social Justice and the Empowerment of Marginalised Communities" in G. Bazemore and M. Schiff, eds., *Restorative Community Justice: Repairing Harm and Transforming Communities* (Cincinnati: Anderson Publishing Co., 2001) 287 at 288.

31 G. Husk, "Making Community Mediation Work" in J. Macfarlane, ed., *Rethinking Disputes: The Mediation Alternative* (Toronto: Emond Montgomery, 1997) at 282.

32 M.L. Hadley, ed., *The Spiritual Roots of Restorative Justice.* SUNY Series in Religious Studies (Albany: State University of New York Press, 2001).

33 Robert Redfield devised the folk–urban continuum, which describes the evolution of a rural community to an urban society and the changes that result. These include the loss of both the original homogeneity and the cohesion of established social practices. Redfield's work is described in I. Schulte-Tenckhoff, *The Concept of Community in the Social Sciences and Its Juridical Relevance* (Ottawa: Law Commission of Canada, September 2001) at 14–15.

34 N. Postman, *Amusing Ourselves to Death: Public Discourse in the Age of Show Business* (New York: Viking, 1985).

35 Marshall, *supra* note 14 at 3.

36 For example, a workshop on program evaluation presented by Dr. Avery Calhoun of the University of Calgary drew a very large crowd at the Canadian Criminal Justice Association's 2002 conference in Gatineau, Quebec.

37 Solicitor General of Canada and the Aboriginal Healing Foundation, *Mapping the Healing Journey: The Final Report of a First Nation Research Project on Healing in Canadian Aboriginal Communities* (Ottawa: Solicitor General of Canada, 2002) at 21.

38 Aboriginal Peoples Collection of Canada, *The Four Circles of Hollow Water* (Ottawa: Public Works and Government Services Canada, 1997) at 10.

39 J. Ryan and B. Calliou, *Aboriginal Restorative Justice Alternatives: Two Case Studies* (Ottawa: Law Commission of Canada, 2002).

40 Premier P. Okalik, Speaking notes, National Aboriginal Policing Conference, 13 October 2000, online: <http://www.gov.nu.ca/Nunavut/English/premier/press/apc.shtml> (date accessed: 17 September 2003).

41 *Supra* note 38, at 7.

42 Aboriginal Peoples Collection of Canada, *The Four Circles of Hollow Water* (Ottawa: Public Works and Government Services Canada, 1997) at 11.

43 E. LaRocque, "Re-examining Culturally Appropriate Models in Criminal Justice Applications" in M. Asch, ed., *Aboriginal and Treaty Rights in Canada: Essays on Law, Equity and Respect for Difference* (Vancouver: University of British Columbia Press, 1997) at 75–76, suggests that there is a "growing complex of reinvented 'traditions' which have become popular even while lacking historical or anthropological contextualization."

44 W. Stewart, A. Huntley and F. Blaney, *The Implications of Restorative Justice for Aboriginal Women and Children Survivors of Violence: A Comparative Overview of Five Communities in British Columbia* (Ottawa: Law Commission of Canada, July 2001) at 28.

45 *Criminal Code*, R.S.C. 1985, c. C-46, s. 718.

46 *Ibid.* at 718.2(e).

47 A conditional sentence is a term of imprisonment that is served in the community. A number of criteria have to be met before an offender can be sentenced to serve his or her term of custody in the community under supervision. First, the sentence cannot exceed two years less one day. Second, if

the offence carries a minimum penalty, the offender cannot receive a conditional sentence. Third, the judge must be convinced that the presence of the offender in the community (rather than prison) does not pose a danger to the public. Finally, the judge must be convinced that a conditional sentence is consistent with the purpose and principles of sentencing that are contained in the *Criminal Code*. For more information see: "What Is a Conditional Sentence?" Conditional Sentencing Series Fact Sheet 1 (Research and Statistics Division, Department of Justice Canada), online: <http://www.canada.justice.gc.ca/en/ps/rs/rep/fs_cs_001e.pdf> (date accessed: 17 September 2003).

48 *R. v. Proulx* [2000] S.C.R. 6, 2000 SCC 5, online: QL.

49 *Ibid.* at para. 22.

50 *Ibid.* at para. 19.

51 Chief Justice Lamer stated that "there may be certain circumstances in which the need for denunciation is so pressing that incarceration will be the only suitable way in which to express society's condemnation of the offender's conduct." But, he continued, "Judges should be wary of placing too much weight on deterrence when choosing between a conditional sentence and incarceration. The empirical evidence suggests that the deterrent effect of incarceration is uncertain." Chief Justice Lamer, in *Proulx* at paras. 106–107.

52 A brief review of recent case law reveals that the courts continue to have difficulty determining when conditional sentences are appropriate. Despite the principle established in *R. v. Proulx*, that no particular offence or set of offences need be excluded from the ambit of conditional sentencing and that offence and offender should each be assessed on their particular circumstances, some judges still see restorative principles as having no relevance to very serious crimes. In some cases, the appeal courts have overruled the decision of the trial judge and substituted incarceration. In other cases, appeal courts have allowed the substitution of a conditional sentence. See, for example, *R. v. Marchment*, [2000] O.J. No. 3559, (Meehan J., aggravated assault case); *R. v. Longaphy*, [2000] N.S.J. No. 376,2000 NSCA 136, (Oland J.,). "[The trial judge] failed to give proper weight to certain objectives of sentencing, particularly denunciation, deterrence, and promoting a sense of responsibility in the offender. Her decision does not mention denunciation. There is only one specific reference to deterrence and that is in her summary of the Crown's submission; she stated that the Crown had urged incarceration in the interest of general deterrence. She herself did not address deterrence as an objective of sentencing in her decision. There is no indication how the sentence she ordered would promote a sense of responsibility in the respondent." (para. 38); *R. v. J.F.* [2001] N.B.J. No. 286. (Larlee J., aggravated assault). "The goals of denunciation and deterrence cannot be sacrificed to the

principle of Restorative Justice. This offender must be separated from society for a long period of time." (para. 16). In *R. v. Wells*, [2000] 1 S.C.R. 207, the Supreme Court refused a conditional sentence to an Aboriginal offender because of "aggravating factors, the nature of the offence, the community context, and the availability of conditions which have the capacity to properly reflect society's condemnation" and that "[i]t was accordingly open to the sentencing judge to give primacy to the principles of denunciation and deterrence in this case on the basis that the crime involved was a serious one." at 287.

53   *Supra*, note 46.

54   For example, the much-recognized efforts of Judge Barry Stuart in the Yukon and the work of a local Justice with the Hollow Water project in Manitoba. See B. Stuart, "Sentencing Circles: Making Real Differences" in J. Macfarlane, ed., Rethinking Disputes: The Mediation Alternative (Toronto: Emond Montgomery, 1997); T. Lajeunesse, *Evaluation of Community Holistic Circle Healing: Hollow Water First Nation*. Volume 1: *Final Report* (Ottawa: Solicitor General of Canada, 1996)

55   The Honourable Justice M.E. Turpel, "Sentencing within a Restorative Paradigm: Procedural Implications of R. v. Gladue" (1999) 4:3 *Justice as Healing* 2. See also J. Savarase, "'Gladue' Was a Woman: Should Sentencing from a Restorative Perspective Also Be Feminist?" (prepared for delivery at the 6th International Conference on Restorative Justice, Simon Fraser University, Vancouver, B.C., June 2003).

56   *R. v. Gladue*, [1999] 1 S.C.R. 688, [1999] S.C.J. No. 19 (para. 61).

57   K. Douglas and D. Goetz, "Bill C-7: *The Youth Criminal Justice Act*" Legislative Summary 356E, (Ottawa: Library of Parliament, Legislative Research Division, 2000).

58   United Nations Economic and Social Council, "Basic Principles on the Use of Restorative Justice Programmes in Criminal Matters" (Vienna: Commission on Crime Prevention and Criminal Justice, 2002), online: <http://www.restorative justice.org/rj3/UNdocuments/UNDecBasicPrinciplesofRJ.html> (date accessed: 17 September 2003).

59   Note that the United Nations Principles were the focus of an online discussion facilitated by the Network for Conflict Resolution in 2002–2003.

60   J. Nadeau, *Critical Analysis of the UN Declaration of Basic Principles on the Use of Restorative Justice Programmes in Criminal Matters* (Leuven, Belgium: University of Leuven, Centre for Advanced Legal Studies, 2001) at 36, online: <http://www.restorativejustice.org/asp>.

61 Several consultations were undertaken over an 18-month period. The reports from these consultations are available online: <http://www.restorativejustice.ca/ NationalConsultation/national.htm>.

62 For a classic description of this VOM process, see M. Umbreit, "Mediation of Victim–Offender Conflict" (1988) 31 *Journal of Dispute Resolution* 84.

63 For example, the now defunct Dispute Resolution Centre of Ottawa–Carleton.

64 For example, the Ottawa Collaborative Justice Project has received the majority of its referrals from pre-trial judges. For more information see online: <http://www.ccjc.ca>.

65 B. Archibald, "A Comprehensive Canadian Approach to Restorative Justice: The Prospects for Structuring Fair Alternative Measures in Response to Crime" (prepared for delivery at the 1998 Conference on Making Criminal Law Clear and Just, Queen's University, Kingston, Ontario, November 1998).

66 In theory, intervention can also occur before the engagement of the formal justice system, for example, if the community becomes alerted to schoolyard bullying issues at a local school. Intervention at this early stage is an important restorative justice principle, but in VOM and VORP, as in other restorative justice processes, this type of early intervention is relatively less common than the four system entry points described above. Intervention can also occur before the engagement of the justice system, but it is more complex to identify, document and evaluate for the purposes of policy development.

67 For example, in Nova Scotia, an extensive new program of restorative justice initiatives builds on the work of alternative-measures programs. See A. Thomson, *Formal Restorative Justice in Nova Scotia: A Pre-implementation Overview* (prepared for delivery at the Annual Conference of the Atlantic Association of Sociologists and Anthropologists, Fredericton: October 1999) at 7, online: <http:// ace.acadiau.ca/soci/agt/justice/restorativejustice.htm> (date accessed: 17 September 2003).

68 M. Peterson, "Developing a Restorative Justice Program: Part One" (2000) 5:3 *Justice as Healing* 1, online: <http://www.usask.ca/nativelaw>.

69 The Ottawa Collaborative Justice Project has issued the clear message that it is "[not a diversion project]—the Collaborative Justice Project works within the criminal justice system. Pleas are entered, convictions registered and sentences imposed. Cases are not diverted out of the system; rather, the Project encourages the involvement of all the parties in a process that assists them to identify their needs and have a voice in designing a satisfying resolution."

Collaborative Justice Project, Final Report on the Collaborative Justice Project for Fiscal Year 1999/2000 (Ottawa: Collaborative Justice Project, 2001), online: <http://www.ccjc.ca/news/collaborative.cfm> (date accessed: 14 October, 2003).

70 Marshall and Merry, reporting on U.K. programs, found that 76 percent of U.K. VOM programs operate post-sentence. See T. Marshall and S. Merry, *Crime and Accountability: Victim/Offender Mediation in Practice* (London: Home Office HMSO, 1990) at 8.

71 See, for example, J. Hudson, A. Morris, G. Maxwell and B. Galaway, eds., *Family Group Conferences: Perspectives on Policy and Practice* (Australia: Federation Press, 1996).

72 See Marshall, *supra* note 35, at 20.

73 Gerry Ferguson points out that in recent history the best-known example of a criminal jury attempting to have input into sentencing was in the trial of Robert Latimer (*R. v. Latimer*, [2001] 1 S.C.R. 3); the jury's request was brushed off by the trial judge. See G. Ferguson, *Community Participation in Criminal Jury Trials and Restorative Justice Programs* (Ottawa: Law Commission of Canada, 2001) at 140.

74 See Stuart, *supra* note 54.

75 M. Peterson notes that Judge Fafard of Saskatchewan has participated in 60 to 70 sentencing circles and has never rejected a circle recommendation. See M. Peterson, *supra* note 68 at 81. For a comprehensive description of the philosophy, rationale and practices of circle sentencing, see the judgment of Justice Stuart, in *R. v. Moses*, [1992] Y.J. No. 50, [1992] 3 C.N.L.R. 116 (QL).

76 Although community panels are part of a more encompassing project called the Restorative Resolutions Project in Manitoba. See G. Richardson, B. Galaway and M. Joubert, "Restorative Resolutions Project: An Alternative to Incarceration" (1996) 20:2 *International Journal of Comparative and Applied Criminal Justice* 209.

77 One study estimates that 17 percent of offenders fail to complete their agreements. See L. Kurki, "Restorative and Community Justice in the United States" (2000) 27 *Crime and Justice* 235.

78 See, for example, the Vermont program described in D.R. Karp and L. Walther, "Community Reparative Boards in Vermont: Theory and Practice" in G. Bazemore and M. Schiff, eds., *Restorative Community Justice: Repairing Harm and Transforming Communities* (Cincinnati: Anderson Publishing Co., 2001)

199; and in Norway, T.B. Nergard, "Solving Conflicts Outside the Court System: Experience with Conflict Resolution Boards in Norway" (1993) 33:1 *British Journal of Criminology* 81.

79 A number of individual schools have implemented restorative justice processes for resolving conflict. In British Columbia, the Fraser Region Community Justice Initiatives agreed to work with a school district to explore how restorative justice principles might be applied throughout the local school system. This project is one of the first of its kind to implement restorative justice as a collaborative effort and in a comprehensive manner throughout an entire school district. See C. Bargen, *Safe Schools: Strategies for a Changing Culture* (prepared for delivery at the 6th International Conference on Restorative Justice, Simon Fraser University, Vancouver, B.C., June 2003).

80 The Youth Canada Association works to understand conflict and promote peace-building through restorative processes among Canadian youth. See online: <http://www.youcan.ca/>.

81 Many examples in the introduction to the recent book by Bazemore and Schiff fall into this fourth category. G. Bazemore and M. Schiff, eds., *Restorative Community Justice: Repairing Harm and Restoring Communities* (Cincinnati: Anderson Publishing, 2001) at 1-4.

82 These programs include Aboriginal treatment and healing programs, Aboriginal healing lodges (currently, eight across Canada), agreements with Aboriginal communities to offer services to Aboriginal offenders, and elders working in institutions and in the community.

83 Kathleen Daly, for example, argues that proponents of restorative justice often overstate the philosophical divide that exists between restorative justice and retributive justice. K. Daly, "Revisiting the Relationship Between Retributive and Restorative Justice" in H. Strang, and J. Braithwaite, eds., *Restorative Justice: Philosophy to Practice* (Aldershot: Ashgate, 2000) 33. See also A. Von Hirsch, J.V. Roberts, A. Bottoms, K. Roach and M. Chiff, eds., *Restorative Justice and Criminal Justice: Competing or Reconcilable Paradigms* (Oxford: Hart Publishing, 2003).

84 J. Braithwaite, "Restorative Justice" in M.H. Tonry, ed., *The Handbook of Crime and Punishment* (Oxford: Oxford University Press, 1998) at 239.

85 T. Wachtel, and G. Gold, "Restorative Justice in Everyday Life" in H. Strang and J. Braithwaite, eds., *Restorative Justice and Civil Society* (New York: Cambridge University Press, 2001) 114.

86 For example, the work of Dave Gustafson with serious crimes at the Fraser Region Community Justice Initiatives. See D. Gustafson and S. Bergin, *Promising Models in Restorative Justice: A Report for the Ministry of the Attorney-General of British Columbia* (Victoria: Ministry of the Attorney-General, 1998); and the work of the Ottawa Collaborative Justice Project, which targets serious crimes, including cases of robbery, robbery with a weapon, weapons offences, break and enter, theft over $5,000, fraud, assault, assault causing bodily harm, impaired driving causing bodily harm or death, and careless driving or dangerous driving causing bodily harm or death. As well, the John Howard Society of Manitoba is in the early stages of developing a restorative justice program for domestic assault. L. Maloney and G. Reddoch, *Restorative Justice and Family Violence: A Community-based Effort to Move from Theory to Practice* (prepared for delivery at the 6th International Conference on Restorative Justice, Simon Fraser University, Vancouver, B.C., June 2003).

87 K. Roach, "Changing Punishment at the Turn of the Century: Restorative Justice on the Rise" (2000) 42:3 *Canadian Journal of Criminology* 249 at 258.

88 For example, the systemic sexism and tolerance of violence against women in some Aboriginal communities is described in W. Stewart, A. Huntley and F. Blaney, *The Implications of Restorative Justice for Aboriginal Women and Children Survivors of Violence: A Comparative Overview of Five Communities in British Columbia, supra* 44, at 26–31.

89 Heather Strang notes that the development of a victims' movement in the 1970s resulted by the end of that decade with a coalition that "encompassed a spectrum of activists from radical feminists to hard line law-and-order conservatives." H. Strang, "The Crime Victim Movement" in H. Strang and J. Braithwaite, eds., *Restorative Justice and Civil Society* (New York: Cambridge University Press, 2001) at 72.

90 Strang, *ibid.* at 81.

91 Tony Marshall and Susan Merry have suggested that the process of face-to-face dialogue between victim and offender can enable victims to explore and sometimes dismantle stereotyping views they held of offenders, in general, and the offender who harmed them, in particular. See Marshall, *supra* note 70.

92 Umbreit, *supra* note 60, at 97.

93 J. Latimer, C. Dowden and D. Muise, *The Effectiveness of Restorative Justice Practices: A Meta-analysis* (Ottawa: Department of Justice, 2001).

94 J. Wemmers and M. Canuto, *Victims' Experiences with, Expectations and Perceptions of Restorative Justice: A Critical Review of the Literature.* (Ottawa: Policy Centre for Victims Issues, Department of Justice Canada, 2001).

95 The results of the program evaluations at the four American sites—Oakland (California), Travis County (Texas), Albuquerque (New Mexico) and Saint Paul (Minnesota)—are published in M.S. Umbreit, R.B. Coates and A.W. Roberts, "The Impact of Victim–Offender Mediation: A Cross-National Perspective" (2000) 17:3 *Mediation Quarterly* 215.

96 M.S. Umbreit, *Mediation of Criminal Conflict: An Assessment of Programs in Four Canadian Provinces* (St. Paul: Center for Restorative Justice and Mediation, School of Social Work, University of Minnesota, 1995.)

97 This study, along with the American and Canadian program evaluations, is reported and consolidated in M.S. Umbreit, *Victim Meets Offender: The Impact of Restorative Justice and Mediation* (Monsey: Criminal Justice Press, 1994).

98 M.S. Umbreit, *supra* note 95, at 221.

99 For a review of the literature on restorative justice evaluations, L. Kurki, "Evaluating Restorative Justice Practices" in A. Von Hirsch, J. Roberts, A. E Bottoms, K. Roach and M. Schiff, eds., *Restorative Justice and Criminal Justice: Competing or Reconcilable Paradigms* (Oxford: Hart Publishing, 2003).

100 See, for example, M. Ruth, Stories of Negotiated Justice (Toronto: Canadian Scholar's Press Inc., 2000); and W. Derksen, *Confronting the Horror: The Aftermath of Violence* (Winnipeg: Amity Publishers, 2002).

101 Umbreit, *supra* note 97.

102 Marshall, *supra* note 70. See also the data reported in J. Braithwaite, "Restorative Justice: Assessing Optimistic and Pessimistic Accounts" (1999) 25 *Crime and Justice* 1 at 23–24.

103 In *Restoring Dignity*, the Law Commission of Canada provides an overview of the qualities of a meaningful apology and the role of meaningful apologies in the justice process. See Law Commission of Canada, *Restoring Dignity: Responding to Institutional Child Abuse in Canadian Institutions*, (Ottawa: Law Commission of Canada, March 2000). See also S. Alter, *Apologising for Serious Wrongdoing: Social, Psychological and Legal Considerations* (Ottawa: Law Commission of Canada, May 1999) at the sections entitled "Acknowledgement of the Wrong Done" and "Accepting Responsibility for the Wrong Done."

104 For example, victim participation in the long-standing Winnipeg project is reported as just 10 percent. J. Bonta, S. Wallace-Capretta and J. Rooney, *Restorative Justice: An Evaluation of the Restorative Resolutions Project* (Ottawa: Solicitor General of Canada, 1998). See also the data presented by David Karp and Lynne Walther on victim participation in the Vermont Community Reparative Boards. Karp, *supra* note 78, at 210–211.

105 T. Lajeunesse, *Evaluation of Community Holistic Circle Healing: Hollow Water First Nation*. Volume 1: Final Report (Ottawa: Solicitor General of Canada, 1996). On the experience of victims in Canadian restorative justice processes, generally, see C.T. Griffiths, "The Victims of Crime and Restorative Justice: The Canadian Experience" (1999) 6:4 *International Review of Victimology* 279.

106 D. Poirier and N. Poirier, *Why Is It So Difficult to Combat Elder Abuse and, in Particular, Financial Exploitation of the Elderly?* (Ottawa: Law Commission of Canada, July 1999).

107 H.B. Eisenberg, "Combating Elder Abuse Through the Legal Process" (1991) 3:1 *Journal of Elder Abuse and Neglect* 65; and C. Spencer, *Diminishing Returns: An Examination of Financial Responsibility, Decision Making and Financial Abuse Among Older Adults in British Columbia* (Vancouver: Gerontology Research Centre, Simon Fraser University, 1996).

108 For a description of "passive" contrasted with "active" responsibility-taking, see M. Bovens, *The Quest for Responsibility* (New York: Cambridge University Press, 1998) at 26–38.

109 Braithwaite, *supra* note 15, at 63–65.

110 Achilles, *supra* note 18, at 91.

111 Braithwaite, *supra* note 15, at 64.

112 A. Morris and G. Maxwell, "Restorative Conferencing" in G. Bazemore and M. Schiff, eds., *Restorative Community Justice: Repairing Harm and Transforming Communities* (Cincinnati: Anderson Publishing Co., 2001) at 182–183.

113 Notable here is the work of John Braithwaite, who developed the notion of reintegrative shaming to explain and justify the effect of restorative processes on the individual offender. Braithwaite argues that we have overlooked the importance of personal shame as a deterrent to crime. He proposes that the two most potent deterrents, accordingly, are social disapproval and individual pangs of conscience. J. Braithwaite, *Crime, Shame and Reintegration* (New York: Cambridge University Press, 1989) at 19.

114 See, for example, the discussion in D. Cayley, "Security and Justice for All" in H. Strang and J. Braithwaite, eds., *Restorative Justice and Civil Society* (New York: Cambridge University Press, 2001) at 211–213.

115 S. Cohen, *Visions of Social Control* (Oxford: Polity, 1985). See also Roach, *supra* note 87, at 255; Braithwaite, *supra* note 102, at 89.

116 D. Moore, "Shame Forgiveness and Juvenile Justice" (1993) 12:1 *Criminal Justice Ethics* 3.

117 Ferguson, *supra* note 73.

118 R. Putnam, *The Decline of Civil Society: How Come? So What?* (prepared for delivery at the John L. Manion Lecture, Canadian Centre for Management Development, Ottawa, 22 February 1996), at 4.

119 Stewart, *supra* note 44.

120 Some sociologists advance the theory that there is a relationship between various communities and the levels of types of crime committed therein. Work under this paradigm explores community influences on individual development. See, for example, P. Wikstrom, "Communities and Crime" in M. Tonry, ed., *The Handbook of Crime and Punishment* (New York: Oxford University Press, 1998) at 269.

121 Wachtel, *supra* note 85 at 116–117.

122 Christie, *supra* note 8 at 3–7.

123 Marshall, *supra* note 14 at 3.

124 If restorative justice is to have a broader societal appeal, it is important that forgiveness is not seen as incumbent upon victims, for religious or other reasons. Another way of conceptualizing forgiveness outside a religious framework is to understand it as a means of "coping" with the stresses of life, "a search for significance in troubled times," an expression coined by Pargament. See K. Pargament, *The Psychology of Religion and Coping: Theory, Research, Practice* (New York: Guilford Publications, 1997). See also: Alter, *supra* note 103.

125 K. Pargament and M. Rye, "Forgiveness as a Method of Religious Coping" in E. Worthington, ed., *Dimensions of Forgiveness: Psychological Research and Theological Perspectives* (Philadelphia: Templeton Foundation Press, 1998) 59 at 60–64.

126 R. Enright, and the Human Development Study Group, "The Moral Development of Forgiveness" in W. Kurtines and J. Gewirtz, eds., *Handbook of Moral Behaviour and Development*, (Hillsdale: Erlbaum, 1991) at 123.

127 T. Tyler, K. Rasinki and N. Spodick, "The Influence of Voice on Satisfaction with Leaders: Exploring the Meaning of Process Control" (1985) 48 *Journal of Personality and Social Psychology* 72.

128 R.A. Bush and J.P. Folger., *The Promise of Mediation: Responding to Conflict Through Empowerment and Recognition* (San Francisco: Jossey-Bass, 1994) especially 84–89.

129 Umbreit, *supra* note 97 at 101.

130 See also the discussion in J. Macfarlane, "Why Do People Settle?" (2001) 45 *McGill Law Journal* 663 at 709–710.

131 John Braithwaite identifies respectful person-to-person dialogue as a core procedural justice value for restorative justice; this is what Llewellyn and Howse describe as "encounter" or "the context in which everything happens." Braithwaite, *supra* note 102 at 41; and *Restorative Justice: A Conceptual Framework* by J.J. Llewellyn and R. Howse, (Ottawa: Law Commission of Canada, 1999) at 57.

132 See, for example, Thibaut, *supra* note 1; T. Tyler, K. Rasinski and K. McGraw, "The Influence of Perceived Injustice Upon Support for the President, Political Authorities and Government Institutions" (1985) 48 *Journal of Applied Psychology* 72; T. Tyler, "The Role of Perceived Injustice in Defendants' Evaluations of Their Courtroom Experience" (1984) 18 *Law and Society Review* 51; and N. Welsh, "Making Deals in Court-connected Mediation: What's Justice Got to Do with It?" (2001) 79:3 *Washington University Law Quarterly* 787.

133 Testing four possible limitations on the satisfaction associated with a high degree of process control, Tyler found that the only factor that significantly reduced or eliminated this satisfaction was when the final decision-maker (where outcomes were imposed) did not appear to give due consideration to the disputants' view. See T. Tyler, "Conditions Leading to Value Expressive Effects in Judgments of Procedural Justice: A Test of Four Models" (1987) 52 *Journal of Personality and Social Psychology* 333.

134 See D.M. Kolb and Associates, *When Talk Works: Profiles of Mediators* (San Francisco: Jossey-Bass, 1994) at chapter 1. This is also sometimes described as a "therapeutic" style of mediation. See S. Silbey and S. Merry, "Mediator Settlement Strategies" (1986) 8 *Law and Society Policy Review* 7; and see also L. Riskin, "Mediator Orientations, Strategies and Techniques" (1994) 12 *Alternatives* 111.

135 R. Albert and D. Howard, "Informal Dispute Resolution Through Mediation" (1985) 10 *Mediation Quarterly* 99.

136 Christie, *supra* note 8 at 14.

137 See, for example, Stuart, *supra* note 54 at 201, 205–229.

138 G. Davis, "The Theft of Conciliation" (1985) 32 *Probation Journal* 7.

139 This was explicitly stated as important to more than half the sample in Umbreit's study of four American VOM programs. Umbreit, *supra* note 97 at 103.

140 Family group conferencing generally uses a community-of-care model to determine who should be present at the circle.

141 S. Retzinger and T. Scheff, "Strategy for Community Conferences: Emotions and Social Bonds" in B. Galaway and J. Hudson, eds., *Restorative Justice: International Perspectives* (New York: Criminal Justice Press, 1996) 315.

142 Despite the fact that some crimes may might relate to domestic relationships, for example, as in the case of spousal abuse.

143 C. LaPrairie, "The 'New' Justice: Some Implications for Aboriginal Communities" (1998) 40:1 *Canadian Journal of Criminology* 61 at 67.

144 See, for example, data on compliance and completion of agreements in Marshall, *supra* note 14 at 18; and in the context of civil mediation, see C. McEwen, and R. Mainman, "Small Claims Mediation in Maine: An Empirical Assessment" (1984) 33 *Maine Law Review* 244.

145 G. Pavlich, *Deconstructing Restoration: The Promise of Restorative Justice* (prepared for delivery at the International Conference on Restorative Justice, Tubingen, Germany, October 2000).

146 For this reason, Dean Peachey, one of the earliest Canadian innovators in restorative justice, argues that restorative justice initiatives should be described as "projects" (connoting ongoing change and responsiveness), rather than "programs" (implying established practices and principles). Professor George Pavlich notes somewhat cynically that "[t]he success of restorative justice is, no doubt, related to its ambiguity and equivocation." D. Peachey, "The Kitchener Experiment" in M. Wright and B. Galaway, B., eds., *Mediation and Criminal Justice* (Newbury Park, CA: Sage, 1989) 15; Pavlich, *supra* note 145 at 4.

Chapter 3 Participatory Justice in a Non-criminal Context: Consensus-based Justice

In Chapter 3, we review the development of participatory justice processes for resolving non-criminal conflicts. Whether in commercial litigation, bankruptcy, landlord-tenant disputes, administrative law, family law or other legal domains, over the past two decades a number of non-adversarial processes have developed with participation as a core value. We use the term consensus-based justice to refer to innovative methods of resolving conflicts in these domains.

Like restorative justice, consensus-based justice often arose as a response to frustrations with the adversarial processes. In traditional systems, the focus is on the event, and the wrongs and rights, as defined by rules and principles—inevitably leading to the construction of stories of personal experience—as processed by professionals.[1] In criminal and non-criminal conflicts, disputants feel that they have been displaced and that they have lost ownership of their conflict and control over its outcome. The course of conflicts is clearly affected by similar escalating factors-for example, a dehumanizing experience, the detached formality of legal process with its technical but rarely emotional or cognitive resolution. A major difference between the two systems may be the extent to which some relationships affected by civil matters are restricted to particular individuals, while the collective community that might be understood as affected by criminal behaviour might be drawn much wider. What is clear is that there are many similarities between the conditions that have led to the development of restorative and consensus-based justice alternatives to the formal justice system.

This chapter will examine innovative methods of conflict resolution in the civil system. Over the past two decades there have emerged a number of promising alternatives to the adversarial processes that have "consensus" as a core value. Most work described as consensus-based justice occurs in relation to conflict outside the criminal sphere, for example, family mediation, community mediation, administrative tribunals, civil court-connected mediation; landlord–tenant disputes; and facilitated dialogue around environmental and other types of policymaking. Just as we have seen with the development of restorative justice initiatives, some of these programs operate inside the formal justice system, and some operate outside or are loosely connected to it. A number of emerging practices illustrate this approach, and some examples are described below.

3.1   THE CONTEXT

Much like the growth of restorative justice in the criminal context, the rise of consensus-based justice processes was the result of several factors. Section 3.1 will review some of the factors that contributed to the rise of consensus-based justice.

3.1.1   The gap between adversarial justice and disputants' conceptions of justice

The history of the inability of formal justice models to provide the types of outcomes that disputants really want and need can be traced back at least as far back as the Middle Ages. The original English "merchant courts" were developed as an alternative to the king's courts by the merchant classes who wanted a speedier and more practical means of resolving their commercial disputes. In the 20th century, the development of commercial arbitration, both domestic and international, emerged as a result of similar dissatisfactions with the civil justice system. Commercial parties seek outcomes to business conflicts that recognize the conventions of business practice and that are developed by adjudicators familiar with these conventions and with the impacts of these disputes on commercial operations. They want solutions that can be implemented without unnecessary delay or cost and that maintain positive on-going relations. Private judging services now exist in many different forms, including binding and non-binding evaluations. Some may question whether commercial arbitration, in its increasingly formalized format, actually meets these needs in the manner originally intended. However, there is no disagreement about the impetus for its growth.[2]

In the 21st century, the same gap persists between the needs of many commercial disputants and what the formal justice system offers them. For example, businesses that deal exclusively or mostly on the Internet have begun to look for Internet-based solutions to their conflicts. Privately contracted online dispute resolution (ODR), which operates outside the world of judicial norms or actors, is a response to the frustrations of this group with the traditional civil court system of dispute resolution.

> "The phenomenal growth of the Internet, both in terms of numbers of users, estimated at 323.7 million users in April 2002, and breadth of use, creates the first pressure point for ODR's [online dispute resolutions] development. ... Another critical force propelling ODR's emergence is e-commerce's economic vortex. Estimates of commercial activity emanating from the Internet are currently in the hundreds of billions of dollars with growth projected upwards to trillions of dollars within a few years. Consider the electronic revitalization of the old-fashioned auction through E-bay, where an estimated four million items are offered for sale each day. With increased economic traffic comes increased consumer and business complaints."
>
> E. Zweibel, "On-line Dispute Resolution," in J. Macfarlane, (ed.),
> *Dispute Resolution: Readings and Case Studies* (2nd ed.)
> (Toronto: Emond Montgomery, 2003),
> citing J. Glasner, "Net Shoppers Still Complaining" (2001), online:
> <http://www.wired.com/news/business/0,1367,44361,00.html> at 520.

In turning to commercial arbitration, private judging, and ODR services, commercial agents express their frustrations with the adequacy and sufficiency of the traditional civil justice system. Another development that exemplifies the dissatisfaction of users with the traditional civil justice model—and appears more clearly influenced by aspirations to consensus-based justice and to restorative, healing, respectful processes and outcomes—is the development of collaborative lawyering for divorcing and separating couples. Increasing numbers of couples are choosing not to use court procedures to formalize their separation, whether for financial reasons (including the reduced scope of provincial legal aid for family matters), or simply because of dissatisfaction with the level of animosity that divorce and separation proceedings frequently generate.

The users of civil legal services have often been frustrated by the failure of adversarial justice to resolve the core problems they face, either in their commercial dealings or in their domestic relationships. There is a widespread desire to take greater control over outcomes than these types of adjudication permit. In addition, a particular theme for restorative and consensus-based justice initiatives is a desire to pay greater attention to the relationship dimensions of disputing dynamics and outcomes.

3.1.2   System costs

A very significant factor in the movement toward alternatives to adversarial justice is the cost of using the existing civil justice system. This cost includes both legal fees and the investment of time required to bring a civil action to trial. While there is increasing public attention to exponentially rising legal costs, early studies in the United States already showed a widening gap between investment in legal services and returns.[3]

Ontario's 1996 Civil Justice Review[4] estimated that the cost of bringing a lawsuit, culminating in a five-day civil trial in the General Division, would be around $35,000—and legal costs have risen considerably over the ensuing years. Even when litigation settles on the eve of trial and legal costs will be lower than if a trial had taken place, they will nonetheless be significant. By this stage, the parties will likely have spent weeks or even months in preliminary questioning when the parties are examined under oath, which will account for a high percentage of total legal costs. As a consequence, lawyers are reporting marked changes in client expectations: they expect their lawyers to make early efforts to resolve cases before undertaking expensive discoveries, and they are demanding regular reporting on, and justification for, costs incurred.

Considerable resources have been put into programming initiatives to encourage the earlier settlement of litigation, with the goal of lowering costs, expediting resolution and possibly restoring (personal, commercial) relationships. Procedural reforms such as mandatory mediation and proactive case management[5] have achieved some success in increasing the rate of earlier settlement.[6]

Efforts to resolve the problem of last-minute settlement must take into account the pivotal role played by lawyers in the present system as the agents of disputing.[7] The practices, strategies and attitudes of lawyers are crucial to finding workable and efficacious solutions. In addition, the role that lawyers understand themselves as playing in the settlement process has its own cultural context, which both defines and constrains it. This has become clear in the mixed reactions of litigators to mandatory mediation in Ontario and Saskatchewan.[8]

> A study funded by the Law Commission of Canada asked commercial litigators about the expectations of their institutional and commercial clients. One responded, "Now more and more clients are asking for an assessment right at the top from a timing stand point, and asking you to analyse what's the best time to get a resolution of the thing and especially with in-house counsel involved. They are very conscious of the costs and they want to know up front where the thing is going."
>
> Another litigator reflected, "I've noticed a few of my commercial clients recently, the old 'just fight-at-all-costs and don't look at it (the legal bill), don't even think about an approach' (i.e., opening negotiations) just doesn't seem to exist anymore."
>
> J. Macfarlane, "Culture Change? A Tale of Two Cities and Mandatory Court-Connected Mediation" 2 Journal of Dispute Resolution (2002) at 241.

There are no clear or easy solutions to the problem of excessive system costs, both in terms of delays and the costs borne by the parties. These types of costs are in themselves enough to persuade many system users that they need to create alternative processes that proceed more rapidly and are less costly than those of adversarial justice. However, expenditures of time and money are not the only or even the most significant costs of using the present civil justice system to manage conflict.

3.1.3   The other costs of conflict

Aside from system costs, there has been growing awareness of the related costs of conflict, whether in the workplace (for example, high rates of absenteeism caused by conflict) or in relationships (for example, fractured family relationships caused by acrimonious divorce proceedings). These further costs of conflict may be reflected in productivity, workplace morale, individual mental health, or family stability, but each is a cost that appears to be at best exacerbated by, or at worst actually created by, the adversarial process. There is increasing awareness among employers of the high number of days lost to absenteeism caused by conflict-related stress. Conflict management strategies in corporate and government settings are moving away from an adversarial, rule-driven approach toward a more inclusive, participatory environment. "Employees today equate fairness with a sense of participation, and failure to create a participative culture could, in the future, have a negative effect on employee commitment."[9] In this context, practical conflict resolution and problem-solving skills are regarded as important management tools more than traditional machismo and toughness.[10]

Realizing the extent of these other costs of conflict has focused researchers' attention on ways of de-escalating conflict at an earlier stage, before it reaches the level of a formal "claim", with its consequent costs. The constraints of the formal justice system often make these types of restorative outcomes difficult to achieve.[11]

3.1.4 The community justice movement

Discontent with monetary and other costs of adversarial justice, as well as a gap between practical, desired outcomes to conflict and those available in a formal win–lose model, have contributed to the momentum of a search for alternatives. Efforts to create alternative processes have often focused on grassroots, community-based initiatives, just as in the development of restorative justice processes. The emergence of a community justice movement that takes on non-criminal issues affecting neighbours and neighbourhoods—for example, landlord-tenant disputes, neighbour disputes, and smaller consumer-merchant conflicts—is a response to dissatisfaction with the resolution of conflict in civil disputes, just as restorative justice initiatives search for an alternative to the formal criminal justice system. The same themes—the desire for community decision-making, a frustration with the bureaucracy of state dispute resolution systems, and a commitment to social justice issues, especially at a local level—are apparent and do not require repeating here. The momentum achieved by the community justice movement in the 1980s has played a critical political and structural role in the emergence of both restorative justice and consensus-based justice models.

3.2   POLICY FRAMEWORK

Statutory provisions to incorporate mediation into conflict resolution processes are common, both at the federal level and at the provincial level. Twenty-two federal statutes contain mediation provisions, and eighteen of them provide substantive mediation requirements as part of dispute or complaint resolution processes. The provinces and territories have also embraced mediation as a tool to varying degrees. New Brunswick and the Northwest Territories have included mediation procedures in a few statutes. Quebec, Ontario and British Columbia each carry mediation provisions on more than twenty of their active statutes. The type of statutes that have most commonly incorporated provisions for mediation include personal information protection acts, human rights codes, statutes related to land disputes, family law acts and numerous pieces of labour dispute legislation.

3.2.1 Federal initiatives

Some acts are more comprehensive than others. At the federal level, the *Farm Debt Mediation Act*[12] lays out a point-by-point process for mediation between insolvent farmers and their creditors. Labour dispute legislation tends to incorporate mediation as a first step in resolving disputes. Other acts also incorporate mediation. The *Canadian Human Rights Act*,[13] for example, includes a provision stating that the Minister, on receiving a request from the Tribunal to decide whether a member should be subject to remedial or disciplinary measures, may "refer the matter to mediation."[14] The *Divorce Act* creates a statutory duty for lawyers to inform a client in divorce proceedings of any "mediation facilities" that might help in negotiating matters.[15]

The *Bankruptcy and Insolvency Act*[16] includes several mediation provisions. Under s. 68(6-10), a trustee or a creditor who disagrees about the amount of the bankrupt's income to be paid to the trustee may request that the matter be determined by mediation; another section allows a dissatisfied bankrupt to make a similar request. The rules for mediation are set out in detail in the regulations to the Act and include provisions for timing, presence of the parties, mediator discretion, and formation of a mediation agreement.[17]

More extensive mediation provisions are incorporated into the *Canadian Environmental Assessment Act*.[18] The Act defines mediation as "an environmental assessment that is conducted with the assistance of a mediator."[19] The mediator must be appointed under s. 30, which stipulates that the Minister must consult with all parties affected to appoint a mediator who is "unbiased and free from any conflict of interest" and who "has knowledge or experience in acting as a mediator." Under the *Canada Labour Code*,[20] the Federal Mediation and Conciliation Service (FMCS) is responsible for providing dispute resolution and dispute prevention assistance to trade unions and employers.[21]

3.2.2 Provincial initiatives

British Columbia has government-directed mediation services. The Mediation and Arbitration Board derives its authority from the *Petroleum and Natural Gas Act*.[22] In 1986, the province created the British Columbia International Commercial Arbitration Centre (BCICAC). The Centre is directly named in the *Nisga'a Final Agreement Act* appendices,[23] which include provisions for a number of licensing agreements. Two British Columbia statutes, the *Commercial Arbitration Act*[24] and the *International Commercial Arbitration Act*,[25] refer commercial disputes to BCICAC. The *International Commercial Arbitration Act* is based on the model set out by the United Nations Commission on International Trade Law (UNCITRAL) and refers to the development history of the *UNCITRAL Model Law on International Commercial Arbitration*[26] for assistance in interpreting the British Columbia statute. Similar statutes have been enacted in other provinces with reference to the UNCITRAL model. Most provincial versions of the international commercial statute contain a provision based on the following:

> 30(1) It is not incompatible with an arbitration agreement for an arbitral tribunal to encourage settlement of the dispute and, with the agreement of the parties, the arbitral tribunal may use mediation, conciliation or other procedures at any time during the arbitral proceedings to encourage settlement.[27]

In June 2002, the *UNCITRAL Model Law on International Commercial Conciliation* was released.[28] It is hoped that the conciliation model will be as well integrated into provincial law as the arbitration model was.

Mediation provisions have been most widely incorporated, as well as being presented in the greatest detail, in statutes pertaining to divorce and family law. In 1997, the Quebec General Assembly introduced extensive amendments to the *Quebec Code of Civil Procedure* that provide a detailed framework for mediation in divorce proceedings.[29] The Code stipulates that

> no application that involves the interests of the parties and the interests of their children may be heard by the court if there is a

dispute between the parties regarding child custody, support due to a party or to the children, the family patrimony or other patrimonial rights arising from the marriage, unless the parties have attended an information session on the mediation process and a copy of the mediator's report has been filed.

The province has made mediation a mandatory part of the divorce process, a legislative action that brought with it the creation of Quebec's Family Mediation Service.

Mandatory mediation in such instances has received considerable criticism because research seems to show that spouses with tangible resources tend to experience an advantage in mediation proceedings; post-divorce depression prevents people from working in their own interests; women's low perception of entitlement affects their negotiating skills; the blending of issues means women will often trade financial benefits for custody, regardless of the potential court outcomes; and of course, serious power dynamic problems exist where there has been a situation of physical abuse.[30] The Quebec legislators have gone to great lengths to mitigate such power imbalances. After an information session, the mediator files a report and the participants have the choice of pursuing mediation or not.[31] Either of the parties can terminate a mediation at any point in the proceedings "without having to give reasons," and mediators also have the power to end a mediation if they consider it "ill-advised."[32] As well, the court may at any time step in and make any "appropriate order to safeguard the rights of parties or children" during the mediation.[33] In addition, a party may refuse to attend the information session and may inform the mediator that their choice is related to "the inequality of the power relationship ... or the physical or psychological condition of the party." A further protection, one common to most provincial family acts, is a confidentiality clause, which prevents any statements made during mediation from being presented to the courts.

Other provincial statutes also provide for mediation in family disputes. For example, the Northwest Territories *Family Law Act*[34] provides that the court may order a mediation on topics of its choice as does the Ontario *Family Law Act*.[35] The Ontario Act directs payment for the mediation to come from the parties, while the

Quebec amendments place the fees for a limited number of sessions with the Family Mediation Service. Clearly, further developments will be forthcoming in this area.

Statutes dealing with conflicts that tend to involve high levels of citizen and government interaction often have incorporated mediation provisions. For example, Alberta's *Municipal Government Act* requires that mediation be attempted for disputes between municipalities and landowners and for intra-municipal disagreements. If mediations fail, the municipalities must submit to the court explanations for the failure to reach a mediated settlement.[36] In British Columbia, the *Local Government Act* allows the Minister to force parties into mediation when there is a dispute that involves the withdrawal of services.[37] The Minister may also order mediation if there are attempts to pass bylaws for service withdrawal but an inspector is not satisfied that the parties to a service have come to an agreement.[38]

3.2.3   Other initiatives

Besides the International Chamber of Commerce and the American Arbitration Association, many organizations provide mediation and arbitration services. For example, the Canadian Commercial Arbitration Centre provides both arbitration and mediation services. Recent developments include services in disputes regarding ".ca" domain names and amateur sports disagreements. The movement is well established at the international level. For example, the Commercial Arbitration and Mediation Center for the Americas was founded in 1995 by national institutions devoted to the development of consensus-based dispute resolution practices in disputes in international commercial agreements.[39]

3.3   MEDIATION ACCREDITATION IN CANADA

A number of professional associations of mediators have emerged both nationally and provincially over the last few years. Nationally, the ADR Institute of Canada (ADRIC) provides training and a national accreditation scheme for mediators and arbitrators. Since its inception ADRIC has developed a strict set of rules and procedures for accreditation, as well as a series of protocols for various forms of mediation.

To attain the designation of chartered mediator with ADRIC, a practitioner must meet educational, practical experience and skills assessment requirements, pass reviews, and obtain the approval of a Regional Institute's Accreditation Review Committee and ratification by ADRIC's National Accreditation Committee.[40] Applicants must also complete a pledge to abide by ADRIC's Code of Ethics.

Also nationally, Family Mediation Canada (FMC) offers three forms of certification: family relations mediator, family financial mediator and comprehensive family mediator. Certification requires a thirty-hour practicum or two years of experience, with references; the submission of a role-play video, which is assessed by a FMC assessor; completion of an exam; and ratification by the FMC Board of Directors. Maintaining certification requires participation in continuing education programs and adequate insurance coverage.

In British Columbia, the Mediator Roster Society admits mediators in civil mediation and family mediation.[41] In the Saskatchewan Civil Mediation Program, mediators are hired by the Dispute Resolution Office on the basis of a combination of training and experience.

Justice Quebec does not dictate who is used as a mediator under their mediation program, but refers parties to professional organizations. The "Institut de médiation et d'arbitrage du Québec" (IMAQ, Mediation and Arbitration Institute of Quebec) has brought together four professional organizations under an agreement to provide a central civil mediation roster.[42]

Under the new mandatory mediation program in Ontario, mediator applicants are chosen and approved by local mediation committees. The committees' guidelines are based on a point system, in which applicants receive points for their experience as a mediator, for training and for education; for their familiarity with the civil justice system and for references. In Nova Scotia, the Barristers Society, in conjunction with the Department of Justice and the local mediation community, established a Civil Mediation Roster that is managed by the Barrister Society and administered by the Civil Mediation Policy Committee.[43]

3.4 CONSENSUS-BASED JUSTICE PROCESSES

It is within this context that a number of innovative, consensus-based justice processes have been developed. These processes cover different types of disputes, including those related to family law, landlord–tenant relations, bankruptcy, administrative law and commercial interests. This section will review some processes that have been developed over the past two decades.

3.4.1 Community mediation

The earliest formal manifestations of community-based mediation services in non-criminal matters were the neighbourhood justice centres that arose during the 1980s. By 1985, there were 182 community justice centres offering informal, consensus-based dispute resolution procedures across the United States.[44] In Canada, an early community mediation service was developed in Kitchener–Waterloo that grew out of an early victim–offender initiative (Community Justice Initiatives).

One model is for a conflict resolution program to attach itself to an existing community centre, with perhaps one or two funded staff with the remainder of the services provided by trained volunteer mediators. The reliance on a combination of short-term project funding and a volunteer pool means that community mediation programs often face instability and insecurity in their operations. Generally, community mediation programs provide a body of volunteer mediators whose diversity—of language and ethnicity—matches that of the local population. A co-mediation model, with substantial effort made in early case development before bringing the parties together, is also common.

The caseload of most community mediation programs is diverse, including both non-legal or pre-legal disputes, such as neighbour, neighbourhood or roommate conflicts, as well as matters that are already following legal procedures, such as landlord—tenant disputes, consumer goods or services complaints or disputes between small businesses. In such cases, if an agreement results from mediation, it may be filed with the court, which will discontinue the action. Some programs have formalized referral links with local small claims courts (for example, the University of Windsor Mediation Service) or with local city services (for example, Community Justice Initiatives of Kitchener–Waterloo or Toronto's St. Stephen's Conflict Resolution Service) or with local police.

The mediation filmed by the National Film Board that is the subject of the DVD attached to this report is a community mediation.

3.4.2 Court-connected mediation

The last decade has seen the successive introduction of new rules of procedures that enable a formal referral from the justice system into a court-sanctioned mediation process. The first example of a mandatory court-connected mediation program in Canada was in the Saskatchewan Court of Queen's Bench, which introduced early mandatory mediation in civil non-family cases in two centres (Regina and Swift Current) in 1994 under the *Queen's Bench Act*.[45] Ontario introduced a mandatory mediation pilot program under a Practice Direction to the Toronto General Division in 1994.[46] In 2000, a new rule of civil procedure made mandatory non-family civil mediation a permanent feature of litigation in Toronto and Ottawa.[47] Similar procedural reforms have been introduced in British Columbia[48] and are being considered in Alberta.

In relation to more familiar pre-trial processes, court-connected mediation generally occurs earlier in the litigation process and is usually (although not always) hosted by a non-judicial officer. Such processes are intended to structure a discussion between the parties over settlement options and if possible, assist in the crafting of a settlement. Where attendance is mandatory, mediation is scheduled for two to three hours, although the parties may choose to continue if they believe the process to be constructive. In mandatory programs such as those of Ontario and Saskatchewan, attendance at a mediation session is required before the matter can proceed through the regular court process.

3.4.3 Judge-led settlement conferencing

Rules of court are allowing more opportunities for judges to play a proactive role in moving the parties toward settlement. Sometimes this intervention takes the form of a broader case management initiative, in which a judge is assigned at an early stage to ensure that a timetable is agreed to.[49] Moreover settlement conferences, which are most commonly used as a means of canvassing settlement options under the evaluative guidance of a judge, are now included in either, or both, family and civil non-family matters in all Canadian provinces.

In 1998, the Quebec Court of Appeal initiated a judge-led conciliation service. The Conciliation Service, which is offered free of charge, is open to all parties involved in civil, commercial or family litigation at the appellate level. Parties to the conflict must agree to participate in the process. Filing for conciliation suspends the appeal proceedings, but any party may abandon conciliation and return to the ordinary appeal process at any time. Confidentiality is crucial to the success of the program. The parties voluntarily commit to keep all matters strictly confidential and refrain from disclosing the substance of all discussions. There are no transcripts or summaries of the conciliation session. If the parties are successful in resolving their conflict, a settlement agreement is drafted. The settlement agreement is ratified by an independent panel of three judges of the Court of Appeal. The judgment is then as enforceable as any other judgment of the court.

3.4.4 Collaborative family lawyering

A final example of the use of consensus-based justice in non-criminal matters is the development of collaborative family lawyering. Collaborative lawyering reflects a commitment by the lawyers and their clients to negotiate an alternative to a litigated or adjudicated outcome. Collaborative lawyering refers to a contractual commitment between lawyer and client not to resort to litigation to resolve the client's problem. The lawyer is retained to provide advice and representation regarding the non-litigious resolution of the conflict and to focus on developing a negotiated, consensual outcome. If the client does decide that legal action is ultimately necessary to resolve the dispute, the retainer stipulates that the collaborative lawyer (along with any other collaborative professionals, such as divorce coaches or financial planners) must withdraw and receive no further remuneration for work on the case.[50]

Originating in Minneapolis in 1990, collaborative lawyering arrangements have flourished in Minnesota, Ohio, California, Texas and Georgia, and now in many Canadian provinces, including British Columbia, Alberta, Saskatchewan and Ontario. Proponents of collaborative law suggest that this approach reduces legal costs; expedites resolution; leads to better, more integrative solutions; and enhances personal and commercial relationships.[51]

3.5   THE OBJECTIVES OF CONSENSUS-BASED JUSTICE

The discussion that follows describes four key value-based objectives for consensus-based justice. The model of consensus-based justice presented here is not simply a descriptive model for negotiation within an adjudicative context. Conventional legal negotiations that

> "By the time litigants arrive at the Court of Appeal, they are firmly gripped by the mindset of the adversarial system. Having had this direct experience at the trial division, the adversarial attitude often settles in and does little to encourage parties to consider resolving their conflict amicably, on their own. Judicial conciliation offers litigants this opportunity to withdraw—voluntarily and temporarily—from the formal adversarial system. It allows them to settle their differences with the active support and assistance of a judge. The process as such presents no risks for the parties who remain free to return to the formal system should a settlement not be achieved."
>
> The Honourable Louise Otis, "The Conciliation Service Program of the Court of Appeal of Quebec," prepared for the NAFTA Advisory Committee on Private Commercial Disputes and presented at the Alternative Dispute Resolution for Judges and Businesses Conference, Mexico City, Mexico, June 1999.

occur between lawyer–agents in the process of litigation often adopt many of the same values and principles as adversarial justice.[52] The concept of consensus-based justice draws on a set of objectives, including a desire to fashion consensual outcomes that meet individual needs; the inclusion of individual disputants as direct participants; and a focus on the relationship dimensions of the conflict, both present and future.

The four key objectives presented are shared among programs and proponents. These objectives are

- clarification of the wrong and an appraisal of its impact;

- distribution and assumption of responsibility;

- relationship transformation; and

- moving forward.

Each of these objectives is discussed below.

3.5.1 Clarification of the wrong and an appraisal of its impact

From a consensus-based justice perspective, the first step in conflict resolution is clarification of the wrong, rather than attributing it to or blaming someone. The relevant question becomes "What happened here?" rather than "Whose fault was it?" This implies an exploratory and investigative element in the dialogue, as well as an appraisal of the actual impact of the harm done by the act.

Traditional civil justice also includes an exploratory and investigative phase during which parties and others are examined under oath. However, the motivation and rationale for gathering information and the use of it are quite different in a consensus-building process than in litigation. In litigation, information is gathered to substantiate a particular version of events.[53] Evidence is generated to enhance a particular rights-based argument, and anything that does not bear on this is deemed irrelevant. Presenting information as evidence means presenting it as "fact" and requires a certain denial of ambiguity, circumstance or context. In this adversarial model, the side with the most complete and well-constructed information file is best placed to carry the day. In adversarial processes, information is for winning, not for sharing.

Where negotiations anticipate an outcome developed by the parties themselves, rather than one in which there is a clear winner and loser, the purpose of information collection is clarification. Instead of being for winning, information is sought and disclosed to build a better collaborative outcome for the parties. This does not mean that tensions do not arise. Nevertheless, in consensus-based justice processes—such as mediation, settlement conferencing and collaborative lawyering—the ability to identify and share information that is essential to early resolution is a critical skill.[54]

A consensus-based justice approach emphasizes value-creating negotiation strategies for creating *power with* rather than *power over* outcomes.[55] Personal, business, practical and emotional issues can be factored into solutions that might include future business arrangements, monetary settlements, an apology or an acknowledgment of responsibility or of unintended impact, or the bestowal of some other valued outcome by one party on the other.[56] Focus shifts away from finding a winning formula toward discovering a good outcome; for this to be possible, there must first be clarification through the sharing of information.

3.5.2 Distribution and assumption of responsibility

The initial gathering of information in a consensus-based justice process has a different purpose and is of a different nature than in an adversarial civil litigation process. More accurate, fair and practical allocation of responsibility will take place following a full disclosure of information, so that the wrong can be clarified.

Based on the information now available, the parties in a consensus-based justice process must assess who assumes responsibility for the harm, and for which part of the harm, caused by the conflict. A degree of flexibility over the distribution of responsibility is possible in a consensus-based justice process. This type of flexibility does not always exist in a conventional litigation model. A consensus-based justice approach to conflict enables factors to be taken into account in responsibility allocation beyond what formal rules of law might suggest.

In consensus-based justice processes, which are concerned with positively impacting actual and perceived relationships, responsibility-taking is important, but it is not a win–lose proposition. In other words, there is no given volume or depth of responsibility that must be assumed by one party. Responsibility is divisible, and it need not add to up 100 percent. The parties can negotiate what responsibilities each has to the other and how these may have been broken, assess the factors relevant to that breach of expectations (including, for example, factors beyond one or the other's control), and eventually determine how much responsibility each must assume and what is the acceptable measure and tone of regret.

3.5.3   Relationship transformation

Each of the objectives listed above works toward the ultimate goal of consensus-based justice processes: the transformation of the relationships damaged or broken by the conflict. **Transformation** refers to a range of possible outcomes, from reconciliation to future avoidance. The important point is that the negative energy that fuelled the conflict is confronted and addressed, even in the most pragmatic of ways (for example, by preventive steps and avoidance).

Some writers and practitioners argue that the central objective of consensus-based justice processes is to significantly change a relationship, whether or not the conflict is actually resolved.[57] This approach acknowledges that different parties in different circumstances may seek different levels of resolution for their conflict and that none is proscribed or prohibited in a party-driven consensus-based justice process. For example, one disputant may simply want another party to stop a behaviour. Another may look to reveal a different understanding of what produced the dispute and why the other person behaved as they did. Yet others may feel that their emotional needs have been met in the resolution.[58]

The model of consensus-based justice proposed here—and which we suggest has the most widespread currency among the many and various manifestations of consensus-based justice—does not assume that the only good outcome of conflict is a better, or at least significantly changed, relationship between the parties, regardless of whether the conflict has actually been addressed and resolved between them.[59] What is highlighted is the importance placed on relationships, as both a symptom and a cause of conflict, and the need to offer process opportunities to the parties to enhance this (business or personal) relationship.

3.5.4   Moving forward

Consensus-based justice processes encourage disputants to take a long hard look at the future, beyond the conflict that is presently consuming them. First, the clarification and appraisal stages of the process are designed to ensure that the parties can move forward to consider the future, including their future relationship, whatever form that might take. Second, the outcomes of consensus-based justice processes anticipate future issues and even conflicts and attempt to address these in a proactive, realistic manner. A good example of this is the difference between an order for custody and access made by a family court judge and the types of detailed, context-specific agreements that may be reached as a consequence of family mediation or collaborative lawyering; or the potential for structuring commercial agreements to enable structured payments, rather than the single judgment order of a court.

Third, consensus-based justice sees the process of dialogue and resolution itself as a rehearsal for the future, whether involving these parties and issues or another context of conflict resolution. The emphasis placed on a fair, accessible and constructive process of dialogue by consensus-based justice models is not simply instrumental, achieving a given end; it anticipates a future in which other conflicts will need to be addressed and offers some tools for that future.

3.6   CORE PROCESS VALUES FOR CONSENSUS-BASED JUSTICE

It is in the domain of process values that the congruence between restorative justice and consensus-based justice is most striking. Both restorative justice and consensus-based justice processes emphasize the importance of giving explicit voice to all those involved and

---

The Objectives of Consensus-based Justice

In summary, the Commission believes there are four objectives that consensus-based justice processes ought to strive for:

- Clarification of the harm and an appraisal of its impact;

- Distribution and assumption of responsibility;

- Transformation of relationships; and

- Moving forward.

---

affected by the conflict in a way that ensures that they can use their own words to describe the impact on themselves.

Each type of process assumes that the form of dialogue that will enable the achievement of its objectives is one that occurs, for the most part, face-to-face, rather than by correspondence or at arm's length. Both restorative justice and consensus-based justice stress respect for all participants as a core process value, as well as respect for the outcomes of the process. Flexibility—of both process and outcomes—is of central importance.

3.6.1 Participation

Much of what has already been said above about restorative justice is equally applicable to consensus-based justice and need not be repeated. Mediators who view mediation as primarily an opportunity to enhance communication focus their efforts on paraphrasing and reframing each party's expression of needs, to provide explicit acknowledgment and validation. Some authors set out an understanding of acknowledgment that they describe as recognition.[60] Recognition by one party of the needs and goals of others is the quid pro quo of personal empowerment. While recognition may be tacit, open recognition of another disputant's needs and interests generally reflects a changed understanding, however subtle, on the part of the speaker and, as a consequence, a reassessment of, or a re-orientation to, the problem that has caused the dispute.[61]

This type of re-orientation may be essential to unleashing the transformative effects of the mediation and other consensus-based justice processes.

3.6.2   Respect for all participants

Respectful listening, acknowledgment and recognition can be expanded into a broader principle of civility and courtesy between all participants in negotiations.[62] It is a key value of consensus-based justice to ensure that all participants are treated respectfully. While always a challenging proposition, respect is perhaps easier to maintain as a structural equality value in non-criminal processes.

3.6.3   Fair treatment

People want to be treated fairly. Perceptions of fair treatment in the process itself are as important as actual outcomes when disputants come to appraise dispute resolution processes.[63] While there is an obvious relationship between a sense of fair process and a welcome outcome, this research suggests that these judgments are independent.[64]

Research shows that perceptions of fair treatment are as important as outcomes when disputants come to appraise dispute resolution experiences.[65] Moreover, research shows that there are higher levels of compliance with court orders when, in the view of the disputants, the process is a fair one[66] and that a feeling of procedural fairness may enhance perceptions of apparently negative outcomes, described as the "cushion effect."[67] Similarly, there are those whose negative experience of process persists, notwithstanding a good outcome.[68] Preference for procedural fairness, as well as the identification of the factors that make up procedural fairness, appears fairly consistent across a range of cultural contexts.[69] Recent work in the mediation field has suggested that for some disputants, having control over a process, especially the expression of their particular voice, has value in itself.[70]

3.6.4   Respect for agreed outcomes

As with restorative justice, a key practical element of consensus-building in a consensus-based approach is the voluntary acceptance of agreed outcomes and compliance with them. In non-criminal matters, there are a variety of ways in which agreements reached in mediation or similar processes can be formalized by court order, enabling the parties to bring themselves within the aegis of judicial enforcement measures. However, since consensus-based justice emphasizes a healthy process, relationship restoration and forward-looking outcomes, many of the elements of an agreed outcome (for example, how these parties will treat one another in the future or how they have agreed to get past their conflict) are not readily monitored or enforceable. This makes an authentic commitment and a desire to maintain the outcomes—perhaps with some self-monitoring—especially important.

3.6.5   Flexibility of process and outcomes

Finally, as with restorative justice, consensus-based justice adopts a commitment to the flexibility and responsiveness of both process and outcomes. This flows naturally from the emphasis placed by both models on the emergence of effective resolution within a pre-existing context. The process of developing a resolution must also reject a rigid procedural approach, both to reduce unnecessary formality and to enable the appropriate process model to emerge for these parties and this conflict.

Process Values for Consensus-based Justice

- Participation

- Fair treatment

- Respect for all participants

- Respect for agreed outcomes

- Flexibility of process and outcomes

3.7   SUMMARY

The growth in consensus-based justice processes in Canada has been quite remarkable over the past two decades. Programs have developed in most jurisdictions and in many different fields. For the most part, these programs have developed in an ad hoc way; in some jurisdictions, for example, mediation of some civil disputes is mandatory, in others it is strongly encouraged, while in still others there are disincentives to enter into mediation. Notwithstanding the ad hoc nature of the development of consensus-based justice, there has emerged a set of objectives and core process values. As in restorative justice, at the root of consensus-based justice processes is the value of participation. Consensus-based justice processes also allow Canadians a choice in deciding how to resolve their conflicts. To this extent, these processes encourage the development of a healthy democracy.

---

[1]   C. Menkel-Meadow, "The Transformation of Disputes by Lawyers: What the Dispute Paradigm Does and Does Not Tell Us" (1985) 25 *Missouri Journal of Dispute Resolution* 1 at 3.

[2]   See, for example, K. Braid, "Arbitrate or Litigate: A Canadian Corporate Perspective" (1991) 17 *Canada–US Law Journal* 465.

[3]   For example, the Civil Litigation Evaluation Project, an extensive empirical study of civil litigation conducted during the 1980s by leading American academics, estimated that 22 percent of plaintiffs who paid their lawyers on an hourly basis paid more in legal fees that they recovered in litigation. See D.M. Trubek, A. Sarat, W. Felstiner, H.M. Kritzer and J.B. Grossman, "The Costs of Ordinary Litigation" (1983) 31 *UCLA Law Review* 72 at 112.

[4]   Ontario Civil Justice Review, *Civil Justice Review: Supplemental and Final Report* (Toronto: Ministry of the Attorney General, 1996).

[5]   For a short review, see E. Zweibel, "Hybrid Processes: Using Evaluation to Build Consensus" in J. Macfarlane, ed., *Dispute Resolution: Readings and Case Studies*, 2nd ed. (Toronto: Emond Montgomery, 2003) at 587–588.

6   See, for example, J. Macfarlane, *Court-based Mediation in Civil Cases: An Evaluation of the Toronto General Division ADR Centre* (Toronto: Ontario Ministry of the Attorney General, 1995) at 4–13; and R. Hann, C. Barr and Associates, *Evaluation of the Ontario Mandatory Mediation Program: Final Report—The First 23 Months* (Toronto: Ontario Queen's Printer, 2001) at chapter 3.

7   R.J. Gilson and R.H. Mnookin, "Disputing Through Agents: Cooperation and Conflict Between Lawyers in Litigation" (1994) 94:2 *Columbia Law Review* 509.

8   See J. Macfarlane, "Culture Change? A Tale of Two Cities and Mandatory Court-connected Mediation" (2002) 2002:2 Journal of Dispute Resolution 241; and J. Macfarlane, *Building on "What Works": An Evaluation of the Saskatchewan Queen's Bench Mediation Program* (Regina: Saskatchewan Justice, 2003).

9   M.L. Coates, G.T. Furlong and B.M. Downie, *Conflict Management and Dispute Resolution Systems in Canadian Non-unionized Organizations* (Kingston: Industrial Relations Centre, Queen's University, 1997).

10   See, for example, the attitudes noted in J. Lande, "Getting the Faith: Why Business Lawyers and Executives Believe in Mediation" (2000) 5 *Harvard Negotiation Law Review* 137; and J. Lande, "Failing Faith in Litigation? A Survey of Business Lawyers and Executives Opinions" (1998) 3 *Harvard Negotiation Law Review* 1.

11   Apology is often assumed to be an admission of liability that would void insurance coverage under standard insurance protocols. Case law on whether an apology is conclusive in establishing liability is inconclusive. In California and Massachusetts, legislative reform has been enacted to ensure that apologies can be made without compromising liability; see *Annotated Laws of Massachusetts*, ch. 233, § 23D and *West's Annotated California Code* § 1160.

12   *Farm Debt Mediation Act*, S.C. 1997, c. 21.

13   *Canadian Human Rights Act*, R.S.C. 1985, c. H-6.

14   *Ibid.*, s. 48.3 (2)(b).

15   *Divorce Act*, R.S.C. 1985, c. 3 (2nd Supp.).

16   *Bankruptcy and Insolvency Act*, R.S.C. 1985, c. B-3.

17   *Bankruptcy and Insolvency General Rules*, C.R.C., c. 368, s. 105(1).

18   *Canadian Environmental Assessment Act*, S.C. 1992, c. 37.

19   *Ibid.*, s. 2.

20   *Canada Labour Code*, R.S.C. 1985, c. L-2, s. 70.1.

21   The Federal Mediation and Conciliation Service (FMCS) is included in evidentiary provisions of the *Status of the Artist Act*, S.C. 1992, c. 33, s. 60(2), and it seems likely that legislated involvement of the FMCS will increase with further uptake of alternative dispute resolution (ADR) mechanisms within federal departments.

22   *Petroleum and Natural Gas Act*, R.S.B.C. 1996, c. 361. The Board has the authority to undertake mediation and arbitration activities over land-access disputes involving mineral extractions in the province.

23   *Nisga'a Final Agreement Act*, S.B.C. 1999, c. 2. Appendices, Article 10.3.

24   *Commercial Arbitration Act*, R.S.B.C. 1996, c. 55.

25   *International Commercial Arbitration Act*, R.S.B.C. 1996, c. 233.

26   *UNCITRAL Model Law on International Commercial Arbitration*, 1985.

27   *Supra* note 25, s. 30(1).

28   *UNCITRAL Model Law on International Commercial Conciliation*, 2002.

29   *Code of Civil Procedure*, R.S.Q. 2001, c. C-25.

30   Gordon, M.L., "'What Me, Biased?' Women and Gender Bias in Family Law" (2001) 19:1 *Family Law Quarterly* 53.

31   *Supra* note 29, s. 814.6.

32   *Supra* note 29, s. 814.8.

33   *Supra* note 29, s. 814.9.

34   *Family Law Act*, S.N.W.T. 1997, c. 18, s. 58(1), s. 58(1).

35   *Family Law Act*, R.S.O. 1990, c. F-3, s. 3(4).

36   *Municipal Government Act*, R.S.A. 2000, c. M-26, ss. 117(2) and 118(1)(a).

37   *Local Government Act*, R.S.B.C. 1996, c. 323, s. 813.09.

38   *Ibid.*, s. 802.3.

39   See also the International Centre for the Settlement of Investment Disputes (ICSID) that administers a program of dispute resolution between countries and investors. Online: <http://www.worldbank.org/icsid/>.

40 ADRIC's educational requirements include the completion of at least 80 hours of mediation theory and skills training in programs approved by the Institute, as well as 100 hours of study or training in general dispute resolution. General programs can include areas such as the psychology of dispute resolution, negotiation, public consultation, mutual gains bargaining, communication, management consulting, conflict management, or specific substantive areas such as law, psychology, social work and counselling. There is also an alternative process for applicants who can show the Regional Accreditation Board that they have satisfied or exceeded the educational requirement through proven skills and competency, longevity in practice and recognition or recommendation by peers. Applicants must also demonstrate practical experience by conducting at least ten mediations in which they were either the sole mediator or at least five separate mediations in which they were the mediation chairperson, and at least five of these had to be fee-for-service activities. ADRIC must also be satisfied that a skills assessment has taken place and that the applicant has demonstrated competency in the process of mediation.

41 To be admitted to the Civil Roster, a mediator must have at least 80 hours of core education in conflict resolution and mediation theory, and skills training; 100 additional hours of training in dispute resolution or in a related field; knowledge of Supreme Court procedures; letters of reference; insurance coverage; and completion of a minimum of ten mediations as the primary mediator. Admission to the Family Roster has similar requirements, but with a concentration in practical family mediation and at least 50 mediations as the primary mediator, in which 40 were family related. An alternative route can be taken by qualifying first with Family Mediation Canada.

42 The four organizations are the Chambre des notaires du Québec (Chamber of Notaries of Quebec), the Ordre des comptables agréés du Québec (Order of Chartered Accountants of Quebec), the Ordre des évaluateurs agréés du Québec (Order of Chartered Appraisers of Quebec) and the Ordre des ingénieurs du Québec (Order of Engineers of Quebec). Qualification and maintenance of the title of accredited mediator requires that an individual have five years of membership in one of the partner organizations, 40 hours of training at an accredited institution, 30 hours of continuing relevant education within five years of becoming accredited, and performance of at least three mediations within five years of becoming accredited. IMAQ is also a regional member of ADRIC.

43 Guidelines detail the role of the Committee and set out the requirements for membership on the Roster. Section 3 lists rules for mediator selection, which include personal qualities that determine mediator effectiveness, a minimum of 80 hours of training in core subject areas, being a member or retired member

of the local bar or showing substantial knowledge of the court process, and having acted as a sole mediator in at least five interest-based mediations over a five-year period. Maintaining a position on the Roster requires that a member has acted as a mediator at least twice in the previous year, provide minimum insurance coverage of $1 million, and attend any continuing education programs as directed by the Committee.

44 D. McGillis, *Community Dispute Resolution Programs and Public Policy* (Washington, D.C.: National Institute of Justice, 1988).

45 Originally an amendment to the Queen's Bench Act, R.S.S. 1978, s. 54(2)(1), and subsequently in the *Queen's Bench Act*, S.S. 1998, c. Q-1.01.

46 Practice Direction Concerning Alternative Dispute Resolution Pilot Project in the Ontario Court, 16 O.R. (3d) 481.

47 Ontario Rules of Civil Procedure, O. Reg. 194/90, Rule 24.1.

48 See the "Notice to Mediate" (B.C. Reg. 127/98) under the *Insurance (Motor Vehicle) Act*, R,S,B,C. 1996, c. 231, s. 44.1.

49 See, for example, O. Reg. 194/90 (Ontario Rules of Civil Procedure), Rule 77, (non-family civil case management).

50 See, for example, P. Tesler, *Collaborative Law: Achieving Effective Resolution in Divorce Without Litigation* (Chicago: American Bar Association Family Law Section, 2001); J. Lawrence, "Collaborative Lawyering: A New Development in Conflict Resolution" (2002) 17 *Ohio State Journal on Dispute Resolution* 431; and T. Sholar, "Collaborative Law - A Method for the Madness" (1993) 23 *Memphis State University Law Review* 667.

51 See J. Lande, "Possibilities of Collaborative Law" [unpublished paper]; and J. Macfarlane, "Collaborating with the Collaborators: Preliminary Results from a Three-year Research Study" (prepared for delivery at the American Association of Law Schools, Washington, D.C., 2003).

52 See, for example, S. Clarke, E. Ellen and K. McCormick, *Court-ordered Civil Case Mediation in North Carolina: Court Efficiency and Litigant Satisfaction* (Chapel Hill: Institute of Government, University of North Carolina, 1995).

53 See also J. Macfarlane, "What Does the Changing Culture of Legal Practice Mean for Legal Education?" (2001) 20 *Windsor Yearbook of Access to Justice* 191.

54 See Macfarlane, *supra* note 8 at 241; J. Lande, "How Will Lawyering and Mediation Practices Transform Each Other?" (1997) 24 *Florida State University*

Law Review 839; and A. Zariski, "Disputing Culture: Lawyers and ADR" (2000) 7:2 *Murdoch University Electronic Journal of Law*. Note that in collaborative family lawyering, the retainer agreement explicitly requires full and complete disclosure of all relevant information.

55 G. Chornenki, "Mediating Commercial Disputes: Exchanging 'Power Over' for 'Power With'" in J. Macfarlane, ed., *Rethinking Disputes: The Mediation Alternative* (Toronto: Emond Montgomery, 1997).

56 See, for example, D. Lax and J. Sebenius *The Manager as Negotiator: Bargaining for Competitive Gain* (New York: Free Press, 1986); and C. Menkel-Meadow, "Towards Another View of Legal Negotiations: The Structure of Problem-solving" 31 *UCLA Law Review* (1984) 754.

57 A view often associated with the transformative models of mediation, epitomized by the work of professors Bush and Folger. R.A. Bush and J.P. Folger, *The Promise of Mediation: Responding to Conflict Through Empowerment and Recognition* (San Francisco: Jossey-Bass, 1994).

58 B. Mayer, *The Dynamics of Conflict Resolution* (San Francisco: Jossey-Bass, 2000).

59 In contrast, some proponents of consensus-based justice would argue that only a significantly enhanced relationship is a satisfactory outcome and that the resolution of the original problem is far less important—a distraction even—from the real purpose of a participatory process. This is the argument made by Bush and Folger (*supra* note 56 at 33–78) and rebutted by Carrie Menkel-Meadow in her review, "The Many Ways of Mediation: The Transformation of Traditions, Ideologies, Paradigms, and Practices" (1995) 11:3 *Negotiation Journal* 217.

60 Bush, *supra* note 56 at 28–40.

61 Bush, *supra* note 56 at 89–92.

62 E.A. Lind and T. Tyler, *The Social Psychology of Procedural Justice* (London: Plenum Press, 1992) at 109. For an unusually explicit professional standard on civility, see Rule 10.035 of the Florida Rules for Court-appointed and Certified Mediators (1998), which reads: "a mediator shall be patient, dignified and courteous to all participants in the mediation."

63 J. Thibaut, L. Walker, S, LaTour and S. Houlden, "Procedural Justice as Fairness" (1974) 26 *Stanford Law Review* 1271; J. Thibaut, and L. Walker, *Procedural Justice: A Psychological Analysis* (New York: Erlbaum, 1975).

64 Similar results are reported from a study asking citizens for their appraisal of (1) the fairness of government policy and (2) their personal benefits (specifically regarding taxation and benefits). See T. Tyler, K. Rasinski and K. McGraw, "The Influence of Perceived Injustices on the Endorsement of Political Leaders" (1985) 15 *Journal of Applied Social Psychology* 700.

65 *Supra* note 62. See also T. Tyler, "The Role of Perceived Injustice in Defendants' Evaluations of Their Courtroom Experience" (1984) 18 *Law and Society Review* 51.

66 See, for example, C. McEwen and R. Mainman, "Small Claims Mediation in Maine: An Empirical Assessment" (1984) 33 *Maine Law Review* 244: and C. McEwen and R. Maiman, "Mediation in Small Claims Court: Achieving Compliance Through Consent" (1984) 18 *Law and Society Review* 11.

67   T. Tyler and E.A. Lind "A Relational Model of Authority in Groups" in M. Zanna, ed., *Advances in Experimental Social Psychology*, vol. 25 (New York: Academic Press 1992); and Thibaut, *supra* note 62.

68 For example, a significant number of litigants in the Ontario General Division interviewed for a 1995 study expressed dissatisfaction with the process, notwithstanding a positive outcome to their cases. More than one-third (36 percent) were dissatisfied with the "fairness" (described as opportunity to provide input to the counsel, time to speak and be heard) of the process. Furthermore, only 8.5 percent described themselves as completely satisfied with the outcome, reflecting perhaps the fact that further enforcement steps were often necessary after securing a favourable judgment. In some cases, this seemed to overshadow the final result. For example, one successful litigant told the interviewer, "It's taken so long, and we're still waiting. It's taken its toll on myself and my family. Nothing could have prepared us for this process." J. Macfarlane, *Court-based Mediation in Civil Cases: An Evaluation of the Toronto General Division ADR Centre* (Toronto: Ontario Ministry of the Attorney General, 1995).

69 See, for example, K. Leung and E.A. Lind, "Procedural Justice and Culture: Effects of Culture, Gender and Investigator Status on Procedural Preferences" (1986) 50 *Journal of Personality and Social Psychology* 1134; E.A. Lind, Y.J. Huo and T. Tyler, "... And Justice for All: Ethnicity, Gender and Preferences for Dispute Resolution Procedures" (1994) 18 *Law and Human Behaviour* 269.; and Lind, *supra* note 61 at 107–111.

70 T. Tyler, K. Rasinki and N. Spodick, "The Influence of Voice on Satisfaction with Leaders: Exploring the Meaning of Process Control" (1985) 48 *Journal of Personality and Social Psychology* 72. See also Bush, *supra* note 56 at 84–89.

Chapter 4   Restorative Justice and Consensus-based Justice: Common Elements, Critiques and Concerns

Restorative justice and consensus-based justice have developed in response to related concerns about the deficiencies of existing adversarial dispute resolution processes. In many ways the differences between a criminal wrong and a civil wrong are arbitrary. Conventional dichotomies (public–private, criminal–civil, state-citizen) explain disputes in the light of applicable legal and procedural rules and principles. But it is sometimes difficult to sustain a fair and logical distinction between wrongs that are always private concerns and those that are always matters for public adjudication. Indeed, these conventional dichotomies themselves are often considered responsible for maintaining boundaries that are antithetical to many contemporary ideals. It is similarly challenging to identify a clear social consensus in a diverse society that designates certain behaviours as wrong and others as right.[1] There may be excellent reasons to treat some conflicts differently from others—for example, impact on the community, degree of harm, relative power of the affected parties—but the conventional dichotomy between criminal matters and civil matters is only one dimension of this differentiation.

Chapter 4 will explore points of convergence and divergence between restorative justice and consensus-based justice.

4.1   POINTS OF CONVERGENCE BETWEEN RESTORATIVE JUSTICE AND CONSENSUS-BASED JUSTICE

This section describes points of convergence between restorative justice and consensus-based justice. Both systems are underpinned by a common vision. These participatory processes are committed to generating outcomes that can be designed and embraced by those affected, rather than imposing outcomes in advance and from the outside. This section provides an overview of a set of values that restorative justice and consensus-based justice hold in common. There are three key areas in which the vision of restorative justice and that of consensus-based justice overlap:

- Conception of harm

- Conception of justice

- Focus on relationships

4.1.1 Conception of harm

In criminal law, an act is assumed to cause harm if it is defined as a crime in the *Criminal Code*: an act that violates the *Criminal Code* is inherently harmful, independent of the type or level of actual impact. If harm is inherent in particular acts, a retributive approach has strong logical appeal. The challenge is to match the harm with an appropriately equal punishment.[2]

Because harm is inherent in a criminal act, the impact of an act on a victim has historically been seen as somewhat irrelevant, exemplified in the virtual exclusion of victims from the process of assessing harm and its consequences. Instead, the central issue is proof that the act took place as claimed and was carried out by (or with the aid of) the defendant. Once proof is established, the question that remains is the level of culpability of the individual defendant.[3]

For both restorative justice and consensus-based justice, the purpose of conflict resolution is to identify the harm and to understand its impact. Restorative justice and consensus-based justice conceive harm as occurring first and foremost against an individual, a breach of a relationship—and secondarily as also having implications for the whole community. Both approaches suggest a vision of harm that is not necessarily inherent in the act itself nor an automatic consequence of a breach of rules, but as arising from its impact on others as individuals and community members. The notion of harm is contextually constructed and thus adaptable to the circumstances of the disputants or the offender and victim, and those who are secondarily harmed by the conflict (for example, the community, the industrial sector, third parties in commercial disputes, or children and other relatives in a marital breakdown).

4.1.2   Conception of justice

Restorative justice is about restoring a damaged relationship to a level of social equality—characterized by respect, mutual concern and dignity—rather than about advancing or protecting an abstract rule.[4] The objectives of formal equality—the maintenance of general rules—are different from those of a system more concerned with establishing or restoring actual equality and respect between particular persons in a given context following a particular set of actions or events.

Some authors describe restorative justice as "equal well-being." To achieve equal well-being, different individuals will have different needs. This notion of needs-responsive justice cannot be proscribed or administered through a particular set of procedures or rules, which often privilege one or another rights holders and may perpetuate patterns of systemic inequality. Instead, equal well-being must be "created or achieved"[5] by those who participate in the process (participation being key to both a cognitive and an affective sense of equal well-being).

An important dimension of achieving justice through restorative justice is the creation of processes that enable different needs to be responded to differentially, without an assumption of same treatment. This vision of justice contemplates not only the resolution of interpersonal conflict and the restoration of those relationships,

---

"[In an ideal state,] everyone feels that his or her present needs have been presented, acknowledged, respected and met, and, therefore, feels justly treated. When these conditions are met, there is an overwhelming sense that justice has, in fact, been done."

D. Sullivan and L. Tifft, "The Negotiated and Economic Dimensions of Restorative Justice" 22(1) *Humanity and Society* (1998) 38 at 40.

---

but also the redistribution of power within society.[6] This vision of justice is resonant of consensus-based justice models on the civil side. The shift away from a rights-centred approach to conflict resolution and toward the use of negotiation and mediation processes in which differences are articulated, needs are clarified, and appropriate norms are created.[7] Where litigation has already commenced, a consensus-based justice approach requires disputants to reconceive their conflict as one in which certain solutions other than a win–lose outcome are possible. To achieve even the possibility of such solutions, disputants must embrace some of the hallmarks of a consensus-based justice vision, including openness, direct dealing and a longer-term vision.

The hands-on creation of fair, consensual outcomes to conflict allows for the differential treatment of individuals and circumstances. Consensus-based justice processes thus have the potential to recognize and address systemic inequalities by changing the ways we relate to one another.[8]

Justice as it is conceptualized and practised in both restorative justice and consensus-based justice traditions is multidimensional. Both approaches reject the idea that a just outcome must only be consistent with pre-existing rules. Instead, the presumption goes the other way—that in almost every case the solution is integrative, rather than winner-take-all. For restorative justice advocates, notions of harm and responsibility are more complex than a simple determination of right and wrong.[9]

4.1.3 A focus on relationships

The nature of an adjudicative system that determines outcomes according to established rules and principles leaves little room to consider relationships. The formal legal system is interested in objective notions of relationships (parent, corporate officer, agent), rather than their subjective realities. Moreover, relationships are considered as they are presently constituted, with the evaluation of future relationships of little or no relevance (other than perhaps in child custody and access litigation). Adjudicators are not charged with mending relationships, only with addressing events and their ramifications.

Within every conflict or criminal behaviour, a relationship or set of relationships is affected. These relationships might be personal and intimate, arm's length and formal, long term or short term, important to the parties or not. However, to neglect to recognize that there are relationship consequences of some kind for every type of conflict or conflict-producing act is to ignore what lies at the heart of personal experiences. Wherever there are people, the possibility of relationship conflict exists, and behind every corporate, institutional or otherwise representative action (including Crown prosecutions), there are real people.

Relationships and their possible transformation—or more often perhaps simply relationship issues and closure—are central concerns of restorative and consensus-based justice processes. Both approaches are committed to exploring the context and impact of harm and creating a sense of justice, rather than adopting pre-determined solutions.

Different types or levels of conflict resolution have different implications for future relationships. Bernard Mayer suggests that there are three possible levels of resolution for conflict:

- Behavioural resolution—in which behaviour is changed, by court order or perhaps by agreement;

- Cognitive resolution—in which there is a change in how the parties perceive the causes and outcomes of the conflict; and

- Emotional resolution—in which there is a difference in how the parties feel about the conflict and about one another.[10]

The adversarial system primarily addresses behavioural resolution; rarely does it address the parties' attitudes toward one another or the causes of their conflict or their emotional needs. Mayer argues that while the potential exists for disputants to choose a different level of resolution, one not purely behavioural, this is the prerogative of the parties themselves and should not be imposed or assumed by any single process or third party.

On one level, restorative and consensus-based justice approaches re-establish the primacy of the personal experience of conflict and its resolution. This is implicit in the emphasis on face-to-face dialogue and "giving voice" and in the commitment to context-sensitive and individually chosen outcomes. In this way, both the restorative justice and the consensus-based justice models attempt to give conflict back to the disputants themselves, reversing the "theft" of their conflict by lawyers, prosecutors and justice officials.[11]

However, restorative justice processes, in particular, encourage the expansion of who we understand to be affected by criminal behaviour. They promote community empowerment and ownership of the causes and consequences of antisocial behaviours. Similarly consensus-based justice approaches, in practice, engage any person or group whose interests might be affected by the conflict, often dispensing with conventional notions of standing, to bring all those affected into the process of dialogue.

4.2   COMMON CONCERNS

There is an evident similarity in the social and political causes that have provided the momentum for restorative and consensus-based justice initiatives, in particular a desire for more self-directed and practical outcomes that are less costly to parties (including victims), both financially and emotionally. What many would see as a vehicle for social and personal transformation may also be utilized as a means to develop private and unregulated business solutions for corporations. Finally, there are fears about the dilution of the vision of restorative and consensus-based justice and their co-optation by institutionalized bureaucracies. These concerns are discussed further below.

4.2.1   Resources and training

In response to the growing recognition of the advantages, both personal and financial, of restorative processes, a myriad of sanctioning associations have sprung up across the country. This has led to considerable variation in prerequisites, educational requirements and practicum expectations. In some cases, family mediation in particular, justice departments have made efforts to ensure that only "qualified" individuals may work as mediators.[12] Although a level of sanctioning uniformity may improve client confidence, it no doubt serves to limit creativity in implementation and to circumscribe local variation in practices.

As previously noted, a major hurdle for restorative process initiatives has been both the limited and fragmented nature of funding programs. The resources needed to organize, including a core group of highly motivated individuals, may be lacking or may not be long lasting. Increased regulation and accreditation requirements threaten the capacity of grassroots organizations to function. Professionalization of any process comes at increased costs for education and training, costs which ultimately filter down to those attempting to bring in innovative programs.[13]

4.2.2 The commitment of the state to protecting all its citizens equally

The introduction of informal and unregulated dispute resolution processes—whether in the context of community conflicts, of grievances arising between individuals, or of allegations of criminal behaviour—has been subject to criticism by those concerned about the protection of especially vulnerable parties.[14] Vulnerable parties may make accommodations and hold back needs because they fear renewed violence or simply because they are intimidated. For example, in a divorce mediation, a woman who has been the victim of spousal abuse may experience pressure from her community to agree to an outcome that does not sufficiently protect her or her children from future harm. In a sentencing circle, the same woman may feel compelled to acquiesce to a sentence that she is not fully comfortable with and that does not adequately address the harm or inequality that has been caused.[15] Even if provision is made for ensuring the safety of the victim, a non-custodial sentence may implicitly send a message of tolerance for wife abuse.[16]

Alternatives to adversarial justice have drawn the fears and suspicions of many groups. Some of these advocates regard restorative and consensus-based justice processes, operating either independently of the formal legal system or behind closed doors without public scrutiny, as dangerous opportunities for getting weaker parties to concede to the tyranny of stronger ones—exactly what the rights-based system seeks to prevent. There is a real fear that rights-based gains for vulnerable or marginalized groups will be negotiated away in these unregulated environments. There are concerns about persons with disabilities being able to fully participate and be heard by the other parties to a conflict.

Authoritative adjudication is often seen as critical to the development of legal protections for the vulnerable or the less popular. The criminal law has developed protections for both those accused of crime (for example, rules on the admissibility of evidence and the protection of the *Charter of Rights and Freedoms*)[17] and victims (for example, the rape shield legislation[18]). These hard-won rights should not be waived in an informal process behind closed doors. The fear is that private, unregulated processes may privilege more powerful parties in ways that—at least in theory—formal, public processes do not.[19] There are worries that cultural and other minorities may be unable to express their differences in the context of consensus-based justice processes.

There are especially concerns that issues of gender inequality will not be taken into account by informal dispute resolution processes. In a civil family context, scepticism has been expressed over the equal bargaining positions of separating spouses, not only in cases in which there has been a history of violence or intimidation, but also, for example, in those cases in which the husband has been the dominant emotional and financial figure in the marriage.[20] It has been suggested that the social pressures on a woman to seek a harmonious outcome—perhaps one that offers some stability for the children—may lead her to settle for less than she should in divorce mediation.[21] Worse, some women may be intimidated by any prospect of face-to-face dialogue with an abusive former spouse. There is a perception that family mediators are not sufficiently sensitive to systemic gender inequalities in family dynamics, and there is evidence to suggest that attitudes toward violence and intimidation are at times unsophisticated and naïve.[22]

Similar fears lie behind the resistance of some groups to the use of circles and non-custodial sentences for physical and sexual abuses carried out by men on women and children. Many women's advocates are apprehensive about the impact of restorative justice principles on the lives of women and children.[23]

AWAN conducted focus groups with Aboriginal women in small communities in British Columbia to assess their thoughts on the value of restorative justice. Many of the women were too intimidated to speak out about violence in their communities. Many women spoke of leaving the reserve to escape violence, yet a similar code of silence was attested to in downtown east side Vancouver, where many Aboriginal people live. A similar dynamic of oppression and silencing undoubtedly exists in some non-Aboriginal communities and families as well.[24]

> "It was evident in many of the accounts that women felt they had less power in their communities than men and that the system was designed to privilege and benefit males. The power imbalances within these communities are usually complex and bureaucratic. Band councils were often cited as reflecting the ways of the colonizer, with men holding power in the communities. Focus group participants expressed tremendous concern with the diversion of cases of violence against women and children because they felt that the majority of support goes to offenders along with a prevalence of victim-blaming mentalities. A lack of concern for the safety needs of women and children, particularly in isolated communities was also cited as a major concern in processes such as 'Victim–Offender Mediation'. In such situations, women must confront her abuser. This could have grave implications, in terms of psychological and physical safety, if the offender were to remain in the community."
>
> W. Stewart, A. Huntley and F. Blaney, "The Implications of Restorative Justice for Aboriginal Women and Children Survivors of Violence: A Comparative Overview of Five Communities in British Columbia," research report prepared for the Law Commission of Canada, July 2001, at 27.

How can communities that reflect systemic patterns of gender-based violence be entrusted with the responsibility to confront these problems or to create an environment free from fear?

The challenge for restorative and other alternatives to adversarial justice is to transform the conditions that created the conflict in the first place. If sentencing circles, for example, simply reproduce the hierarchies of power and oppression of violent gender relations, they can rightly be criticized as no better—and for some vulnerable parties, possibly even worse—than the traditional processes they seek to replace. However, many of those most concerned about the vulnerability of disempowered groups in informal dispute resolution processes would also acknowledge the lack of success of rights-based advocacy to change underlying social attitudes toward systemic inequities.[25] Our efforts, therefore, should be directed toward providing process safeguards to ensure voluntariness, information and freedom from coercion in both restorative justice and consensus-based justice processes.

Rather than assuming that power differences and imbalances can be addressed by guarantees of sameness in treatment and procedural requirements, it is important to regard every situation in which conflict arises—whether private contractual, public order, family and domestic, governance, corporate or any other—as one already affected by unequal social and economic structures. This may be as a result of prevailing social attitudes toward a particular type of crime (for example, white-collar crime or domestic violence), the position of individuals or groups (such as well-resourced litigants, impecunious litigants, parties with strong and supportive reference groups, parties with no reference groups, and so on), and in each case, the values reflecting the current status quo, perhaps replicated in the legal system. These differences cannot be eliminated by a conflict resolution process. But recognizing them explicitly would enable the construction of just outcomes that do not assume sameness to be the equivalent to fairness. Processes and outcomes should instead respond to particular circumstances and needs.

4.2.3 Vigilantism, punitiveness and exclusivity

A related critique made consistently of restorative and consensus-based justice programs is that delegating the power to develop solutions to the communities, even to the parties themselves, assumes that these are healthy communities or people whose decision-making will be fair and balanced.

In the case of some troubled communities, this means going even further and assuming a healed community.[26] Critics question why there is an assumption that the goodwill and good sense directing these processes are necessarily preferable to a judge-directed, legally formulated outcome. For example, it is possible to imagine offenders accepting a greater degree of punishment—or at least a greater degree of public humiliation—than they might have been subject to had they entered a plea of not guilty and taken their chances at trial. It is possible to imagine a defendant in a civil law suit settling for less monetary compensation than a court might award, or even a plaintiff paying out more than a court might have ordered. Are the agreed outcomes of community panels, group conferences and mediations really "better"—in the sense of fairer and more just—than the comparable decisions of a court? One author chillingly points out that "society's response can be even more terrifying than crime itself," pointing to the rise in gun sales and vigilantism that followed the Los Angeles riots of 1992.[27]

If a perception of harm to the community is the trigger for intervention in a restorative model, there is also a fear that the community might take this intervention into inappropriate areas, such as those of personal privacy and family life. If such interventions are also legitimized and buttressed by the authority of the state, the danger of net-widening becomes a very real threat.[28] Again the issue is: Who decides when and what type of community intervention is

> "Restorative justice envisions the community taking significant responsibility for conducting programs. The creation of new positions of authority creates concern about the participation of diverse community members and how their views will be included. The dynamics of communities involve relationships of power ... [W]e cannot assume that communities are healthy and safe, or are concerned with creating an equitable status for all their residents."
>
> Provincial Association Against Family Violence, *Making It Safe: Women, Restorative Justice and Alternative Dispute Resolution* (St John's, Nfld. and Lab.: Provincial Association Against Family Violence, 2000) at 12.

necessary? And how willing are we to offer this responsibility to communities, with all their flaws?

The notion of communitarianism implicit in restorative justice is generally understood as a means of extending and entrenching community control. However, a traditional conception of communitarianism is essentially a unifying strategy that inevitably separates "insiders" (who buy in) and "outsiders" (who are alienated from the community or who are simply less comfortable with collective solidarity). This raises fears about the potential for the community— or powerful individuals within the community—to act oppressively toward outsiders or those less powerful than themselves. How practically able are homogeneous communities to tolerate and include views highly divergent from their own? How hospitable will communities be toward outsiders?

Even those who argue that community stewardship can be supported and grown acknowledge that there should be controls and safeguards on decision-making by communities. These controls and safeguards can be ensured by a relevant state with a responsive regulatory framework, and constitutional limits on the discretion of community decision-making.[29] This relationship will be discussed further in Chapter 8, where the regulatory role of the state in relation to restorative justice and consensus-based justice will be explored in further detail.

4.2.4   Co-optation

A quite different concern—and sometimes criticism—of restorative and consensus-based justice practices is that their original innovative vision could be corrupted through integration into institutional and bureaucratic structures. This is a quite different kind of critique because it presupposes that restorative and consensus-based justice models are worth preserving in their pure form.

There is a real tension between the need for new forms of dispute resolution to be related to the formal justice system (thereby achieving legitimacy)[30] and the need to be independent from it (thereby ensuring that its original principles do not become diluted). Some of those who advocate either restorative justice or consensus-based justice do so with a vision that it will ultimately replace the formal justice system, not simply modify or supplement it with new alternative processes. However, as long as the formal justice system exists, restorative and consensus-based justice programs can only function entirely independently of it if they limit their interventions to conflicts at an early stage (for example, before pleadings are issued or before charges are laid) or to conflicts outside the context of legal claims. While some researchers' data suggest that formal litigation accounts for only a very small proportion of all dispute resolution processing,[31] drawing these disputes into a community-based dispute resolution program is far from easy.[32]

Therefore, a balance must be struck between the need to coordinate the efforts and preserve the flexibility and creativity of the different processes. We come back to this difficult equilibrium in Chapter 7.

Restorative justice and consensus-based justice attract very similar critiques. Both face comparable challenges in ensuring that the benefits of community-based, informal dispute resolution processes do not produce greater unfairness and inequities than the traditional justice systems they seek to substitute or supplement. Any integrated model must operate with a strong awareness of the critiques that concern those who might otherwise be supportive of alternatives to adversarial justice.

---

[1] The Law Commission addresses the normative question of what a crime is in its discussion paper Law Commission of Canada, *What is a Crime? Challenges and Alternatives*, (Ottawa: Law Commission of Canada, 2003).

[2] Even where one might feel that no real harm is being caused by a single individual act, traditional deterrence theory has argued that nonetheless standards need to be maintained for the greater good of the community. Retributive theories of justice also see criminal acts as harms that extend beyond the individual to the whole community, and the justification for assigning and ceding to punishment as laying in the notional "social contract" to which citizens subscribe. J.J. Llewellyn and R. Howse, *Restorative Justice: A Conceptual Framework* (Ottawa: Law Commission of Canada, 1999) at 33.

[3] Llewellyn and Howse describe this in terms of a focus on individual guilt. *Ibid.* at 34–35.

[4] *Ibid.* at 28.

[5] D. Sullivan and L. Tifft, "The Negotiated and Economic Dimensions of Restorative Justice" (1998) 22:1 *Humanity and Society* 38 at 40.

[6] See, for example, H. Zehr, *Changing Lenses: A New Focus for Crime and Justice* (Waterloo: Harold Press, 1990) at 52–57, 203–204; see especially R. Quinney, "The Way of Peace: On Crime, Suffering and Service" and H. Pepinsky, "Peacemaking in Criminology and Criminal Justice" in H. Pepinsky and R. Quinney, eds., *Criminology as Peacemaking* (Bloomington: Indiana University Press, 1991).

[7] E. Waldman, "Identifying the Role of Social Norms in Mediation: A Multiple Model Approach" (1997) 48 *Hastings Law Journal* 703.

[8] This is Bush and Folger's "transformation story," which suggests higher ends and goals for collaborative processes than the resolution of a particular lawsuit. R.A. Bush and J.P. Folger, *The Promise of Mediation: Responding to Conflict Through Empowerment and Recognition* (San Francisco: Jossey-Bass, 1994) especially 20–22.

[9] In non-criminal matters, where it is easy to see many conflicts as being less about values and principles and more about resource allocation, this is even more clearly the case. See V. Aubert, "Competition and Dissensus: Two Types of Conflict and Conflict Resolution" (1963) 7 *Journal of Conflict Resolution* 26.

[10] B. Mayer, *The Dynamics of Conflict Resolution* (San Francisco: Jossey-Bass, 2000) at 98–108.

[11] The analogy of "theft" most memorably developed by Nils Christie in relation to criminal matters. See N. Christie, "Conflicts as Property" (1977) 17:1 *British Journal of Criminology* 1.

[12] Quebec, for example, has certified five professional organizations which may designate mediators for the purpose of Family Mediation. *Code of Civil Procedure*, R.S.Q. 2001, c. C-25, r. 2.1 (Regulation Respecting Family Mediation).

[13] Correction Services Canada provides an extensive list of restorative justice and mediation training programs from accredited universities and government justice departments. Very few are from grass-roots or non-profit organizations: "Canadian Resource Guide to Restorative Justice and Conflict Resolution Education Programs", online: <http://www.csc-scc.gc.ca/text/prgrm/ rjust_e.shtml> (date accessed: 17 September 2003).

14 See, for example, R. Delgado, C. Dunn, P. Brown, H. Lee and D. Hubbert, "Fairness and Formality: Minimizing the Risk of Prejudice in Alternative Dispute Resolution" (1985) 6 *Wisconsin Law Review* 1359, especially 1387–1389; P. Bryan, "Killing Us Softly: Divorce Mediation and the Politics of Power" (1992) 40 *Buffalo Law Review* 441; L. Lerman, "Mediation of Wife Abuse Cases: The Disadvantageous Impact of Informal Dispute Resolution on Women" (1984) 7 *Harvard Women's Law Journal* 57; and see, generally, R. Abel, *The Politics of Informal Justice: The American Experience* (New York: Academic Press, 1982).

15 See the findings of W. Stewart, A. Huntley and F. Blaney, *The Implications of Restorative Justice for Aboriginal Women and Children Survivors of Violence: A Comparative Overview of Five Communities in British Columbia* (Ottawa: Law Commission of Canada, July 2001).

16 See, for example, T. Grillo, "The Mediation Alternative: Process Dangers for Women" (1991) 100:6 *Yale Law Journal* 1545 especially 1590–1593.

17 Section 24 of the *Canadian Charter of Rights and Freedoms* excludes any evidence obtained in violation of Charter rights. *Canadian Charter of Rights and Freedoms*, Part I of the *Constitution Act*, 1982, being Schedule B to the *Canada Act* 1982, (U.K.), 1982, c. 11.

18 Section 277 of the *Criminal Code* (which, unlike s. 276, survived the challenge of Seaboyer) excludes any evidence being admitted in a rape trial that discloses the previous sexual history of the complainant if its purpose is to challenge the credibility of the complainant. See P. Kobly, "Rape Shield Legislation: Relevance, Preference and Judicial Discretion" (1992) 30 *Alberta Law Review* 988.

19 Kent Roach addresses the power imbalance between men and women and notes that feminist opposition to restorative justice could discredit it as a meaningful and non-discriminatory response to serious crimes. K. Roach, "Changing Punishment at the Turn of the Century: Restorative Justice on the Rise" (2000) 42:3 *Canadian Journal of Criminology* 249 at 273.

20 For two powerful critiques from a feminist perspective, see M. Bailey, "Unpacking the 'Rational Alternative': A Critical Review of Family Mediation Movement Claims" (1989) 8 *Canadian Journal of Family Law* 61; and J. Rifkin, "Mediation from a Feminist Perspective: Promise and Problems" (1994) 2 *Law and Inequality* 21.

21 Grillo, *supra* note 16 at 1545.

22 This issue is analyzed and discussed in E. Kruk, "Power Imbalance and Spouse Abuse in Divorce Disputes: Deconstructing Mediation Practice via the 'Simulated Client' Technique" (1998) 12:1 *International Journal of Law, Policy and Family* 1. See also the results of a recent Halifax study: Transition House Association of Nova Scotia (THANS). *Abused Women in Family Mediation: A Nova Scotia Snapshot. A Report Prepared by The Transition House Association of Nova Scotia* (Halifax: THANS, 2000), online: <http://www.nicr.ca>.

23 W. Stewart, A. Huntley and F. Blaney, *supra* note 15.

24 On victim-blaming, see also J. Braithwaite and D. Roche, "Responsibility and Restorative Justice" in G. Bazemore and M. Schiff, eds., *Restorative Community Justice: Repairing Harm and Transforming Communities* (Cincinnati: Anderson Publishing Co., 2001) at 74.

25 See, for example, the analysis in D. Bell, *Faces at the Bottom of the Well: The Permanence of Racism* (Basic Books, 1993); and R. Delgado, "Conflict as Pathology: An Essay for Trina Grillo" (1997) 81 *Minnesota Law Review* 1391.

26 W. Stewart, A. Huntley, and F. Blaney, *supra* note 15 at 28.

27 R. Abel, "Contested Communities" 22(1) *Journal of Law and Society* (1995) 113 at 118.

28 Roach, *supra* note 19 at 259-262.

29 J. Braithwaite, and D. Roche, "Responsibility and Restorative Justice" in G. Bazemore and M. Schiff, eds., *Restorative Community Justice: Repairing Harm and Transforming Communities* (Cincinnati: Anderson Publishing Co., 2001) at 69.

30 See, for example, N. Rockhill, *Building the Caseload: Report from the Conflict Resolution Service* (Toronto: Fund for Dispute Resolution, 1993), (pointing out that formal alliance with agencies and justice systems enabled St. Stephen's Community Mediation Service to develop a healthy caseload); and J. Benoit, J. Kopachevsky, S. Macdonald and G. MacDonald, *Evaluating the Effects and Methods of Mediation: A Summary Report* (Halifax: Institute of Public Affairs, Dalhousie University, 1986) at 8, (noting that community-based services struggle for legitimacy and cases, arguing that "the best way to organize a mediation centre which relies on police referrals is to establish it within the police department").

31 For example, the Civil Litigation Research Project, using a survey of 5,000 households, found that only just over 11 percent of the disputes that respondents identified were processed using litigation in the court. See D.M.

Trubek, A. Sarat, W. Felstiner, H.M. Kritzer and J.B. Grossman, "The Costs of Ordinary Litigation" (1983) 31 *UCLA Law Review* 72, 85–87; see also R. Miller and A. Sarat, "Grievances, Claims and Disputes: Assessing the Adversary Culture" (1980-81) 15 *Law and Society Review* 525 at 566.

32 S. Merry and S. Silbey, "What do Plaintiffs Want? Re-examining the Concept of Dispute" (1984) 9:2 *The Justice System Journal* 151.

Part III — The Future of Participatory Justice

Chapter 5 Toward Participatory Justice

A central premise of the models of dispute resolution set out in earlier chapters is that every conflict—its circumstances, its players, its impact-is unique. Participatory processes, unlike the traditional adversarial processes, do not strive for a uniform set of rules and principles with which to achieve, consistency and certainty (in any case, more of a theoretical goal than a realizable objective for formal justice systems). While we have distilled some of the common values and principles of both approaches, it would run counter to their core assumptions to regard these as universally applicable to all types and contexts of dispute. This chapter considers the relationship between the characteristics of any one conflict or set of conflicts—the issues, the affected relationships, the community within which the conflict arises—and the appropriateness of new approaches to conflict resolution. Are some conflicts ever suitable for a restorative or consensus-based justice approach?[1]

Research has not yet established a convincing correlation between case type—the area of law in which the conflict falls, the character of the disputants, the issues at stake, and so on—and successful resolution using consensus-building approaches.[2] However, it is useful to identify those dispute characteristics that suggest that an informal, consensual approach might be inadequate to ensure that fairness is achieved or that the goal of transforming relationships is achieved.

5.1 DIFFERENT TYPES OF CONFLICTS

Criminal and non-criminal matters raise similar concerns about the appropriateness of dialogue and consensus-building processes, but these are often expressed somewhat differently. A first set of issues relates to the personal safety of victims and, more generally, the less powerful parties in a conflict. Circles, Victim–Offender Mediation, family mediation in which there is a history of domestic violence, or any civil mediation in which one party appears likely and capable of intimidating the other, raise concerns about the vulnerability of weaker parties and the impact on the authenticity and constructiveness of the process.[3] There is a special concern about processes that are mandatory (for example, mandatory court-connected mediation) or implicitly coercive (involving pressure on victims to agree to a restorative process).[4]

Program evaluation data tend to be predominantly quantitative, providing statistics for numbers of cases (often grouped according to dispute type) that have been settled. There are a number of methodological problems with such comparisons. Numeric data on outcomes generally do not examine variables such as whether the parties chose this process voluntarily and without pressure, how the parties felt about their role in the dialogue, and whether their particular needs and interests were met by the outcome. Apparently higher numbers of resolutions in any one case-type category can often be explained by contextual factors. For example, the Ontario Pilot Evaluation found that a higher number of wrongful dismissal cases were settled in mediation than other case types. It was hypothesized that the explanation for this was that a higher percentage of wrongful dismissal cases were mandated to mediation and, that as a consequence, the wrongful dismissal attorneys had become skilled at dealing with cases in mediation, as well as that the legal issues involved in wrongful dismissal cases were fairly well settled and the contentious issue was limited to determining the award. The aspiration of proponents of these new methods of conflict resolution is to provide respectful processes for developing fair and accepted outcomes. Quantitative program evaluation data on formal outcomes tell only part of this story.

A second but closely related set of concerns arises in relation to the health and tolerance of the communities within which disputes arise, especially if those communities will play a crucial role in the development and implementation of outcome agreements, whether as mediators, as circle participants, or perhaps as members of a community panel.

Another set of critical questions arises in relation to the potential for the abuse of a consensual process by parties who do not act in good faith or in the spirit of the process, or who may denigrate the integrity of the process and its credibility in the eyes of a significant community.

Finally, some would argue that some conflicts are simply too serious, too complex, or perhaps too socially repugnant to be dealt with in private processes. Instead, these types of conflicts require pubic adjudication and the application of formal rules to ensure fairness in outcomes. In the criminal arena, this argument has focused on the severity of crimes that should be dealt with in restorative processes. Programs limited to minor offences and perhaps first-time offenders tend to win public acceptance more easily than those that tackle more serious crimes. In the civil context, a parallel debate often centres on the need for adjudication if other individuals are actually or potentially affected. Each of these issues will be dealt with below.

5.1.1 Personal safety and the ability to bargain free from fear

The most obvious group of disputes in which informal consensual processes may be deemed inappropriate are those in which there is no possibility of equal dialogue, either because of the level of intimidation and fear in the relationship between the parties or because the history of the relationship indicates that equal bargaining is impossible. Where these factors are present, the more vulnerable party is unlikely to be a willing participant in the process. Even if the more vulnerable party is willing to be present, it may be that this person will be unable to speak freely during the dialogue.[5] The dialogue that participatory processes aim to encourage and support may be missing entirely or dominated by one party only. Victims' groups have expressed great concern over the use of mediation or circles under such circumstances.[6] This concern is further heightened by a perception that many mediators are inadequately trained and unprepared to anticipate and manage issues of domestic violence.[7]

The unique nature of every conflict and the relationships involved in the conflicts mean, however, that it is important not to exclude all disputes with these variables. Indeed, mediation has been used with careful safeguards in some cases of domestic and other sexual violence with positive results. In addition, a circle setting where there is no pressure on the victims can offer them an opportunity to address their abusers in a safe environment where it can be an empowering experience.[8]

Rather than excluding all cases in which there has been violence or intimidation from the possibility of restorative or consensus-based justice processes, a better approach is to emphasize voluntariness, which requires the adequate provision of information and counselling to ensure that all dimensions of a decision to proceed are understood.

Some programs apply careful screening questions at the intake stage in an effort to identify disputes in which fear and especially fear of violence may exist.[9] For example, the Collaborative Justice Project in Ottawa spends much time working separately with victims and offenders to prepare each for a face-to-face meeting. Even after a long period of preparation, some victims and offenders choose not to meet directly. Clearly, where there is fear of coercion, pressure or intimidation, exiting from a participatory justice process must be straightforward and easy for the fearful party.[10]

In addition, even when an individual genuinely volunteers to participate in a process, it is incumbent on a trained mediator to assess the situation independently and, ultimately, make a decision about whether to proceed with a dialogue. Some offenders may volunteer for a dialogue for purely strategic reasons. In these instances, a face-to-face dialogue may not be the most effective restorative justice process to use.

We will return to the question of intake practices, including case screening, in Chapter 6.

5.1.2 The need for healthy and tolerant communities

To meet the goals of participatory processes, it is critical that the community that is asked to take ownership of both the conflict and its solution is itself healthy, respectful of diversity and committed to finding fair and meaningful outcomes to conflicts. Are these processes appropriate if the community has a history of oppression or intolerance?[11] We identify and differentiate between certain groups of victims and offenders who are regarded with more or less social approbation. Communities create hierarchies of crime and approbation.[12] This may be especially marked in some communities where hierarchical relationships between men and women, leaders and followers, and adults and children have resulted in a level of tolerance and acceptance of certain types of crime and conflict inherently oppressive to the victims. It is essential that communities can both offer safety to those confronting victimizing behaviour and ensure that the victim is not placed under any (explicit or tacit) pressure to participate in a dialogue when they are feeling fearful or disempowered.

At the same time, the dialogue and openness offered by restorative and consensus-based justice processes may offer a unique means for a troubled community to heal itself. An example is the use of circles to address long-standing and widespread sexual abuse among members of a Manitoba Aboriginal community. The Community Holistic Circle Healing (CHCH) process began as an effort by an interdisciplinary community team to better understand and address the systemic problems of a small Aboriginal community. The discovery of widespread sexual abuse within the community led to the development of a healing process to uncover and address the harms perpetuated by child sex abuse.[13] By an agreement with the Manitoba Department of Justice and the federal Aboriginal Justice Directorate, Hollow Water established a structure for referral of all sexual abuse charges brought against Hollow Water community members to a community circle program.

This procedure permitted the development of a series of steps—involving the victim, the victimizer, and friends and family—leading to the eventual determination of a three-year plan for the rehabilitation of the offender and protection of the victim (in effect, a three-year probation order with the CHCH acting as the supervisory body). The evaluation of the Hollow Water program in 1996 noted that "there is no doubt that CHCH is making advances in creating a safer community."[14] In the extensive data collected from program workers, victims and their families and victimizers, there is no challenge to the idea that even such a serious matter as child sex abuse can be dealt with responsibly in this forum, providing that adequate safeguards (in particular the proper monitoring of the "probation" period) are ensured. There is clear acceptance within the community that despite a history of denial and a painful and continuing process of disclosure and confrontation, the only way forward for this community is dialogue, forgiveness and eventually healing.

> "[F]orgiveness is the hardest thing for people to do for people, but it is the natural way to healing. As long as you have anger, it will make you sicker and sicker."—Hollow Water resident
>
> T. Lajeunesse, *Evaluation of Community Holistic Circle Healing: Hollow Water First Nation*. Volume 1: Final Report (T. Lajeunesse, and Associates, 1996) at 75.

5.1.3   Process abuse

There is a fear—which may grow with the potential seriousness of the offence or complaint—that offenders can abuse restorative and consensus-based justice processes by presenting themselves as remorseful, simply to reduce the severity of their punishment. This fear can be countered by evidence that many offenders find a circle or mediation process far more painful and personally demanding than a court appearance.[15] Nonetheless, this concern persists and underscores the importance of having trained mediators who are able to utilize their judgment when determining the desirability of a meeting between a victim and an offender.

In civil matters, there is ample evidence of the strategic use of negotiation and mediation by lawyers who sometimes choose to use these processes to gather information rather than as good faith

> Restorative justice is not a soft option. Many offenders find it hard to face the real impact of their crime. For victims, restorative justice may not be about forgiveness, but a desire to tell the offender how the crime has affected them and their family, or getting information that only the offender can give.
>
> D. Blunkett, "Foreword from the Home Secretary" in *Restorative Justice: The Government's Strategy*, (London: The Home Office, 2003) at 5.

opportunities for bargaining and possible settlement. Research on the attitudes of litigators using mandatory mediation in Toronto and Ottawa confirms this. The "instrumentalist"[16] regards mediation and mediators as a process or a tool to be captured and used to advance the clients' mostly unchanged adversarial goals. Mediation is regarded as a procedural tool to be efficiently utilized or, alternatively, avoided or neutralized (by showing up but not engaging). Another commonly described strategy for process abuse is to use mediation as a delaying tactic.

The response of some American jurisdictions has been to legislate a requirement of good faith of participants in civil mediation,[17] although there is continuing debate about the effectiveness of such requirements.[18] This approach has not found favour in Canada. A better approach may be to seek to change the climate of credibility and legitimacy of consensual processes so that good faith—at least in the sense of regarding informal processes as important opportunities to constructively advance resolution—will follow. In such a climate bad faith is internally censored and disapproved of, and good faith becomes the norm.[19] Government has an important role to play in advancing the public credibility and acceptance of these processes. This will be discussed further in Chapter 8.

5.1.4 Repugnant acts

Are all types of disputes amenable to participatory justice processes? Some argue that very serious infractions of community norms and values should be excluded from restorative justice processes.

Some restorative justice processes only accept offenders who have committed minor criminal offences or first-time offenders, or they tend to focus on young offenders.[20] Other models have provoked considerable debate over whether there should be limits on the types of criminal offences that are eligible for a restorative justice program. In New Zealand, for example, all offences committed by juveniles, excepting only murder and manslaughter, must lead to a family group conference, which the victim is entitled to attend and which occurs before the court proceeds to deal with the case. The conference is an opportunity to discuss the needs of the young people and their families and to develop plans that will provide access to funds for services and programs intended to achieve these goals.[21]

The Fraser Region Community Justice Initiatives program in British Columbia has for some time been working with more serious offenders.[22] There are also examples of projects that deal with serious sexual abuse, such as Hollow Water. The Collaborative Justice Project provides another example of a program that has explicitly identified more serious crimes as its focus. The Collaborative Justice Project is not a diversion project; rather, a formal guilty plea is entered and the offender will ultimately be sentenced by a judge who may—or may not—accept the recommendations of a restorative process (for example, a circle or VOM). Moreover, along with making reparations to the victim, offenders can receive the full range of legal punishments, including a period of incarceration. It may be easier to make the argument for extending the range of offences for which restorative alternatives are available if these cases remain within the formal justice system—and offenders receive a criminal record, whatever the outcome.

It is important to recognize, however, that "a serious offence does not necessarily mean a serious offender."[23] Results from an evaluation of the Collaborative Justice Program showed that while a majority of offenders who participated in the project had committed a serious offence, 51 percent of the offenders were first-time offenders, and the evaluation indicated that the majority of offenders were offenders with a low likelihood of re-offending.

"Unique in its focus on serious criminal behaviour, the Collaborative Justice Project (CJP) deals with adult and youth cases of robbery, robbery with a weapon, weapons offences, break and enter, theft over $5000, fraud, assault, assault causing bodily harm, impaired driving causing bodily harm or death, and careless driving or dangerous driving causing bodily harm or death ... Cases are accepted when all three criteria are present:

- the crime is serious and the Crown is seeking a period of custody;

- the accused person displays remorse, is willing to take responsibility for and work to repair the harm done;

- there is an identifiable victim who is interested in participating."

Year End Report on the Collaborative Justice Project, March 31, 2002, online: <http://www.ccjc.ca>.

5.1.5 Disputes involving the public interest

Arguments similar to those made in relation to serious crimes are often made over the importance of requiring strict public accounting of those whose civil actions have caused harm to a wide group of people, for example, environmental disputes, or whose behaviour challenged a fundamental value of our society, such as a Canadian Charter of Rights violation. Should some types of conflict—for example, disputes raising Charter or other human rights issues—be declared to be in the public domain and excluded from the realm of private settlement?

The principle of self-determination that lies at the heart of participatory processes implies that if the parties prefer a private consensus-building strategy to public adjudication, they must be allowed to make this choice. It would be unfair to deny litigants the benefit of a participatory process because their claim involves a human rights argument. In fact, in many human rights cases, a

> Mediation has enormous potential to resolve most complaints of discrimination.(…) [I] n the majority of cases, mediation offers a non-adversarial context in which the parties can get beyond positions of right and wrong and address the needs and interests that are key to finding a solution. Mediation is a more humane approach: it promotes understanding between the parties and has the power to heal, something of particular value where the relationship between the parties is ongoing.
>
> M. Gusella, Chief Commissioner, Canadian Human Rights Commission, "New Approaches to the Protection of Human Rights" speech delivered at the Canadian Association of Statutory Human Rights Agencies 25–28 May 2003, Winnipeg, online: <http://www.chrc-ccdp.ca/Legis&Poli/CASHRASpeech_DiscoursACCCDP.asp?l=e>.

participatory process may allow the victims to articulate a better remedy that fulfills their need and respects their dignity.

As discussed earlier, there may be cases in which the imbalance of power between the parties is such that a participatory process may not be adequate. At other times, the parties themselves may wish for a public adjudication to contribute to changes in the law. Possible still is the disclosure of the terms and results of the participatory process to respond to a need for public transparency and accountability. In Chapter 7, we give examples of processes that have been developed to balance the need for public scrutiny and the ability of parties to come to an understanding that satisfy them.

5.2   PARTICIPATORY JUSTICE IN DIVERSE COMMUNITIES

Some people have argued that participatory justice models are best suited to closely knit, non-urban communities with some of the characteristics of a traditional community. They argue that participatory justice models premised on meaningful interaction between individuals cannot be sustained in urban areas where individuals are socially disconnected from one another. Section 5.2 will examine the possibility of participatory justice in diverse communities.

5.2.1   Aboriginal communities

Principles and values of participatory processes often seem to better reflect the cultural mores of Aboriginal communities. For example, the acceptance of collective responsibility for conflict within the community—counterintuitive for an individualistic Western model of disputing—appears closer to how many Aboriginal communities approach conflict. In many Aboriginal teachings there is no distinction between the pain or the disgrace of one individual and the harm caused to the whole community.[24] In addition, dialogue processes emphasizing consensus-building through participation are the cultural heritage of Aboriginal communities, despite the huge changes that contact with Western culture has wrought in their traditional way of life. The model of "circles" derives from Aboriginal practices in many parts of the world.[25] Therefore, there is familiarity with dialogue as a means of resolving conflict, although it is important to note that Western legal culture has made significant inroads into this tradition.[26]

In addition, there is a strong desire in many Aboriginal communities—a desire that is widely recognized by the Department of Indian and Northern Affairs—to bring justice and decision-making back to their local roots and traditions.

An impressive number of successful restorative justice initiatives have taken root in Aboriginal communities. These include the original circle sentencing projects in the Yukon, pioneered by Judge Barry Stuart, clarified in his landmark judgment in *R. v. Moses*,[27] and now established in Aboriginal communities in the Yukon. The circle is used with criminal cases of chronic offenders. Separate healing circles are held for the victim and the offender. Accountability is a strong component of the latter. The sentencing circle includes the judge, prosecutor, defence lawyer, victim, offender, their supporters and any other community members who want to attend. The members of the circle participate as equals in determining the sentence. The process may last for several weeks. Similar initiatives are now in place across Canada, particularly in western Canada. In addition, circles operate in urban environments, for example, Aboriginal Legal Services of Toronto operates a Community Council

Dogrib Law Before Contact with Europeans

"[T]raditionally, social control was enforced by adult members of the society in order to maintain harmony among people, the animals, the spirits. Dogrib laws existed and were taught carefully so all members of the group knew them and understood the consequences if they breached them. Minor offences were dealt with by ridicule, more serious ones by shaming and the most serious ones by banishment. Camp leaders dealt with minor and some medium offences. If the offender were not compliant with the conditions for reparation set down by the camp leader, then all adults in camp were involved in resolving the matter through the circle process. Shaming and shunning were used as mechanisms to bring the offender back into line and reparation and reconciliation followed when the consequences had been met. If the crime were truly serious, then all the camps moved to a gathering place where the senior male leader facilitated a circle in which all adults participated and came to consensus as to what might be an appropriate remedy if there was one. If there wasn't a remedy, then the offender was banished."

J. Ryan and B. Calliou, "Aboriginal Restorative Justice Alternatives: Two
Case Studies," paper prepared for the Law Commission of Canada,
January 2002, at 23-24.

Program, and the Vancouver Aboriginal Friendship Centre Society runs the Vancouver Aboriginal Restorative Justice Program.

5.2.2 Non-Aboriginal communities, including metropolitan settings

Some argue that participatory processes can only work in small, homogeneous communities. For example, the successful Farm Mediation Program in Saskatchewan in the 1980s and 1990s reflected the central importance of farming to the economy and the values shared among both farmers and financial institutions in maintaining

Vancouver Aboriginal Restorative Justice Program

"On the evening of April 27ᵗʰ [2000], the Vancouver Aboriginal Restorative Justice Program (VARJP) held its first ever Community Council forum. Three Community Council members, an Elder, the offender and two of his family members, joined in a circle with VARJP Coordinator, Christine Smith-Parnell, to discuss the offence and the underlying causes of the behaviour which led to it.

The victims, employees of a Canadian corporation, while not in attendance, provided information during a pre-forum interview that was shared by letter during the actual forum. This information was of great assistance in helping the offender to understand the consequences of his actions. It also aided the Council members who were challenged with the task of coming up with a healing-focused plan that addressed both the offender's and victim's needs.

Feedback from forum participants was extremely positive. The offender stated that he was very grateful to have an opportunity to deal with the matter within the Aboriginal community and away from the court system. He was particularly happy about the presence of two Council participants who shared the same First Nations background as [he]. The family members who accompanied the offender for support were very excited to see him take responsibility for his wrongdoing and move towards addressing his negative behaviour.

When contacted with the results of the forum, the victims also expressed satisfaction. They were pleased that the offender came to understand that the victim was not just a corporation, but also a group of people who work within it. In addition, they appreciated that the offender was going to take steps toward improving himself.

(continued)

> Overall, with the help of the Community Council, the terms "victim" and "offender" appeared to fade away as both parties began to see each other as human beings who, like all people, are deserving of respect and understanding."
>
> For more information visit the Vancouver Aboriginal Friendship Centre Society's website: <http://www.vafcs.org/>.

a strong agricultural base. Interestingly, there is also plenty of evidence of successful initiatives in much larger and more diverse metropolitan settings (for example, the Ottawa Collaborative Justice Project; neighbourhood mediation projects such as St. Stephen's Community Resolution Centre and Downsview Community Mediation Services, both in Toronto). Perhaps the key concept is the existence of a "community of care" with shared needs and interests, which creates community ties and a sense of motivation to resolve difficulties locally and to apply local knowledge. Such a community might be a group of homeowners in a gated community who are concerned about crime, a loose association of small business owners trying to protect themselves against larger business, or a residents' group lobbying for environmental cleanup in their neighbourhood. Such groups are increasingly recognized by sociologists as "a key organizing principle of contemporary life."[28]

Susan Merry has noted that communities that include pre-existing organizations, professional groups and institutions are more likely to embrace community-based dispute resolution models—what she describes as "those pockets of [American] society which retain the social characteristics of urban villages," where community mediation pro-grams can build on existing "patterns of informal social control."[29] Such programs are often organized around a strong volunteer core. For exam-ple, the Mennonite community took the lead in establishing the first Canadian victim–offender projects in Kitchener–Waterloo; Winnipeg Mediation Services was built on an originally Mennonite volunteer base; and the Church Council of Canada now plays a major role in a variety of projects, including the Ottawa Collaborative Justice Project.

Threshold Requirements for a Participatory Justice Process

- Community motivation to address conflict in a way that will serve individuals and the community better than conventional justice processes

- Local champions within the community

- The support of key players, particularly for referrals (courts, Crown, municipality, police, community organizations, schools)

- A group of core individuals who will work directly to build the program (this must include at least a few able practitioners with relevant training and experience)

- The potential for building a stable group of volunteers

- Access to conflict resolution training

5.2.3 Enhancing the capacity of communities to provide participatory processes

It is much more difficult to build credible and sustainable justice projects where the community lacks some unifying characteristics. For example, communities with high levels of transition—people moving in and out—are also those where collective spirit is harder to develop and maintain. The resources needed to organize, including a core group of highly motivated individuals, may be lacking or may not be long lasting. The creation of a stable volunteer group may be difficult or even impossible under such circumstances. Moreover, a large group of volunteers is essential for avoiding "volunteer burnout" syndrome, which affects many community justice projects.

For planning the development of a justice project in the form of a community mediation service, a VOM program, a program of healing circles, or a community panel process, the following resources appear to be threshold requirements.[30]

5.3   SOME CONCLUSIONS

Three conclusions emerge with some clarity from our discussion. One is that restorative justice and consensus-based justice appear most suitable for disputes where each party participates voluntarily and has sufficient capacity to engage fully in a process of dialogue and negotiation. Perhaps most importantly, process design must reflect local conditions and individual circumstances. For example, face-to-face dialogue may not be appropriate in every case. Instead, separate caucuses may be more appropriate. Whereas in restorative justice processes, victims and offenders may require time to deal with the aftermath of the crime, and many victims and offenders may not wish to enter into a dialogue. In some communities, there may be a need to constrain or monitor in some way the outcomes of community decision-making, to ensure that intolerance and vigilantism do not surface. The need for justice processes to be flexible and responsive to the unique conditions of each conflict is discussed further in Chapter 7 as a key design principle.

But while participatory processes are not universally applicable to all types of conflicts, experience suggests that a dialogue-based, consensus-seeking approach may be an appropriate tool in a wide range of conflict settings (wider than currently used). Despite fears about intimidation and coercion in disputes involving family violence, offering mediation as an option for separating or divorcing spouses can sometimes give a historically disempowered partner an opportunity to find a voice and control the outcome of a marriage dissolution in a way that traditional litigation cannot. Similarly, where the victims of violent crimes have chosen to participate in restorative justice processes they often describe relief and a renewed sense of control over their lives when the process is complete.[31]

There are examples of criminal justice projects in which communities have confronted collective demons and emerged stronger and healthier as a consequence. Even sceptical litigators have come to embrace court-connected mediation in cities where a culture of legitimacy has begun to develop around the use of mediation— marked in part by a generalized rejection of more instrumental and abusive uses of the mediation process to advance purely adversarial goals. Sometimes, under the most unlikely circumstances, restorative, consensus-based justice has the greatest impact because of its potential to transform people, relationships and local culture.

Asking whether some disputes and dispute settings are appropriate for participatory processes is highly relevant to the question of where government should target resources to initiate and support such programs. But appropriateness is not the sole consideration. Government must balance concerns over the suitability of some matters for consensual dispute resolution processes with other important reasons to invest in the innovative enhancement of settlement processes in a particular area of disputing (wrongful dismissal claims, insurance claims, minor assault charges), particular communities (Aboriginal communities, isolated rural communities), or particular groups of disputants (neighbours, family members, young offenders). Government might wish to target one of these areas because of a dismal record of satisfaction or a history of largely unsuccessful outcomes within the traditional justice model (for example, the inability of the justice system to change behaviours in terms of compliance or recidivism). Even where there are characteristics within a target group that raise concerns about the suitability of participatory processes, government may still wish to proceed with new programs but rely on enhanced regulatory measures for monitoring funded programs. The issue of government oversight is the subject of further discussion in Chapter 8.

---

1 Answering this question raises further questions about voluntariness and compulsion in transformative processes. While this discussion cannot be detached from consideration of which disputes should be encouraged to use transformative processes, the question of voluntariness will be considered in more detail in Chapter 7 in relation to process design.

2 See, for example, D.M. Trubek, A. Sarat, W. Felstiner, H.M. Kritzer and J.B. Grossman, "The Costs of Ordinary Litigation" (1983) 31 *UCLA Law Review* 72 especially 95–97.

3 For example, see the results from focus groups convened by the John Howard Society of Manitoba to determine the suitability of a family group decision-

making program in Winnipeg, Manitoba: L. Maloney and G. Reddoch, *Restorative Justice and Family Violence: A Community-based Effort to Move from Theory to Practice* (prepared for delivery at the 6th International Conference on Restorative Justice, Simon Fraser University, Vancouver, B.C., June 2003).

4   See the further discussion in relation to the principle of voluntariness in Chapter 7.

5   T. Grillo, "The Mediation Alternative: Process Dangers for Women" (1991) 100:6 *Yale Law Journal* 1545.

6   See, for example Provincial Association Against Family Violence, *Making It Safe: Women, Restorative Justice and Alternative Dispute Resolution* (St John's: Provincial Association Against Family Violence, 2000); W. Stewart, A. Huntley and F. Blaney, *The Implications of Restorative Justice for Aboriginal Women and Children Survivors of Violence: A Comparative Overview of Five Communities in British Columbia* (Ottawa: Law Commission of Canada, July 2001).

7   For a highly critical report, see: Transition House Association of Nova Scotia (THANS). *Abused Women in Family Mediation: A Nova Scotia Snapshot. A Report Prepared by The Transition House Association of Nova Scotia* (Halifax: THANS, 2000).

8   For the use of mediation in sexual abuse cases, see F. Titley and T. Dunn, "Mediating Sexual Abuse Cases" (1998) 10:1 Interaction 6; and for the use of mediation in domestic abuse cases, see D. Ellis, *Evaluation of the Hamilton Family Court Pilot Mediation Project* (Hamilton: Ellis and Associates, 1994).

9   For a number of examples, see the survey in J. Pearson, "Mediating When Domestic Violence Is a Factor: Policies and Practices in Court-based Divorce Mediation Programs" (1997) 14:4 *Mediation Quarterly* 319. This article also highlights the many different forms that domestic violence takes and the lack of alternative processes for women who are victims of spousal abuse.

10   In contrast, see the decision in *G.O. v. C.D. H.*, [2000] O.J. No. 1882, where there was a presumption that mediation should be used, despite the objections of the fearful party.

11   See the discussion regarding the challenges faced by some Aboriginal communities in W. Stewart, A. Huntley and F. Blaney, *supra* note 6.

12   See the analysis in D. Sullivan and L. Tifft, "The Transformative and Economic Dimensions of Restorative Justice" (1998) 22:1 *Humanity and Society* 38.

13   It is important to note that the Hollow Water community was facing other very

significant challenges, including high unemployment, inadequate housing and widespread substance abuse. See T. Lajeunesse, *Evaluation of Community Holistic Circle Healing: Hollow Water First Nation*. Volume 1: Final Report (Ottawa: Solicitor General of Canada, 1996) at chapter 3.

14 *Ibid.* at 238. See also R. Ross, *Returning to the Teachings* (Toronto: Penguin, 1996) especially chapter 2.

15 For example, Yves Tessier, an offender who appeared on the Law Commission of Canada's video on restorative justice, said that having to meet with his victim's family was much more difficult than serving time in prison. See Law Commission of Canada, *Communities and the Challenge of Conflict: Perspectives on Restorative Justice* (video) 2000.

16 J. Macfarlane, "Culture Change? A Tale of Two Cities and Mandatory Court-connected Mediation" (2002) 2002:2 *Journal of Dispute Resolution* 241 at 256–257.

17 See, for example, the extensive review in J. Lande, "Using Dispute Systems Design Methods to Promote Good Faith in Court-connected Mediation Programs" (2002) 50:1 *UCLA Law Review* 69 at 78–85.

18 Lande, *ibid.* at 86-107.

19 For example, the Bar in Ottawa has apparently embraced mediation in civil cases to the extent that it is now counter-culture to use the process for instrumental reasons only. Ottawa lawyers complain that they experience process abuse only when they mediate opposite a Toronto litigator, where the culture still supports bad faith and process abuse. See Macfarlane, *supra* note 16 at 300–301 and 315–316.

20 M.S. Umbreit, *Victim Meets Offender: The Impact of Restorative Justice and Mediation* (Monsey, NY: Criminal Justice Press, 1994) at 44–56.

21 G.M. Maxwell and A. Morris, "The New Zealand Model of Family Group Conferences" in C. Alder and C. Wundersitz, eds., *Family Conferencing and Juvenile Justice: The Way Forward or Misplaced Optimism?* (Canberra: Australian Institute of Criminology, 1994).

22 For more information about the Fraser Region Community Justice Initiative, see online: <http://www.cjibc.org/>.

23 "Risk" was measured using the Level of Supervision Inventory. T.A. Rugge and R. Cormier, Department of the Solicitor General of Canada, *Restorative Justice in Cases of Serious Crimes: An Evaluation* (prepared for delivery at the 6th

International Conference on Restorative Justice, Simon Fraser University, Vancouver, B.C., June 2003).

24 See, for example, the Aboriginal teachings outlined in P. Lane, J. Bopp and M. Bopp, *The Sacred Tree* (Lethbridge: Four Worlds Development Press, 1986); and see the discussion in B. Stuart, "Sentencing Circles: Making Real Differences" in J. Macfarlane, ed., *Rethinking Disputes: The Mediation Alternative* (Toronto: Emond Montgomery, 1997) at 206–207.

25 The initial development of "circles" within a formal justice setting is usually attributed to the Maori model of circle dialogue. See R. Ross, *Returning to the Teachings* (Toronto: Penguin, 1996) at 19.

26 Well illustrated by the description of the renewed Navajo peacemaking courts and their struggle to return to traditional Navajo values in P. Bluehouse and J.W. Zion, "Hozhooji Naat'aanii: The Navajo Justice and Harmony Ceremony" (1993) 10:4 *Mediation Quarterly* 327.

27 *R. v. Moses*, [1992] Y.J. No. 50, was a landmark decision by Justice Stuart, setting out for the first time in a written judgment the rationale for using sentencing circles within Aboriginal communities, as well as a description of their process mechanics.

28 B. Wellman, *The Persistence and Transformation of Community: From Neighbourhood Groups to Social Networks* (Ottawa: Law Commission of Canada, 2001) at 27. See also C. Fisher, "Towards a Sub-culture of Urbanism" (1975) 80 *American Journal of Sociology* 1319.

29 S. Merry, "Defining 'Success' in the Neighborhood Justice Movement" in R. Tomasic and M. Feeley, eds., *Neighborhood Justice: Assessment of An Emerging Idea* (New York: Longman, 1982) at 172–177.

30 For an example of the challenges faced by a group in Victoria to establish a restorative justice program, see M. Dhami and P. Joy, *Challenges to Establishing Community-based Restorative Justice Programs: The Victoria Experience* (prepared for delivery at the 6th International Conference on Restorative Justice, Simon Fraser University, Vancouver, B.C., June 2003).

31 See, for example, the experience of the VOM program operated by the Mediation and Restorative Justice Centre in Edmonton, Alberta. A. Edwards and J. Haslett, *Domestic Violence and Restorative Justice: Advancing the Dialogue* (prepared for delivery at the 6th International Conference on Restorative Justice, Simon Fraser University, Vancouver, B.C., June 2003).

Chapter 6 Designing and Evaluating Models of Participatory Justice

One of the objectives of this report is to identify best practices in conflict resolution across Canada. Chapter 6 offers some principles for the design of participatory processes, drawing on the most promising outcomes seen in current restorative justice and consensus-based justice initiatives.

6.1 THE HALLMARKS OF BEST PRACTICE IN PARTICIPATORY PROCESS DESIGN

To achieve the goals of a participatory process, design principles for participatory justice processes must be faithful to both core values and practical constraints.[1] Good practice now includes careful design planning, both at a general level (for example, determining the type of interaction that might occur between parties to a conflict, and whether the outcome is final or can be re-opened in another process) and at an individual level (for example, determining who should participate and what role they should be prepared to play, and the rules or understandings on confidentiality, future admissibility, and the publication of outcomes). Publication of outcomes is especially important in relation to evaluation and monitoring, but it also raises fundamental questions regarding the public scrutiny of informal processes such as mediation, circles and group conferencing.

The process design principles proposed below are responsive to the three ways in which participatory processes are clearly distinguishable from conventional dispute-processing strategies: a conceptualized notion of harm; a concept of justice as equal well-being, in full recognition of existing systemic inequities; and a focus on the relationship dimensions of conflict. First, it is instructive to take brief note of some of the major themes that have emerged in scholarly and practical work, now commonly known as dispute systems design (DSD), not least because these themes underpin our thinking in this area.

6.1.1 Building in disputant choice

Choice is a design principle that has emerged as key in the last decade of experimentation. Proponents argue that providing choices empowers the participants. Providing choices allows people to decide which process can respond better to their needs. Choice has implications for the principle of voluntariness that will be reviewed later.

6.1.2 Community ownership

The development of conflict resolution processes should include consultation and participation of the client groups that will be affected. The involvement of those directly affected in the design and implementation of these new dispute resolution processes is increasingly regarded as essential, enhancing both the credibility and the longevity of such initiatives. Participation may take place at the planning stage, at the implementation stage (for example, during the training of mediators), and at the evaluation stage (for example, through focus groups, surveys and other data collection techniques). Client-centred design allows designers and policymakers to avoid cultural assumptions in developing community-based programs— instead, the design of the program can reflect the cultural demography of the community—and encourages a sense of ownership for the initiative among community members.[2] At a minimum, community participation should include an offer of training to community members on the principles of participatory processes that will form the cornerstones of the new program.[3] As the process design takes shape and a program emerges, community members may choose to play key roles, such as volunteering as community mediators, participating in circles, or sitting as a member of community panels.

6.2 TWELVE GUIDING PRINCIPLES FOR THE DESIGN OF PARTICIPATORY PROCESSES

There is some tension between setting out even general principles for process design and meeting the needs of those who participate in participatory processes. Justice is above all a highly subjective experience.[4] Can the principles of restorative and consensus-based justice be used to generate applicable recommendations for the design of overall systems that support consensus-building and healing? The most important principle for participatory processes may be that any process or system should be sufficiently flexible to take account of individual needs and goals. What works for one dispute will not necessarily work for another, however superficially similar they might appear. Individual expectations, motivations and values—and how the parties have constructed their "reality" of the conflict—are different in every dispute.

Nonetheless, some general principles do emerge and should guide the design of future participatory processes. Each of the 12 design principles that follow reflects the earlier discussion of the core objectives and process values of restorative and consensus-based justice initiatives in Chapters 2 and 3, as well as the fundamental characteristics of participatory processes (a conceptualized understanding of harm, justice as social well-being, a focus on relationships and relationship restoration). The 12 design principles are:

- Early intervention
- Accessibility
- Voluntariness
- Careful preparation
- Opportunities for face-to-face dialogue
- Advocacy and support
- Confidentiality
- Fairness
- Relevant and realistic outcomes
- Flexibility and responsiveness
- Efficiency
- Systemic Impact

6.2.1 Early intervention

A first guiding principle is an emphasis on early intervention and pre-charge or pre-litigation options for non-criminal matters. It seems clear that the earlier that non-threatening, constructive, participatory interventions can be made, the more likely that a conflict may quickly de-escalate. This principle is exemplified in restorative justice processes that operate as a caution for young people who otherwise could be at risk for future criminal behaviour. It is also exemplified in school-based programs that encourage good conflict resolution skills and practices among schoolchildren. In civil matters, early intervention would enable landlords and tenants to seek early mediation assistance when problems arise and their relationship begins to deteriorate, and it would not be delayed until the landlord obtained an order for eviction.[5]

It is interesting to speculate on how this public and political culture might change if people could expect assistance with conflict resolution before a formal criminal charge is laid or a litigation has commenced.[6] There are obvious benefits both for individual disputants themselves and for the community at large. Participatory processes should be designed with an awareness of the benefits of early intervention. Participatory processes should consciously aspire to the creation of a culture in which early problem diagnosis and proactive intervention are widely accepted, in much the same way as the medical community uses early identification and diagnosis of health problems.

The principle of early diagnosis and intervention wherever possible should not discourage the important development of post-adjudication processes—for example, post-incarceration Victim–Offender Mediation or the use of talking circles in a workplace after the adjudication of a grievance. Such processes serve many helpful functions for the participants and contribute to the resolution of long enduring conflicts and the reduction of the costs of those conflicts for our society.

6.2.2 Accessibility

If participatory processes are to be utilized by community members and justice system officials, it is critical to design them to be easily accessible, user-friendly and not overly bureaucratic. A number of factors appear to be significant in designing programs to maximize accessibility and participation. The first is that the program must be located in a place that is considered unthreatening and welcoming to potential users. For this reason, some programs (especially restorative justice initiatives working with offenders and victims) take place outside a courthouse or formal justice venue. A second consideration is that potential users should be able to access information about the service with assurances of complete confidentiality.[7]

Where the consent of a justice system official—for example, a Crown prosecutor, or a judge—is needed before a participatory process can be utilized by the parties, it is important that decision-making is timely and transparent.[8]

6.2.3 Voluntariness

The fears expressed that some members of marginalized and disempowered groups will be coerced to participate in informal dispute resolution processes and perhaps agree to unfair outcomes must be taken very seriously. Genuine voluntariness seems to be more than a desirable principle in the design of participatory processes; indeed, it is fundamental. To ensure that parties to a dispute genuinely volunteer to participate in a program, they must be provided with full information about the process and its alternatives and all the assistance necessary to make an informed choice.[9] This does not mean that each person who chooses a participatory process over a more traditional rights-based approach will do so with no concerns or fears, but that they should do so with authentic voluntariness, having appraised it as a good option for the resolution of the conflict at issue.

Choice must be respected. Participatory processes assume that individual parties are best suited to determine whether a consensual approach is suitable for the resolution of their conflict, whether this lies in the criminal domain or in the civil domain. At the same time, however, the mediator must exercise judgment when considering whether to proceed with a mediation, particularly when issues of fear and violence are present.[10]

Introducing mandatory mediation programs in the civil courts has been criticized on the grounds that requiring the parties to mediate corrupts the concept of voluntary bargaining. Others argue that this is the only way to ensure that clients, rather than their legal representatives, decide whether mediation is appropriate and to enable their legal representatives to experience a process that is otherwise unfamiliar and perhaps counterintuitive to legal training. What emerges from these debates is the need to design programs in such a way that they ensure that disputants themselves actively decide whether to use a participatory process to address a conflict. Attention must also be directed at removing the disincentives to using participatory processes that currently exist in our system of justice, for example, the absence of full legal aid coverage.

Is there a case for requiring some form of participation in consensus-building processes, as, for example, in mandatory court-connected mediation programs? Mandatory requirements vary widely. Some jurisdictions require that the parties and their counsel simply meet to negotiate the most appropriate process (mandatory consideration rules).[11] An argument can be made that mandatory mediation is sometimes appropriate to expose both disputants and their legal representatives to a process that they would otherwise likely decline.[12] Moreover, research now shows a correlation between actual experiences of mediation and positive attitudes toward the usefulness of the process.[13] Research also shows no significant differences in satisfaction between participants in voluntary processes and those in mandatory processes.[14]

Can the same arguments be applied to participatory processes in the criminal context? The debate over voluntariness in restorative justice processes appears to be centred on ensuring exit routes for those who feel coerced into participating (for example, for the victims experiencing pressure from their communities to participate), rather than on any suggestion that either victim or offender should be compelled to attend a circle or community panel instead of a traditional trial process. Nonetheless, an equally strong case can be made from both civil and criminal matters requiring that legal counsel—and perhaps their clients—attend an orientation or information session describing the alternative process and its possible value.

Any suggestion of compulsion or coercion to participate in a mediation, circle or similar process clearly contradicts the principle of voluntariness, which appears intrinsic to participatory processes. It is the view of the Commission that such mandatory programs are to be reserved for non-criminal conflicts, for a time-limited period, alongside accessible training and information opportunities for participants, and with the possibility to refuse to participate for reasons of fear of intimidation or coercion.

It is proposed, therefore, that mandatory participation programs be considered only under the following conditions:

1. Where a requirement of mandatory participation is introduced for a time-limited period, in order to expose the local lawyers and their clients to dispute resolution services and to educate them about the potential alternatives to a traditional justice model.

2. Where a requirement of mandatory participation is introduced alongside accessible training and information opportunities for lawyers and their clients.

3. Where easily accessible exit routes can be provided for those identifying themselves as vulnerable to intimidation or coercion.

The debate over mandatory mediation ought not to detract from the very real issue of the existing disincentives to using participatory processes. Within both the criminal and non-criminal justice systems, many rules, practices and customs make it more difficult or costly for parties who might consider participatory processes. Throughout its consultations, the Commission had heard from many professionals and non-professionals who describe how the rules on costs or on access to legal aid, for example, prevented a serious exploration of participatory alternatives. Many invisible barriers to developing and recognizing alternatives to the traditional adversarial system continue to exist. The Commission hopes that this report and the continued work of the many institutions involved in the justice system will serve to uncover and remove current impediments to wider recourse to participatory processes.

6.2.4 Careful preparation

Another design principle that must coexist, however uneasily, alongside voluntariness in participatory processes is particular attention to disputant relationships that suggest fear or intimidation. An example of a set of minimal standards for screening is provided by the Ontario Ministry of the Attorney General policy for funded mediation services at the Family Court.

Note, however, that point five assumes that when the intake worker believes that mediation is inappropriate, mediation should be refused, even if the party wishes to proceed. This seems incompatible with the emphasis on self-determination in processes and suggests a focus on protecting the intervener, rather than on achieving the best interests of the client. This principle does, however, recognize that it is not always appropriate for parties to meet, even when they want to. Throughout its consultations, the Commission heard that mediators ought to be in a position to evaluate particular cases to determine whether a meeting would be constructive or destructive. The Commission suggests that in cases in which fear and a history of violence are present, but the client wishes to pursue consensual dispute resolution, there should be joint decision-making between the disputant and the mediator. In addition, best practice in design might assign an external mentor to review such a case as it proceeds through the chosen process to ensure that there is no actual or perceived intimidation.

Intake processes should also build in adequate preparation time. A critical part of preparation is considering what documentation and other material needs to be made available to all participants before a meeting. Leaving this to the initiative and discretion of individual participants is sometimes inefficient, especially when counsel are constrained by conventional approaches to information exchange.

Instead, programs should ensure that an early substantive discussion takes place, if necessary facilitated by a program staff person, regarding the exchange of relevant information before a circle, mediation, panel hearing or other process.

Many informal dispute resolution processes move slowly. For example, it may take a great deal of preparatory work to ready participants for a circle; parties, for a face-to-face mediation; or

---

Ontario Ministry of the Attorney General Policy for Government-funded Mediation Services at the Family Court

Mediation services are required to commit to the following goals:

1. the identification of violence in the family/abuse;

2. the safety of victims of violence in the family/abuse;

3. ensuring that mediation is offered only when it is truly voluntary;

4. to give clients who have been disempowered by violence in the family/abuse the support and safety they need to refuse to mediate;

5. to suggest cases which are not suitable for mediation and to refuse mediation in these cases [and to suggest alternate courses of action];

6. to encourage assertiveness of victims of violence in the family/abuse; and

7. to provide clients with information about community resources which can be of assistance to them and their children.

Ontario Ministry of the Attorney General, "Policy for Government-Funded Mediation Services at the Family Court," online: <http://www.attorneygeneral.jus.gov.on.ca:80/english/family/policies.asp>.

---

spouses, for the first substantive four-way negotiation in collaborative law. It is important to invest the time and resources required to adequately prepare disputants for a process. Experience suggests that if this preparatory work is done, these processes appear to proceed much more successfully and quickly toward an acceptable conclusion.

6.2.5 Opportunities for face-to-face dialogue

This report has already dealt with the importance of face-to-face dialogue for both restorative justice and consensus-based justice processes. A key design principle for participatory processes must be the creation of opportunities for face-to-face dialogue in which personal experiences of justice can be created. During its consultations, the Commission heard from many people who are actively involved in restorative and consensus-based justice initiatives. Practitioners told the Commission that there will be occasions when face-to-face dialogue may be inappropriate or ill-advised: it may be rejected by one or more of the parties to the conflict or it may simply not be feasible because of time and distance constraints. Under these circumstances there must be sufficient flexibility to enable a dialogue to take place—through shuttle diplomacy, conference call, video-conferencing or other means—if the parties firmly believe this to be constructive.

While face-to-face dialogue has the potential to offer the greatest impact on victims and offenders, research indicates that even when victims and offenders do not meet, levels of satisfaction, particularly with the process, remain high.[15]

6.2.6 Advocacy and support

The Commission's consultations with practitioners underlined the need for advocacy and support. The experience of these practitioners suggests that program design should ensure a clear place and functional role for supporters. "Supporters" can be lawyers, family members, friends or others who might provide advice and offer emotional support throughout the conflict resolution process. It is important that the role of the supporter be clarified in advance and that participatory processes remain within the ultimate control of the disputants.

Many individuals whom the Commission consulted suggested that the presence of lawyers undermines the participatory nature of the process, as they bring with them their adversarial culture, particularly in criminal cases. The history of mandatory mediation in civil cases reveals that this fear of lawyers undermining a participatory process may be overstated. There is some evidence that when lawyers attend mandatory civil mediation with their clients, the discussions are dominated by counsel who sometimes instruct their clients to leave the talking to them.[16] On the other hand, research conducted for the Commission by Julie Macfarlane showed that many lawyers involved in mandatory mediation come to realize the value of the process. These "true believers" embrace the principles of participatory justice and are open to allowing their clients to assume a leading role in the conflict resolution process.

To ensure that participatory processes retain a focus on the disputants themselves, rather than on their agents, advocates should be briefed on the need for their clients to speak for themselves wherever possible, to participate actively, and with full advice from counsel, to reach their final decisions independent of outside parties who might seek to influence them. As the Commission recommends in Chapter 8, the principles of participatory justice ought to be taught in universities and, in particular, in law schools and reaffirmed by law societies so that lawyers come to understand the value of these processes and the types of skills the processes require so that their potential is fully realized.

There has been a lot of discussion over whether disputants need legal advice in order to reach fully informed decisions in consensual processes. When legal rights and obligations are negotiated, it is good practice to ensure that the parties have access to independent legal advice.[17] At present, not all participatory processes qualify for paid legal representation under provincial legal aid schemes. This is particularly the case in the criminal justice system. Because many legal aid plans do not apply to restorative justice processes means, there is a disincentive for lawyers to recommend these processes to their clients. This is an

"True Believers" in Mandatory Mediation

"The True Believer has made a strong personal commitment to the usefulness of the mediation process which goes further than simply reorienting their practice strategies to new client expectations and requirements. The True Believer speaks about mediation in terms that suggest that it has had a significant impact on his attitudes towards practice, clients and conflict. He may even use quasi-religious metaphors like 'converted' or 'transformed' ('I got religion;' 'I think you'll find that I'm a person who has now converted and I admit to being a believer in mediation') to describe this process of personal and professional change. He sees mediation as having a transformative effect on relationships, outcomes and on the role of the advocacy itself which goes beyond an instrumental use of the process. One True Believer described 'a completely different form of adversary process.' Another in comparing mediation to traditional settlement negotiations asserted, '...[M]y role has significantly changed. All of those things are done quite differently at the mediation.'

The True Believer identifies what he thinks are signs of systemic change in the litigation environment and is perhaps more conscious or preoccupied with these than any of the other attitude types. The True Believer even sometimes takes on the role of proselytizer; for example, 'I've got into the practice of taking on the education of the lawyers on the other side with respect to mandatory mediation.' Because of his changed perspectives on conflict resolution and the role of counsel, the True Believer sometimes experiences a strong feeling of tension between his adversarial role and his settlement role."

J. Macfarlane, "Culture Change? Commercial Litigators and
the Ontario Mandatory Mediation Program,"
report prepared for the Law Commission of Canada, 2001.

important dimension of legitimating participatory processes and ensuring that those who choose this approach to dispute resolution are not disadvantaged compared with those who choose to remain within a conventional adjudicative process.

6.2.7 Confidentiality

The assurance of confidentiality, which is usually provided for processes working toward agreed outcomes, seems critical to their efficacy. Guaranteeing the confidentiality of information disclosed, explanations given and, perhaps, acknowledgments made during mediation, circles or group conferences enable participants to be open and at the same time protects this openness. Disclosures made in the course of participatory processes are generally understood to be inadmissible in future legal proceedings. During the course of the Commission's consultations, some people suggested that from time to time Crown counsels have used information disclosed during the course of a restorative justice process to prosecute the offender in court. These types of abuses of confidentiality ought to be carefully examined. Confidentiality is one of the core elements of participatory processes and ought to be guarded carefully.

Good practice suggests that participants read and sign a written statement before they begin a process. Ideally, confidentiality is discussed during the intake and preparatory stages. Intake procedures should explain both the legal status of disclosures and the importance

Standard Confidentiality Agreement

The parties acknowledge and agree that mediation is a confidential settlement process intended to explore possible compromises or accommodations and alternative solutions or designs to resolve the dispute, and they are participating in the process with the understanding that anything discussed in the mediation process cannot be used in any court or any other proceeding.[18]

of treating disclosures as confidential among participants. In consensus-based justice processes, the former is usually taken care of by standard clauses in mediation agreements.

There is sometimes confusion over the practical import of confidentiality clauses. Clauses such as the above are designed to exclude the repetition of anything said by another party under the cone of confidentiality. They do not restrict in any way a party from repeating a statement she or he has made in mediation or during a circle or conferencing process, nor do they restrict the same party from bringing forward the same information (including documents) again.

It is also important to anticipate certain limitations on confidentiality, both among the parties and on the part of any other participant. These include any disclosure that suggests a threat or danger to life and the ill-treatment or abuse of children. While the Canadian courts have generally been respectful of the confidential nature of conflict resolution discussions, it is also practical to recognize that a judicial order could in theory compel disclosures.[19]

A more difficult question is how to design processes that ensure that the second component of confidentiality—treating what is said as confidential among the participants—is taken seriously and observed honourably. Clearly, members of a circle or parties to a mediation are likely to discuss what was said with others outside the group, for example, with family and friends. This can sometimes lead to problems within small, close-knit communities. It is suggested that program designers and third parties stress the need to ensure that the private discussions that take place within these processes do not spread throughout the wider community, bringing embarrassment and possibly mistrust into the process and undermining the continuation of such processes.

Finally, it is important to distinguish confidentiality within the process from the confidentiality of outcomes, which raises different issues. These are discussed below.

6.2.8 Fairness

While outcomes should be "what matters" to the individual participant,[20] a balance needs to be struck between community autonomy, personal self-determination and the regulatory role of the state. For the design of participatory processes, this raises questions of external scrutiny, review and appeals.

The decision to voluntarily engage in a participatory process should include a commitment to accepting an agreed outcome as a final resolution of the dispute. Whereas allegations of coercion in reaching an agreed outcome must be taken very seriously, it is appropriate to ask participants to agree at the outset that any outcome to which they consent shall be final and without recourse to an appeal body. The essence of a participatory process is that the parties have considered all the circumstances and have agreed to a particular outcome—a very different commitment than submitting to the imposed judgment of a third party. For this reason, Canadian courts have been unwilling to re-open mediated agreements on the civil side or to substitute their judgment for the apparent voluntary consensus of the parties, unless there is evidence of coercion or oppression in reaching that conclusion.[21]

This does not, however, remove the need to monitor the quality of the outcomes of participatory processes. Where there are clear legal standards (for example, child support guidelines in the case of family disputes), there is additional pressure to ensure that these standards are followed and that parties are not agreeing to less than their entitlement. While it is important to satisfy critics that agreed outcomes do not undermine legal principles or diminish the rights of a particular group—for example, single mothers with custody of their children—the principles of participatory processes require that the parties themselves ultimately make the decisions regarding what they can accept as "fair."

If the outcomes of a program are monitored to check for settlement patterns that suggest unfairness, an additional practical problem for designers and evaluators of consensus-based justice programs in civil situations is that outcomes are often regarded as confidential. This problem is removed in criminal diversion cases, for which outcomes must be reported to the court. In many other processes, including family mediation, human rights mediation and some pre-charging processes, there is sometimes a requirement to report outcomes, as these are not generally regarded as private by the parties.

Whether and how outcomes might be made public in processes that are otherwise private is an important design consideration for participatory processes. In some conflicts the accessibility to and publication of the outcome are critical to achieving systemic long-term change (for example, in some human rights and discrimination cases). At the same time, for some parties the opportunity to fashion a private solution to a problem may be an important motivation for them to agree to a participatory approach. These needs and interests must be balanced, but there are clearly instances in which the public interest requires that outcomes should be public, even if anonymity is preserved and some details are omitted.[22] At a minimum, public reporting of the outcome and the form of such reporting should be discussed and possibly negotiated during the process so that participants know in advance what to expect.

6.2.9   Relevant and realistic outcomes

While participatory processes leave the solution to the problem in the hands of the participants, it is important that outcomes be relevant and realistic and, if possible, durable. This is important for the credibility and long-term viability of participatory processes. In criminal matters, this means ensuring that resources are available in the system to provide for community services, probation, drug rehabilitation, anger management education, and so on. When an agreement calls for the payment of monies, program staff should have the resources to follow up to ensure that payments have been made. Some programs may choose to work closely with the civil courts, for example, asking a small claims court judge to rubber-stamp an agreement and thereby give the agreement the force of a court order. If a program prefers that compliance measures be informal only, this should be made clear to all participants at the outset, as well as the steps that the program will take as follow-up.[23]

Compliance is an important indicator of the effectiveness of participatory processes. It is important that program designers anticipate some means of monitoring the durability of outcomes. This may mean that a sample of cases is followed up three (or six) months after agreement, in order to generate compliance data. If problems with compliance and durability become evident, the program should review the types of options that are commonly considered by participants to ensure that these are realistic and appropriate.

More important, failure to comply with agreements that are reached may reflect a failure on the part of some of the participants to take the processes and their outcomes seriously. In this case, program staff should consider renewing efforts to undertake sufficient preparatory work with the parties, to ensure that future outcomes are regarded as serious commitments.

6.2.10 Efficiency

Attempts to measure the cost of court processing time for civil and criminal disputes are unsatisfactory because of the difficulty associated with measuring variables, such as whether a matter returns to court, the economic costs incurred when an individual is placed on probation or incarcerated, or the social costs incurred when a landlord evicts a tenant who is then forced to find new housing. Moreover, it is difficult to quantify the economic benefits that accrue from even one successful victim–offender or landlord–tenant mediation. Advocates of participatory processes argue that the worth of these processes is not directly translatable into any reduction in processing costs but must be seen in long-term benefits to the community. Clearly, it is important that costs not be measured solely in monetary terms, since conflicts have many other costs. Nonetheless, processes that place increased long-term costs on either disputants or the state are unlikely to be acceptable. Efforts must, therefore, be made to use the meeting time efficiently and allow parties to know in advance what is expected of them.

A Cost-Benefit Analysis of the Hollow Water Community Holistic Circle Healing Process

The Native Counselling Services of Alberta conducted a cost-benefit analysis of the Hollow Water Community Holistic Circle Healing (CHCH). Over the course of ten years, CHCH received about $3 million in funding from the federal and Manitoba governments. This money was used for victim and offender services. The Native Counselling Services estimated that if the program did not exist, the cost to the federal and provincial government of providing services would be considerably higher.

CHCH	$3,000,000
Provincial costs	$3,751,414
Federal costs	$2,461,318–$12,150,471
Total costs to governments	$6,212,732–$15,901,885

According to the Native Counselling Services report, the benefit of the CHCH program is significant. The CHCH cost $3 million over ten years. If the program did not exist, it is estimated that the cost to government for providing the services to the victims and the offenders would be between $6.2 million and $15.9 million. At a minimum, the CHCH saved government $3,212,732 over the past ten years.

As the Native Counselling Services report says, "for each dollar Manitoba spends on CHCH, it would otherwise have to spend approximately $3.00 for policing, court, institutional, probation and victims' services. For each dollar the federal government spends on CHCH, it would otherwise have to spend a minimum of $2.00 for institutional and parole services."

Native Counselling Services of Alberta, *A Cost-Benefit Analysis of Hollow Water's Community Holistic Circle Healing Process* (Ottawa: Ministry of the Solicitor General; Aboriginal Healing Foundation, Ottawa, 2001).

6.2.11 Systemic impact

Participatory processes move decision-making into the hands of individual disputants and their communities. The potential for developing what is sometimes described as "social capital" is obvious. The development and implementation of participatory projects build the community's capacity to deal with problems collectively and consensually. This capacity-building can be further enhanced by incorporating training for volunteers into program design, equipping these individuals with conflict resolution skills they can use in the future in their workplaces and communities. Offenders and victims who have participated in participatory processes may be encouraged to return as volunteers in the program. Programs initiated to respond to particular needs and problems within the community—for example, a widespread drug culture or high rates of breaking and entering—might develop related social action projects to tackle the causes of these problems. Education programs—such as anger management programs—can be developed to create systemic impact from the work undertaken in conflict resolution.

In the design of participatory processes, this means ensuring that participants clearly understand what is expected of them in advance

"Every time citizens participate in community-based processes like circles, neighborhood panels or family group conferencing, they communicate their expectations, their standards for behavior. Each incident involves only a small portion of the community in the discussion, but the cumulative effect of using these processes on a regular basis is widespread citizen involvement in decisions which require thinking about values and standards. These processes require citizens to struggle with the questions: How should we treat one another? How should we work through conflict?"

K. Pranis, "Engaging the Community in Restorative Justice," (Balanced and Restorative Justice Project, June 1998) at 16.

and that meeting time is used effectively as discussed above; providing easy access to renewed negotiation processes at any future point in litigation or trial proceedings; and providing appropriate follow up to ensure that matters discussed and resolved are implemented.

6.2.12 Flexibility and responsiveness

The principles described here are suggested as the hallmarks of good practice in the design of participatory processes, on the basis of Canadian experience to date. However, the essence of participatory processes is to provide personal experiences of conflict resolution—in the form of both process and outcome—that are meaningful to the individuals involved. This requires constant flexibility and responsiveness to the particular needs of each unique conflict. This means that programs should foster a spirit of responsiveness and respect for the unique circumstances of each conflict that passes through the process. Rigid structures and rules that unnecessarily reduce participant choices should be avoided if at all possible. The assumption of self-determination that lies at the heart of participatory processes for individuals and communities alike means that affected persons can and must be trusted to make appropriate decisions over the design details of their own processes—such as who should be present, how long the meeting should last, what will be discussed, and what types of solution or outcomes should be considered.[24]

6.3   ANTICIPATING PROGRAM EVALUATION

The evaluation of conflict resolution processes is a developing area for social science research. There is increasing interest in developing best practice approaches to program evaluation to ensure integrity in results and relevant information for policymakers and community members.[25]

Efficient design includes planning for evaluation; deciding whether it will be formal or relatively informal and anecdotal. The core objectives and values of a process are important resources for evaluators, as they offer direction on the problems the new process aims to address and its internal benchmarks for successful change. In this way, the guiding principles for program design outlined above provide a basis for program evaluation. There are three key considerations with respect to evaluation.

6.3.1   Implementation evaluation

An evaluation of implementation assesses how far the program under examination meets the threshold standards of these guiding principles by reviewing program documentation, such as staff manuals and information provided to users, and by surveying or interviewing a sample of program users and staff. Satisfaction surveys are often used in this context. It is important to consider that initial satisfaction with a process may not prevail over time. Some evaluations may provide a better assessment by using longer term analysis and data collection.

6.3.2   Identification and measurement of evaluation priorities

The second task of the evaluator is to work with program staff to identify the program's priority goals. For example, a program may wish to concentrate on increasing case referrals, in which case the priority goal will be enhanced accessibility by strengthening referral links, public education and outreach. There may have been complaints about parties being pressured to participate without being properly informed about their choices at the outset or without being empowered to withdraw, in which case the focus for an evaluation may be intake practices. Experience with low compliance may lead a program to prioritize durable outcomes, so the program's "success" at this time is framed to some extent in terms of outcome compliance. Alternatively, a program may have reached a stage of development at which its priority becomes systemic change, measured by the long-term impact of the program on the wider community.

In each case, the evaluator must identify tangible and credible outcome measures that permit an assessment of this priority. For example, in the case of accessibility, the number of case referrals that continue through the conflict resolution may be important indicators. Similarly, focusing on compliance will probably require collecting follow-up data on cases that have reached agreement over the evaluation period. In contrast, appraising intake and screening practices may require qualitative research, including interviews with parties reporting pressure. Finally, assessing the systemic impact of a program on a community probably involves both quantitative data (for example, local crime rates and recidivism rates from this program) and qualitative data (for example, interviews with community leaders and law enforcement agents about trends and changes they have observed).

6.3.3   Selection of an appropriate evaluation methodology

The third task of the evaluator is to assist in selecting an appropriate evaluation methodology that will provide useful data for the program users, the program staff and the policymakers. The evaluation of dispute resolution systems and processes presents many methodological challenges, both conceptual and practical. For example, it is difficult to develop an objective definition of "satisfaction" (often an important criterion in program evaluation). The extent to which parties feel "satisfied" with dispute resolution processes is usually a reflection of their past experiences and their expectations for this particular process—all entirely subjective. To properly take account of the personal nature of experiences of satisfaction, evaluators should gather information by using open-ended questions from a range of sources and not depend solely on structured surveys with preset answer categories.

Another challenge for evaluation methodologies is the volume of variables present in the implementation of any given process designed to expedite settlement. Comparisons between processes that are informally regulated and those controlled by a mediator or facilitator whose particular role and style will be critical to the outcome are especially problematic. Similarly, within any classification of case type, there are inevitably many variables—for example, how much money is at stake, whether disputants are acting in person or in a corporate capacity, what the quality of legal representation is—that may critically affect settlement outcomes. An external classification of dispute type also overlooks the fact that the disputants themselves may "redefine" the issues if they choose to settle the conflict consensually.[26]

In light of these significant methodological challenges, the evaluator should determine, along with program staff and users:

- What type of data can be collected.

- What data would provide the most useful information for the priority evaluation questions.

- What forms of data would be most authentic.

- What types of data would be most credible to program staff, users, community members and funders.

---

1   See, for example, B. Pearce and S. Littlejohn, *Moral Conflict: When Social Worlds Collide* (Newbury Park: Sage, 1997); G.W. Cormick, N. Dale, P. Emond, S.G. Sigurdson and B.D. Stuart, *Building Consensus for a Sustainable Future* (Ottawa: National Round Table on the Environment and the Economy, 1996); C. Costantino and C. Merchant, *Designing Conflict Management Systems* (San Francisco: Jossey-Bass, 1996); J. Macfarlane, ed., *Dispute Resolution: Readings and Case Studies*, 2nd ed. (Toronto: Emond Montgomery, 2003) at chapter 6; W. Ury, J. Brett and S. Goldberg, *Getting Disputes Resolved* (Boston: Program on Negotiation, Harvard University, 1993); M. Rowe, "The Post-Tailhook Navy Designs an Integrated Dispute Resolution System" (1993) 9:3 *Negotiation Journal* 203; J.P. Conbere, "Theory Building for Conflict Management System Design" (2001) 19:2 *Conflict Resolution Quarterly* 215; and C. Bendersky, "Culture: The Missing Link in Systems Design" (1998) 14:4 *Negotiation Journal* 307.

2   C. Constantino, "Using Interests-based Techniques to Design Conflict Management Systems" (1996) *Negotiation Journal* 207.

3   In the same way as the RCMP has made training in facilitating community forums and conferences widely available to its officers. See *Restorative Justice: A Fresh Approach*, online: <http://www.rcmp-grc.gc.ca/ccaps/restjust_e.htm> (date accessed: 17 September 2003).

4   For a compelling account of justice through the eyes of a series of individual subjects, see S. Silbey and P. Ewick, *The Common Place of the Law: Stories from Everyday Life* (Chicago: University of Chicago Press, 1998).

5   For example, legal clinics consistently report that a high percentage of the tenant clients they see seek assistance only after an order has been made to evict them.

6   Susan Silbey and Susan Merry suggest that at an early stage of conflict many people are embarrassed to find themselves in a dispute and prefer to ignore or hide this from others. See S. Merry and S. Silbey, "What do Plaintiffs Want? Re-examining the Concept of Dispute" (1984) 9:2 *The Justice System Journal* 151.

7   This may also affect the physical location of the program. Workplace programs that identify a particular individual as the first step in a conflict resolution process have often experienced resistance among employees who are reluctant to attend in full view of colleagues.

8   Constantino and Merchant warn against the over-bureaucratization of a decision to access ADR services and argue for the principle of subsidiarity. C. Costantino and C. Merchant, *Designing Conflict Management Systems* (San Francisco: Jossey-Bass, 1996) 130.

9   For a discussion of the ethics of informed choice, see J. Macfarlane, "Mediating Ethically: the Limits of Codes of Conduct and the Potential of a Reflective Practice Model" (2002) 39:4 *Osgoode Hall Law Journal* 78.

10 See, for example, the discussion in E. Kruk, "Power Imbalance and Spouse Abuse in Divorce Disputes: Deconstructing Mediation Practice via the 'Simulated Client' Technique" (1998) 12:1 *International Journal of Law, Policy and Family* 1.

11 For example, Minnesota General Rules of Practice for the District Courts, Rule 114. See further discussion in Chapter 8.

12 C. Hart and J. Macfarlane, "Court-annexed Mediation: Rights Instincts, Wrong Priorities?" *Law Times*, April 28-May 4, 1997 at 5.

13 See, for example, J. Lande, "Getting the Faith: Why Business Lawyers and Executives Believe in Mediation" (2000) 5 *Harvard Negotiation Law Review* 137 at 171–176; and M. Medley and J. Schellenberg, "Attitudes of Attorneys Towards Mediation" (1994) 12 *Mediation Quarterly* 185.

14 R.L. Wissler, "The Effects of Mandatory Mediation: Empirical Research on the Experience of Small Claims and Common Pleas Courts" (1997) 33 *Willamette Law Review* 565. See also the discussion about the ambiguous concept of party "satisfaction," in dispute resolution program evaluation.

15 T.A. Rugge and R. Cormier, Department of the Solicitor General of Canada, *Restorative Justice in Cases of Serious Crimes: An Evaluation* (prepared for delivery at the 6th International Conference on Restorative Justice, Simon Fraser University, Vancouver, B.C., June 2003).

[16] See N. Welsh, "The Thinning Vision of Self-Determination in Court-Connected Mediation: The Inevitable Price of Institutionalization?" (2001) 6 *Harvard Negotiation Law Review* 1.

[17] There may be other important factors besides legal advice in parties choosing a particular outcome, including concern about a future relationship, a desire for a timely outcome, and the need for closure.

[18] There is continuing debate over whether it is feasible to exclude information from future discoveries. The Ottawa mandatory mediation program suggests the following clause: "Mediation is a confidential, off-the-record process. The objective of confidentiality is to protect an environment in which frank and open discussion can take place without the fear of future prejudice. This means that while not restricting any party's right to pursue alternative remedies if mediation fails to produce a settlement, all statements made in mediation, documents (or copies thereof) produced in mediation, notes taken and any other communication during the mediation cannot be relied upon in evidence by the other party in any judicial, arbitral or tribunal proceedings, current or future, unless such information is otherwise discoverable without reliance on any confidential statement, material or communication made during mediation."

[19] The following is an example of a clause from a mediation agreement, setting out standard exemptions for the purposes of confidentiality:

The mediator shall not disclose to anyone who is not a party to the mediation anything said or any materials submitted to her, except:

    i. to any person designated or retained by any party;

   ii. where ordered to do so by a judicial authority or where required to do so by law;

  iii. where the information suggests an actual or potential threat to human life or safety.

[20] J. Braithwaite, "Restorative Justice: Assessing Optimistic and Pessimistic Accounts" (1999) 25 *Crime and Justice* 1 at 6.

[21] Except in cases where there has been clear pressure on one or more parties or some other type of mediator misconduct. See J.L. Schulz, "Mediator Liability in Canada: An Examination of Emerging American and Canadian Jurisprudence", 32 *Ottawa Law Review* (2001) 269.

[22] See the discussion and recommendations in J. Macfarlane and E. Zweibel, *Systemic Change and Private Closure in Human Rights Mediation: An Evaluation of the Mediation Program at the Canadian Human Rights Tribunal* (Ottawa: Canadian Human Rights Tribunal, 2001).

23 Failure to comply with voluntarily assumed obligations is a frequent criticism by clients of mediation processes, and it impacts negatively on program credibility. See J. Macfarlane, *Building on "What Works": An Evaluation of the Saskatchewan Queen's Bench Mediation Program* (Regina: Saskatchewan Justice, 2003).

24 For a practical example of the potential of informal processes to respond to context and be modified accordingly, see H. Ganlin, "Mediating Sexual Harassment" in B. Sandler and R. Shoop, eds., *Sexual Harassment on Campus* (Toronto: Simon and Schuster, 1997) at 191.

25 Two excellent resources relating to program evaluation are C. Morris, "Conflict Resolution and Peacebuilding: A Selected Bibliography," online: <http://www.peacemakers.ca/bibliography/bib25evaluation.html> (date accessed: 17 September 2003); and C. Church and J. Shouldice, *The Evaluation of Conflict Resolution Interventions: Framing the State of Play* (Ulster: International Conflict Research, 2002); and C. Church and J. Shouldice, *The Evaluation of Conflict Resolution Interventions, Part II: Emerging Practice and Theory* (Ulster: International Conflict Research, 2003).

26 For a discussion of some further methodological challenges in measuring the success of dispute resolution programs, see, for example, R.A. Bush, "Defining Quality in Dispute Resolution: Taxonomies and Anti-taxonomies of Quality Arguments" (1989) 66 *University of Denver Law Review* 381; and M. Galanter and M. Cahill, "Most Cases Settle" (1993-94) 46 *Stanford Law Review* 1339.

Chapter 7 Balancing the Role of Government and Community Autonomy

Chapter 7 explores the changes necessary to make participatory justice processes part of the mainstream of conflict resolution practice in Canada without losing their creative elements. The opening section of this chapter reviews some examples of best practice in a range of areas, including criminal, civil, administrative, family and extralegal conflicts. It is presented as a way of building on the current Canadian experience of participatory processes. The chapter then considers the role of governments in relation to community-based justice initiatives. Community participation is key to participatory justice initiatives and many proponents regard government as undermining their work. At the same time, as long as the traditional justice system operates as the hub of dispute processing, community justice initiatives must develop structural relationships with the criminal, administrative and civil justice systems.

7.1 BUILDING ON CURRENT PARTICIPATORY JUSTICE PROCESSES

The application of participatory models to many areas of disputing has demonstrable benefits for individuals and their communities. Canadian experience with consensus-building processes—in both civil and criminal matters and in both court-connected and community settings—suggests many positive outcomes from these initiatives. The following is a review of some of the processes that exist in Canada. Many others also prosper. The following list gives an indication of the breath of current Canadian participatory initiatives:

- Civil mediation programs in Saskatchewan,[1] Ontario[2] and British Columbia[3] have resulted in high levels of user satisfaction. In Ontario, a 1995 study found that 89.5 percent of clients surveyed described themselves as either "somewhat" or "very" positive about the mediation process, following their experience of mandatory court-connected mediation, with fully 95 percent stating that they would use mediation again in the event of a conflict. Notably, these high figures include clients whose cases did not settle at mediation. Ongoing evaluation of the Saskatchewan Queen's Bench Mediation Program indicates widespread acceptance, among lawyers and both institutional and individual litigants, of early mediation as an appropriate response to conflict.[4]

- Civil mediation programs have demonstrated significant savings of cost and time to individual litigants. A 2001 evaluation of the Ontario program found that 80 percent of lawyers estimated major cost savings to their clients as a result of mediation.[5] Cost savings for the system presumably flow from earlier case disposition.

- Where the option of mediation has been introduced into proceedings before administrative tribunals—such as the Canadian Human Rights Tribunal, the Canadian Human Rights Commission, the Ontario Human Rights Commission, the Ontario Residential Tenancies Tribunal, the Public Service Staff Relations Board, and the Canadian Immigration and Refugee Board—reactions and results have been mixed. This may reflect the unresolved relationship between the public mandate of these agencies and the private settlements reached in mediation.[6] Nonetheless, program development and evaluation are continuing in these and other administrative agencies, indicating that mediation continues to be regarded as an appropriate dispute resolution mechanism for some cases in such settings.[7]

- Community mediation programs often collect feedback from client users. The biggest problem confronting community mediation services has been lack of case referrals, but not the enthusiasm of those who have chosen to use their services.[8] Moreover, community mediation programs have clear potential for the development of strong communities in which levels of conflict are reduced and peace and order are widely promoted.[9]

- Early restorative justice projects in Aboriginal communities were welcomed by many, though not all, members of these communities and in some cases have produced very significant results (see, for example, the earlier discussion of CHCH). Even those who raise the dangers of restorative justice processes do not reject their use; instead, they press for more information to be provided to potentially vulnerable participants, a strong emphasis on the dynamics of family violence, and the development of broader antiviolence initiatives.[10]

- Restorative justice processes in non-Aboriginal communities have recorded high rates of participant satisfaction.[11] A 1995 evaluation of four Canadian victim–offender programs—the Ottawa–Carleton Dispute Resolution Centre, Mediation Services Winnipeg, Victim–Offender Reconciliation Langley, B.C. (part of the Fraser Region Community Justice Initiatives), and the Youth

---

Evaluation of the Collaborative Justice Project (CJP)

"A preliminary review of the post-program interviews, with both victims and offenders, indicated that CJP participants, for the most part, are very happy with the Collaborative Justice Project. The majority of participants interviewed expressed satisfaction and concluded the interviews with the endorsement that this program should be continued. Participants praised the CJP staff for making this program possible, and being committed to providing ongoing support in a compassionate, understanding and non-judgmental manner. In general, participants expressed positive thoughts on meeting the other party, specifically the victims being able to address the offenders, and obtain answers for their questions. Furthermore, victims also voiced satisfaction about being involved in the overall justice process. Finally, participants appreciated the sense of closure that the program allowed them."

From the Collaborative Justice project website:
<http://www.ccjc.ca/news/march2002.cfm>.

Advocacy and Mediation Services Program in Calgary—found consistently high rates of satisfaction among users. Parties who used mediation were significantly more satisfied with their experience of the criminal justice system than those who did not use mediation (78 percent compared with 48 percent, among victims; 74 percent compared with 53 percent, among offenders).[12] Similar results were reported in the RCMP's 1999 evaluation of its Community Justice Forums initiative (used for minor crimes, such as theft, assault, drug use and possession, and directed mainly at youth offenders). That internal evaluation reported that 96 percent of participants in these forums found the process to be "very" or "quite" fair; 89 percent of victims rated the agreement or outcome as "very" or "quite" fair, compared with 77 percent of offenders. Another restorative justice project, the Ottawa Collaborative Justice Project, is currently being evaluated by the Corrections Research and Development Division of the Department of the Solicitor General.

- Restorative justice processes consistently report high rates of agreement. The 1995 study reported that agreements were reached in 92 percent of cases surveyed across the four sites.[13] Greater concern arises in relation to compliance, which may reflect the low level of resources currently available for monitoring and follow-up. However, note that the RCMP's Community Justice Forums initiative reports compliance at 85 percent.[14]

- Community interest in participatory justice has increased markedly over the past few years. Academic institutions have also supported a number of centres of excellence across Canada which conduct research and support program development. These include:

  - *Conflict Resolution Network Canada*—This broad-based conflict resolution organization develops, promotes, and extends the use of conflict resolution and restorative justice processes, such as negotiation, mediation, consensus-building and peacemaking circles.

- *Native Counselling Services of Alberta*—This non-profit organization employs approximately 150 full-time staff throughout Alberta. A board of directors, which is made up of Métis and Non-Status and Status Indians, governs the organization. The mission of the organization is to contribute to the holistic development and wellness of the Aboriginal individual, family and community. By respecting differences, it promotes the fair and equitable treatment of Aboriginal people. In addition, by developing and maintaining strong partnerships and honouring those relationships, the agency is committed to evolving proactively with the changing environment.

- *Regroupement des organismes de justice alternative du Québec* (ROJAQ)—This provincial non-profit organization promotes the development of alternative justice organizations in Quebec. ROJAQ also promotes community participation in the administration of youth justice; it supports training and exchanges of services between alternative justice organizations in Quebec; and it supports the development of youth justice community intervention programs.

- *Conflict Resolution Co-op of Prince Edward Island*—This cooperative promotes using and accepting non-violent approaches to conflict. It also fosters, develops, and communicates information on conflict resolution processes for individuals, families, organizations and communities and provides opportunities for education, skills development and understanding conflict issues.

- *Peacemakers Trust*—This Canadian charitable organization is dedicated to research and education on conflict resolution and peace-building.

- *YouCAN!* (Youth Canada Association)—This national non-profit charitable organization is dedicated to empowering youth and building a culture of peace among youth today. The organization helps young people develop the skills needed to build peace, resolve conflicts, and participate actively in youth issues.

- *The Centre for Restorative Justice, Simon Fraser University*—In partnership with individuals, the community, justice agencies and the university, the Centre exists to support and promote the principles and practices of restorative justice. The Centre provides education, innovative program models, training, evaluation and research through a resource centre and meeting place that facilitates outreach, promotion, dialogue and advocacy.

- *The Restorative Justice Diploma Program, Queens Theological Program, Queens University*—The Restorative Justice Diploma program is a theologically grounded exploration of the vision of, the reshaping of relationships through, and the action of restorative justice. A three-week intensive study program combined with a 200-hour supervised field placement, this program can also form a concentration for graduate level studies.

- *The Church Council on Justice and Corrections*— This national coalition of faith-based individuals and churches acts as a shining light for a more humane way of doing criminal justice. The Council has been working toward a restorative model of justice for over 25 years.

These programs and many more throughout Canada constitute the backbone of participatory justice. Further initiatives to strengthen our commitment to participatory justice must build on the support and expansion of the current experience developed through the existing programs.

7.2   A PROACTIVE GOVERNMENT ROLE

Despite the demonstrated benefits that flow to citizens and communities from participatory initiatives, these programs often remain secondary, marginalized, or alternatives to the dominant justice model. The network of participatory justice programs that now stretches across Canada relies heavily on the enthusiasm and commitment of local volunteers and year-to-year project funding. Even court-based programming is often sustained on a pilot basis, while efforts are made to secure its continuity.[15] Relying wholly or primarily on community initiative and public demand might not move participatory initiatives into the mainstream of conflict resolution processes. Because the status quo lies elsewhere—in the traditional criminal justice and civil litigation systems—a more intentional government strategy may be needed to achieve significant change in our habitual response to conflict and conflict resolution.

Public education about alternatives to conventional dispute resolution processes continues to be vital. The best efforts of a network of largely autonomous community projects cannot effect the type of change in public knowledge and disputing habits that is necessary to move participatory processes into the mainstream of Canadian life. The continued expansion and strengthening of participatory processes in both community and court settings requires instead that government play a part in the growth of stable, credible and successful programs that manage and resolve conflict consensually and through dialogue.

There are good reasons for looking to government to play a stronger role in sustaining existing programs and developing new initiatives. Those who work in community-based programs currently spend a large percentage of their time and energy seeking and then maintaining funding. Funding is piecemeal, from many different sources, and is frequently related to short-term projects. St. Stephen's Community House Conflict Resolution Services in Toronto, one of the oldest community mediation programs in Canada, is a typical case. St. Stephen's is currently funded by the Toronto municipal government, the Ontario Ministry of Citizenship and Culture, Ontario Ministry of the Attorney General, Heritage Canada, and the federal Department of Citizenship and Immigration. In addition, community mediation services are sometimes able to obtain funding from the National Crime Prevention Strategy, the Department of Justice Canada and the Solicitor General of Canada, and provincial victims' services departments. This patchwork of funding sources means that community programs face constant uncertainty and must continually search out new sources of potential funding. This often requires the organization to adjust its goals and service provision to meet the needs of the funding provider.[16]

"Having small grants from many sources means having to please many masters, each with different reporting demands ... [M]aking different reports to many funding agencies can be time consuming and resource demanding. Compare this to other projects funded by a single government department or a central agency ... with one report to make and usually a consistent contact person who understands the program and may even advocate for it."

G. Husk, "Making Community Mediation Work," in J. Macfarlane (ed.),
Rethinking Disputes: The Mediation Alternative
(Toronto: Emond Montgomery, 1997) 281 at 290.

Some programs have found that referral links to traditional justice agencies are critical to establishing their credibility within the community, at least at an early stage in their development, as well as in maintaining an adequate case-referral base.[17] Partnerships between participatory processes and local agencies, such as a police department or a small claims court, are presently negotiated on an individual basis and often rely on a particular police officer or small claims court judge to encourage participatory dispute resolution. Such arrangements sometimes require years of careful nurturing. A clearer and stronger government commitment to participatory processes would render these negotiations more straightforward and certain.

Finally, it must not be forgotten that there are real concerns, described earlier in this report, that allowing dispute resolution programming to operate completely autonomously, without government oversight might mean that some programs become tyrannical, intolerant or careless of the needs of marginalized individuals. The absence of external scrutiny and accountability might permit the development of closed systems in which those aggrieved with their experience in a restorative or consensus-based justice program would have nowhere to complain except to the program itself.

> The Australian National Alternative Dispute Resolution Advisory Council concluded that while the climate of reform suggested that government regulation should be seen as a principle of "last resort," and there was little evidence of public dissatisfaction with alternative dispute resolution (ADR) services, nonetheless "there is a strong public interest in promoting ADR, and a purely free market approach would be unlikely to manage the risks associated with ADR or to enhance community confidence in ADR."
>
> D. Syme, "Challenges for Mediation Practice in Australia: Standards for ADR: The Balancing Act," National Alternative Dispute Resolution Advisory Council (Australia), commenting on the proposed Standards for ADR, online: <www.http://www.nadrac.gov.au/www/disputeresolution>.

7.3 STRIKING A BALANCE: AUTONOMY, OVERSIGHT AND SUPPORT

If some type of government role is essential to ensure that participatory processes retain their vibrancy, impact and influence, just what should that oversight look like? The challenge of finding an appropriate structure raises questions of control and autonomy familiar to community activists and policymakers alike. The community justice movement—as well as some of the programs and leaders that have emerged from that tradition—has often regarded the involvement of government in community justice initiatives as detrimental and counterproductive. It is sometimes contended that giving government a role in the development of these programs will lead to a dependence on government-driven structures and resources that will ultimately undermine the ability of communities to make good decisions for themselves and their members. But without some role for government in legitimating and promoting participatory processes, these initiatives may simply cease to grow and flourish. The answer seems to lie in the creation of a partnership between state and communities that would combine the vitality and local knowledge of community-based initiatives with the accountability and resources offered by government.

The concerns of those who fear that government involvement would defeat the objectives of participatory processes must be addressed in any proposed regulatory framework. As well, the interests of government must be met in developing a regulatory approach that satisfies the contemporary context. In the discussion of how to strike this delicate balance, the following guiding concerns provide a useful benchmark.

1. How can government support participatory initiatives in a way that recognizes and celebrates the diversity of the field?

2. How can government support participatory initiatives in a way that protects the public interest in fair, non-coercive dispute resolution processes?

3. How can government support participatory initiatives in a way that values local knowledge and respects communities?

4. How can government support the outcomes of participatory processes, while monitoring their fairness and integrity?[18]

7.4   ROLES FOR GOVERNMENT IN THE PROVISION OF PARTICIPATORY JUSTICE

Governments may choose from a variety of possible roles to support the development and enhancement of innovative conflict resolution processes. Government may cast itself in the role of regulator or of coordinator. Regulation envisages a more proactive role for government in standard-setting and oversight, while coordination limits the role of government to facilitating the organization of programs for accountability and to supporting them with expert advice (for example, training or assistance with program design) and funding. Governments can also support participatory justice in their role as participants in conflicts and in their role as providers of conflict resolution services. Government litigators can advance the development of participatory justice by choosing participatory processes to resolve their disputes. Finally, governments can promote participatory processes through information to citizens. These roles are not mutually exclusive.

Each of these possible strategies for the greater involvement of government in participatory initiatives will be considered in turn, drawing on current experience and models operating elsewhere.

7.4.1   Government as provider

Governments provide participatory justice processes in various ways. They currently offer mediation and conciliation services in various departments and through the justice system. For example, the Federal Mediation and Conciliation Service (FMCS) is responsible for providing dispute resolution and dispute prevention assistance to trade unions and employers under the jurisdiction of the *Canada Labour Code*. FMCS, which is part of Human Resources and Development Canada, offers a number of services to assist employers and unions in resolving industrial relations disputes and in improving labour-management relations. These services include conciliation, mediation, preventive mediation and grievance mediation.

Recently, the Canadian Human Rights Commission also decided to put a stronger emphasis on using mediation techniques to resolve human rights complaints. The mediation provides a non-adversarial context in which parties can address their needs and interests and find a solution. Mediation is now offered at every stage of the complaint process. In addition, several federal government departments have taken advantage of a Dispute Resolution Fund to develop mediation programs. These are some examples.

- The Early File Review Project—Officials at Human Resources Development Canada took on a 2,000-case Canada Pension Plan disability case backlog, identified 900 cases for review, and settled 202 cases.

- Canadian Environmental Assessment Agency—The Dispute Resolution Fund provided support for implementation of the Canadian Environmental Assessment Agency's (CEAA) dispute resolution strategy, including creation of a dispute resolution specialist position, building capacity for and acceptance of dispute resolution processes within CEAA; and for a pilot project that will use dispute resolution in the environmental assessment process.

- Citizenship and Immigration Canada—A new initiative was developed to design and develop dispute resolution models and processes for use throughout Citizenship and Immigration Canada. This initiative occurred concurrently with the implementation of the *Immigration and Refugee Protection Act.*

Governments must continue to offer mediation services to their citizens. As governments develop new programs where disputes between citizens or between citizens and government are likely to occur, they should create participatory processes along the lines defined in Chapter 6. Ideally, these mediation services should not be late developments or add-ons to the existing dispute resolution mechanism, but constitute an integral part of the approach to conflict resolution proposed by governments.

In addition, governments can encourage the development of participatory justice by actively developing a culture of participatory justice within their organization. For example, the Correctional Service of Canada (CSC) has attempted to take a leadership role in using the principles of restorative justice to help resolve conflicts within prisons. CSC has advanced restorative justice and dispute resolution approaches to address various types of conflict including those that involve staff and inmates. Access to trained resource people is made possible through the use of peer mediation, shared mediators from other government departments and professional facilitators. In addition, facilitated processes are being used to resolve some policy issues and in departmental decision-making.

A culture of participatory justice cannot develop in isolation from the dominant culture of an institution. To be able to resolve disputes with citizens in a non-adversarial way, civil servants must have experienced it within their work environment. It is therefore recommended that governments continue to actively provide participatory processes to resolve conflicts within their institution, in their disputes with citizens and when they provide conflict resolution services, such as in the court system or in administrative tribunals.

7.4.2 Government as coordinator and promoter

To date, government efforts to coordinate the development and delivery of alternatives to adjudicative justice have been limited to establishing offices to coordinate intra-governmental activities. For example, both Ontario and British Columbia now have a dispute resolution office, in each case located within the provincial ministry of the attorney general. These units offer training to government employees; promote the design of internal dispute resolution processes using interest-based approaches and consensus-building; and provide recommendations for mediators and interveners in specific disputes. In Quebec, ROJAQ exists to coordinate and promote the actives of those engaged in participatory justice processes.

The federal Department of Justice has also established the Dispute Resolution Services (DRS), which promotes and coordinates dispute resolution initiatives within federal government departments and sometimes facilitates discussion between departments and interest groups (for example, Justice and the plaintiff groups in the residential schools lawsuits; and fishers, resource managers and the Department of Fisheries and Oceans).

These dedicated government offices are important signals that government regards the development of policy in the area of dispute resolution to be a priority. However, none of these offices currently has a mandate to coordinate existing programs outside government (either court-connected or community-based) or to comprehensively promote participatory dispute resolution to the public.

In the United States, most participatory justice models are regulated by an office within the judicial branch of government. However, some state offices coordinate and support community-based resolution programs. For example, Nebraska's Office of Dispute Resolution (ODR) oversees the development of all dispute resolution programs (both court-based and community-based) and has developed a public-community partnership that allows ODR to work collaboratively with Nebraska's community mediation centres. This partnership operates across six regions served by community mediation centres but is adapted to the needs of each. The partnership enables shared decision-making, programming, training and fund-raising. The result has been a growing caseload at community mediation centres and the establishment of program policies and procedures for dispute resolution services provided by community groups. ODR also provides oversight of program quality through a Policy Manual and Training Institute Standards and Guidelines. Each centre submits quarterly reports, which ODR uses for a state-wide quarterly report of all system activity.

The Florida Dispute Resolution Center was established in 1986 as the first state-wide centre for education, training and research in alternative dispute resolution (ADR). Today the Center coordinates court-connected mediation programs in the Florida Supreme Court, certifies mediators and mediation training programs, provides introductory mediation training to volunteer mediators working in county court mediation programs, and provides technical assistance to state courts developing new program alternatives to conventional adjudication. The Center, which operates as a joint court-university initiative, also administers and coordinates the Supreme Court Committee on ADR Policy, which advises the state on matters of ADR policy.

For further information see the website:
<www.flcourts.org/osca/divisions/adr>.

However they are organized, each of these agencies includes programs of public education, which strongly promote alternatives to traditional dispute processing. Public education on the issue of participatory justice processes is key.

It is recommended that governments assume a greater coordinator and promoter role in participatory justice and undertake the following:

- Coordinating sources of public funding.

- Actively promoting participatory processes through public education and accessible training.

- Providing specialized training for interveners and program staff.

- Facilitating networking and information exchanges among various programs.

- Sponsoring research and evaluation.

7.4.3   Government as regulator

The most delicate role that governments can assume is to assume a regulatory function in the context of participatory justice. In the traditional role of regulator, governments become gatekeepers for the development and maintenance of programs, linking their contributions to program resources to oversight and monitoring. The role of regulator opens up two separate but related tasks for governments: developing new programs and processes, and overseeing and monitoring initiatives.

Program development—The most direct approach to program development is for government to adopt a strategy that requires participation in particular programs, which are themselves closely regulated by procedural rules and requirements. Some examples of this approach include mandatory mediation schemes that have developed in provincial jurisdictions;[19] mandatory case management that has been established by procedural rules of court in a number of provinces; and participation in mediation as a prerequisite for family legal aid.[20] In New Zealand, family group conferences are mandatory for all cases involving young offenders, with the exception of murder and manslaughter offences.

Several jurisdictions have developed mandatory mediation schemes. As discussed earlier under the requirement of voluntariness, this strategy is only appropriate for certain types of programs for given periods of time. Any mandatory requirement should operate alongside extensive public and lawyer education programs, to reduce the gap between conventional expectations and the experience of participatory justice. The strategy should be to persuade, not to punish, in response to non-compliance.

A slightly less directive approach is to make it mandatory to offer participatory processes. An example of this approach in the context of court-connected mediation can be seen in the rules of procedure applied in Minnesota,[21] where counsels are required to meet to decide which dispute resolution approach, including mediation, will be most suitable for the progress of the case.

Another alternative is the new restorative justice initiative in Nova Scotia where justice officers must consider the potential for referral to an alternative-measures process at four stages: pre-charge, charge, pre-sentence and post-sentence,[22] and police officers are required to complete a "restorative justice checklist" for all cases involving minor offences.[23] While the "participation rate" (the number of cases diverted in restorative justice processes) will still depend on the willingness of justice officers to consider this alternative, there is now strong government and institutional (through a new restorative justice community agency) support for at least an initial appraisal to be made of the appropriateness of a restorative justice strategy in each case.

The least interventionist approach to program development is for government to offer a range of support and incentives both to communities wishing to develop participatory projects and to individuals wishing to access these programs. Examples of support and incentives to communities and projects could include the following:

- Easily accessible grant programs;

- Provision of local training (and trainers);

- Assistance with design advice for new or expanding programming; and

- Access to networking and dialogue.

Encouragement for members of the public to at least consider consensus-seeking approaches may operate even more informally. For example, many family mediation projects operating in the courts offer mediation on a voluntary basis, but in practice many family court judges in those courts will ask parties if they have considered mediation, and if they have not, will ask them to do so.

Additional structural incentives for individuals to use participatory processes should include:

- Accessible public information and education.

- The availability of professional advice outlining the various alternatives for dispute resolution in any particular dispute and locality and the ramifications of each.

- Access to legal counsel and other advocates. It is essential that those who choose to use these processes should have the same access to legal counsel and other forms of advocacy support as those who choose to remain in the traditional adjudicative system. For example, present legal aid rules do not always compensate counsel for participating in circles or appearing before community justice panels.

Oversight and monitoring—The oversight function of government as regulator can also take many different forms. Traditionally, government oversight of professional services has taken the form of accreditation and qualification restrictions placed on service providers, albeit often devolved through self-regulation. Self-regulation depends on a bargain between the service providers and the government, in which the former are granted autonomy and privileges (through accreditation) to offer their services, while in return the state receives a guarantee that services will be provided with competence and integrity. Each party to the mutual promise or agreement may hold the other to account: the state, by demanding that service professionals develop credible internal procedures to respond to public criticism (at the risk of losing their independence from government oversight); and the profession, by reminding government that it possesses the greater wisdom and experience in ensuring its services are delivered effectively.[24]

Assuming that some type of regulatory or oversight framework is necessary to strengthen and build existing programs, self-regulation offers participatory initiatives the greatest degree of autonomy from government. There is some logic, perhaps, to adopting the same regulatory model for dispute resolution programs operating outside the conventional justice model as that applied to professionals operating within the traditional adjudicative model.[25]

However, there are a number of difficulties with adopting self-regulation in participatory justice services. The most common criticism of self-regulation is that it cannot ensure that the public interest is placed before the private aspirations of the members of the group. Participatory processes have developed significantly from community projects and community empowerment. In a participatory model, the needs of the community (or individual disputants) are in many respects the same as those of the process facilitators: good outcomes that enable a reduction of the costs of conflict, closure, and perhaps even forgiveness and peace. To place the regulation of such a practice in the hands of a professional body would in many ways show a misunderstanding of the work that is being done in victim–offender programs, in community mediation services, and even in some court-connected programs.

Characteristic of all self-regulation schemes is that the body given statutory responsibility to regulate must assume and exercise very wide powers over those whom it regulates. The nature of participatory justice practice, as it is presently developing through

> "Without some minimal standard of training, we risk causing harm to communities, instead of restoring harmony through joint problem-solving in a caring, respectful environment. We also risk losing credibility for this relatively recent restorative approach itself."
>
> "A Report on the Evaluation of RCMP Restorative Justice Initiative: Community Justice Forums as Seen by Participants," online: <www.rcmp-learning.org/restjust/docs/ccap0004.htm>

court and community groups, is that there is so much variegated and decentralized growth—perhaps localized in successful and highly credible court programs or voluntary services—that it is hard to imagine a single regulatory body. The debate over qualifications and standards in the conflict resolution field has a long history and remains unresolved in Canada where there is a patchwork of private qualifications offered commercially, but no provincial or national accreditation. Because of this history of the qualifications debate, this chapter will not consider the role of government in accreditation, although it recognizes that accreditation constitutes a possible regulatory strategy that government could choose to adopt.

A far more appropriate approach is to consider state–community partnerships providing oversight of local programs. In this framework, oversight could take the form of broad threshold standards, leaving the projects themselves to determine their specific operating practices, according to local conditions. These could be as diversified and need-specific as possible, as long as threshold standards of good practice can be maintained.

An example of a recent government–community collaboration occurred in British Columbia, where a group of practitioners and academics developed a model of self-regulation for restorative justice practitioners. The purpose of the document is to articulate what guides their work, practice and commitment to restorative justice. The *British Columbia Charter* is meant to be a "living, breathing document—a continuous work in progress." It was developed following discussions with "various practitioners in the field of restorative justice in the Province of British Columbia and beyond."

Government can gain from the experience of established programs by encouraging the development of flexible standards. These standards should cover areas such as:

- Process intake and screening practices (for example, taking special care when reviewing cases in which there appears to be the possibility of fear or intimidation or where one or more parties has expressed this concern);

- Conduct of the process itself (whether mediation, panels, circles or other processes), to ensure clarity regarding rules on confidentiality and participation, as well as any limits on possible outcomes;

- Procedures for enforcing compliance with outcomes; and

- Any stipulations regarding the qualifications (and any potential disqualifications) of those conducting the process (whether as mediators, facilitators or Keepers of the Circle).

This report contains a number of possible models for such standards, including the articulation of the values, principles and objectives of participatory processes; and the 12 guiding principles for program design elaborated earlier. These models reflect the

---

British Columbia Charter for Practitioners of Restorative Justice

"The purpose of this document is to articulate that which guides us in our work, practice, and commitment to restorative justice. The following is a Charter for Practitioners of Restorative Justice that is a living, breathing document—a continuous work in progress. This draft is based on the discussions and contributions of various practitioners in the field of restorative justice in the Province of British Columbia and beyond. We wish to recognize the many tributary streams that fed our dialogues and honour all who have taught us. We respectfully acknowledge that restorative practices strive to embody values and principles that are akin to and informed by holistic peace and justice making processes in many First Nations communities. We gathered as a group with history and experience, not to attempt to set the standard for the field, but to carefully consider the ethics surrounding our personal practice."

Available at Simon Fraser University's Centre for Restorative Justice website: <http://www.sfu.ca/cfrj/current.html#resources>.

---

present state of knowledge and experience in the field and provide a starting point for the collaborative development of generic, as well as project-specific, standards in partnerships between government and service providers.

A regulatory strategy based on collaboratively developed standards would enable government to have some knowledge and oversight of participatory initiatives, work cooperatively with program providers to maintain high standards, and encourage good practice. This approach may require establishing a government agency that would have responsibility for facilitating the development and review of program standards. Programs themselves could then be charged with self-evaluation and regular reporting, perhaps with periodic external evaluations. Alternatively, the standards could be used simply as an internal evaluation measure for the programs and users themselves. Individual programs should be encouraged to provide a means for concerns and complaints to be brought forward that can be addressed in program evaluation. Carriage of unresolved complaints could be a further function for a government agency; concerns and issues that surface consistently should drive future research and evaluation projects sponsored by government. The DVD produced by the National Film Board that accompanies this report provides an example of a self-evaluation exercise by mediators that could be used.

The regulatory model proposed is, therefore, one of persuasion by modelling, praise and encouragement of good practices, rather than rule-making and sanctions.[26] This shifts responsibility to the programs themselves to apply standards in a contextually responsive manner, recognizing the unique services they provide. This approach not only recognizes the expertise of existing participatory processes and the importance of local knowledge, but also may be more efficacious.[27] It is more important that authentic monitoring take place with the full cooperation of the programs themselves than that evaluation occur mechanically to satisfy a set of external rules.

This approach to standard-setting would be in the spirit of collaboration, flexibility and responsiveness to diversity, but would nonetheless allow governments to take leadership in monitoring and disseminating good practices.

7.5   A PARTNERSHIP BETWEEN GOVERNMENT AND COMMUNITIES

The roles set out above require that there be a partnership between government and participatory processes. This partnership strategy enables government to have oversight of dispute resolution programs, but in cooperation with service providers—courts, and community agencies. A co-regulatory partnership should also involve public interest groups by including representatives of the consumers of dispute resolution services, advocates' groups and others who play a role outside court or community programs.[28]

In practice, co-regulation can operate across a continuum of interventions by government. This would mean a proactive government role in the building of participatory initiatives within communities and courts, consisting of both the regulation and the coordination of services.

The final component of this proposed new strategy is the intentional creation of a relationship between government and those communities that both deliver and access alternative processes. There are already within the field many excellent examples of partnering arrangements that have evolved naturally from local circumstances. For example, the John Howard Society of Manitoba has taken the initiative in developing Victim–Offender Mediation programs in some communities, and these programs have gradually become institutionalized in the local courts. Further examples can be seen in community mediation programs that have developed referral links with local police departments, courts and schools.

In the context of participatory processes, the components of a government-community partnerships might look like this:

- Government would explicitly endorse the development of initiatives that offer choices to disputants other than those of traditional adjudication, in both civil and criminal matters.

- Government would address the current piecemeal resourcing of such initiatives by coordinating funding and investing in core activities.

- Communities would take primary responsibility for management, program design and delivery.

- Government and communities would collaboratively develop standards for program design and delivery, for example, along the suggested model of the 12 guiding principles for the design of participatory processes.

- Government and communities would collaboratively develop evaluation and monitoring mechanisms for programs, along the model outlined in Chapter 6.

- While government would expect to receive assurances that core principles were being adhered to (for example, the principle of voluntariness), programs would be afforded considerable flexibility in adapting evaluation to local needs and conditions.[29]

---

1   Currently regulated under the *Queen's Bench Act*, S.S. 1998, c. Q-1.01; originally introduced in the *Queen's Bench Act*, 1994.

2   Currently regulated under O. Reg. 194/90, Ontario Rules of Civil Procedure, Rule 24.1.

3   Currently regulated under BC Reg 127/98, Notice to Mediate Regulation, authority for which is contained in the *Insurance (Motor Vehicle) Act*, R.S.B.C. 1996, c. 231. No evaluation data are currently available, although a study is in progress.

4   J. Macfarlane, *Building on "What Works": An Evaluation of the Saskatchewan Queen's Bench Mediation Program* (Regina: Saskatchewan Justice, 2003).

5   R. Hann, C. Barr and Associates, *Evaluation of the Ontario Mandatory Mediation Program: Final Report-The First 23 Months* (Toronto: Ontario Queen's Printer, 2001) at 55–58.

6   Critics argue that ADR methods "amount to a private justice system that does not always protect the public's interest in procedural fairness or disclosure of how disputes were resolved." See T.A. Kochan, B.A. Lautsch and C. Bendersky, "Massachusetts Commission Against Discrimination Alternative Dispute Resolution Program Evaluation" (2000) 5 *Harvard Negotiation Law Review* 233.

7   See, for example, the following evaluation reports: L.H. Macleod and Associates, *Assessing Efficiency, Effectiveness and Quality: An Evaluation of the ADR Program of the Immigration Appeal Division of the Immigration and Refugee Board* (Ottawa: Immigration and Refugee Board, 2002); J. Macfarlane and E. Zweibel, *Systemic Change and Private Closure in Human Rights Mediation: An Evaluation of the Mediation Program at the Canadian Human Rights Tribunal* (2001); and J. Macfarlane, J. Manwaring and E. Zweibel, *Negotiating Solutions to Workplace Conflicts: An Evaluation of the Public Service Staff Relations Board Grievance Mediation Pilot* (Ottawa: Public Service Staff Relations Board, 2001).

8   See G. Husk, "Making Community Mediation Work" in J. Macfarlane, ed., *Rethinking Disputes: The Mediation Alternative* (Toronto: Emond Montgomery, 1997) at 287.

9   A report for the government of Scotland on three community mediation programs concluded that "[C]ommunity mediation could be developed as an important component of a comprehensive strategy to promote civility and social integration, to reduce conflict, to deal with some offences which arise in the course of neighbourhood disputes, and to prevent the escalation of disputes at an early stage." R.E. Mackay and A.J. Brown, *Community Mediation In Scotland: A Study Of Implementation* (Dundee, Scotland: University of Dundee, Department of Social Work, 1998).

10 W. Stewart, A. Huntley and F. Blaney, *The Implications of Restorative Justice for Aboriginal Women and Children Survivors of Violence: A Comparative Overview of Five Communities in British Columbia* (Ottawa: Law Commission of Canada, July 2001) at 41-43.

11 For a state of the art review of empirical studies on restorative justice and mediation, see M. Umbreit, R.B. Coates and B. Voss, *Restorative Justice Dialogue: Annotated Bibliography Of Empirical Studies On Mediation, Conferencing And Circles*, (St. Paul: Center For Restorative Justice Peacemaking, School of Social Work, University of Minnesota, 2003).

12 M.S. Umbreit, Mediation of Criminal Conflict: *An Assessment of Programs in Four Canadian Provinces* (St. Paul: Center for Restorative Justice and Mediation, School of Social Work, University of Minnesota, 1995) at xi.

13 Umbreit, *ibid.*

14 Royal Canadian Mounted Police, *A Report on the Evaluation of RCMP Restorative Justice Initiative: Community Justice Forums as Seen by Participants*, online: <http://www.rcmp-learning.org/restjust/docs/ccap0004.htm> (date accessed: 17 September 2003).

15 For example, the Hamilton Unified Family Court operated a "pilot" mediation program for eight years before it became a permanent feature of the courthouse, despite a very favourable evaluation; see D. Ellis, *Evaluation of the Hamilton Family Court Pilot Mediation Project* (Hamilton: Ellis and Associates, 1994). In Ontario, a debate over the development of a permanent Rule of Civil Procedure for court-connected mediation was conducted in the Civil Rules Committee for two years before the introduction of Rule 24.1 (O. Reg. 194/90).

16 Personal communication with Peter Bruer, Director, St. Stephen's Community House Conflict Resolution Services, 8 January 2003.

17 J. Benoit, J. Kopachevsky, S. Macdonald and G. MacDonald, *Evaluating the Effects and Methods of Mediation: A Summary Report* (Halifax: Institute of Public Affairs, Dalhousie University, 1986).

18 Substantially adapted from Evaluation, Audit and Review Group, *Regulatory Reform Through Regulatory Impact Analysis: The Canadian Experience* (Ottawa: Treasury Board, 2002).

19 Saskatchewan: *Queen's Bench Act*, S.S. 1998, c. Q-1.01; Ontario: O. Reg. 194/90, Ontario Rules of Civil Procedure, Rule 24.1.

20 This has been the policy at the legal aid offices of London and Windsor.

21 Rule 114, Minnesota General Rules of Practice. And see the evaluation of that rule in B. McAdoo, The Impact of Rule 114 on *Civil Litigation Practice in Minnesota* (Minneapolis: Minnesota Supreme Court, Office of Continuing Education, 1997).

22 D. Clairmont, "Restorative Justice in Nova Scotia" (2000) 1:1 *Isuma: Canadian Journal of Policy Research* 145.

23 A. Thomson, *Formal Restorative Justice in Nova Scotia: A Pre-implementation Overview* (prepared for delivery at the Annual Conference of the Atlantic Association of Sociologists and Anthropologists, Fredericton, October 1999).

24 See, generally, the discussion by C. Schneider, "A Commentary on the Activity of Writing Codes of Ethics" (1985) 8 *Mediation Quarterly* at 83.

25 For example, the Law Society of Upper Canada is regulated under the *Law Society Act*, R.S.O. 1990, and this statute empowers the benchers elected by the Society's members to govern the profession "in the public interest." *Law Society Act*, R.S.O. 1990, c. L-8, s. 10.

[26] J. Braithwaite, "Restorative Justice: Assessing Optimistic and Pessimistic Accounts" (1999) 25 *Crime and Justice* 1 at 9-11; and see, generally, Ayres, *supra* note 27.

[27] For a discussion of a persuasion strategy in nursing home regulation compared with a traditional rule-based regulatory regime, see J. Braithwaite and T. Makkai, "Trust and Compliance" (1994) 4 *Policing and Society* 1. For a wider exposition of these ideas in relation to regulatory policy, see J. Braithwaite, "The New Regulatory State and the Transformation of Criminology" (2000) 40:2 *British Journal of Criminology* 222.

[28] For a detailed discussion of tripartism, its rationales and implications for regulatory policy, see Ayres, *supra* note 27 at chapter 3.

[29] Another possible model here is the existing funding agreement between Indian and Northern Affairs Canada and Aboriginal communities, which defines minimal accountability standards for a five-year block grant but allows Aboriginal communities "to redesign programs to meet specific community needs, subject to maintaining minimum delivery standards." Indian and Northern Affairs Canada, Funding Agreements, online: <http://www.ainc-inac.gc.ca/ps/ov/agre_e.html> (date accessed: 17 September 2003).

Part IV — Recommendations: Toward a Culture of Participatory Justice

Chapter 8   Recommendations

This Report sets out a number of recommendations for the continued development and improvement of participatory justice processes in Canada. The objective is to work toward achieving a culture of participatory justice within our society. Chapter 8 summarizes the recommendations under three headings: Developing Fair Participatory Processes (8.1), A Proactive role for governments (8.2) and Strengthening a Participatory Culture (8.3).

8.1   DEVELOPING FAIR PARTICIPATORY PROCESSES

The Commission believes that participatory processes are a positive development for our justice system. They represent a way of engaging Canadians in the resolution of their conflicts and offer many benefits. After study and consultation, we believe that they ought to be encouraged in all sectors provided that there are appropriate safeguards and awareness of the potential abuses that could occur.

The Law Commission of Canada considers that:

1.   Participatory initiatives, community or court-based, operating in criminal and non-criminal settings, offer many benefits for both individuals and their communities. These benefits include the peaceful de-escalation and resolution of conflicts; the development of long-term strategies to deal with community problems; a response to the needs of victims; the reform of individual offenders; the restoration of business and personal relationships; and strong procedural satisfaction for participants.

2.　Participatory processes are appropriate for all types of conflict—monetary, biparty or multiparty, about private concerns or public policy, involving harms defined as criminal or civil.

Special care and attention is needed when applying participatory processes to disputes in which one or more parties express fear or intimidation; when communities are at risk of making decisions resting on systemic bias and intolerances; or where there is a risk of process abuse.

Even in these cases, however, a participatory approach may be appropriate, given careful safeguards, authentic voluntariness on the part of participants, special training of mediators or facilitators and consideration of the potential for publishing outcomes.

3.　Participatory processes as alternatives to adversarial justice have potential value for all types of Canadian communities, urban and rural, Aboriginal and non-Aboriginal.

Participatory processes have flourished in communities with a strong collective spirit, especially Aboriginal communities with a history of conflict resolution through dialogue. The successful use of processes that build consensus is also possible in diverse communities that have sufficient motivation and commitment to seek peaceful long-term solutions to shared problems. This includes metropolitan communities and other communities that have shared needs.

4.　It is appropriate for all levels of government and community agencies to consider developing new programs and enhancing those that already exist.

Different circumstances—including the severity of the behaviour, the impact it has had, how broadly the impact has been experienced, and the cultural context of the parties and the behaviour—may require different intake processes, dialogue procedures and degrees of formalized outcomes. Sponsoring organizations are thus encouraged to develop conflict resolution services that encompass a range of dispute types and processes.

The Law Commission of Canada recommends that:

5. Programs offering participatory justice processes, in the context of both criminal and non-criminal disputes, reflect the following guiding principles:

i. Early intervention

Early intervention aims at providing assistance when a problem first arises. Examples of early intervention are pre-charging restorative justice processes, or school-based programs that aim to inculcate good conflict resolution skills and practices among schoolchildren, or assistance for landlords and tenants to seek early mediation when a problem first arises and their relationship begins to deteriorate.

Nevertheless interventions that occur post-adjudication (for example, victim–offender meetings) should continue to be encouraged as important contributions to the objectives of participatory processes.

ii. Accessibility

Processes should be easily accessible, user-friendly and not overly bureaucratic. This includes giving consideration to location (a place that is considered unthreatening and welcoming to potential users) and ensuring that all potential users are guaranteed anonymous or confidential access to information about the service.

iii. Voluntariness

Genuine voluntariness in entering dispute resolution processes must include full information about this process and about alternatives and all the assistance necessary for an informed choice. The participatory model assumes that individual parties are the best judge of whether a consensual approach is suitable for the resolution of their conflict, whether this lies in the criminal or the non-criminal domain.

Currently, there exist many disincentives to the use of participatory processes. Cost recovery mechanisms do not always provide sufficient recognition of the uncertainty of participating in a mediation. More must be done to reflect on the invisible obstacles both in the criminal and non-criminal systems that prevent parties from choosing participatory processes. More must be also done to create incentives for adopting participatory processes. Certainly leadership must be exercised to support the development and use of participatory processes. There may be times when a compulsory program may be needed. It is the view of the Commission that such mandatory programs are to be reserved for non-criminal conflicts, for a time-limited period, alongside accessible training and information opportunities for participants and with the possibility of refusal for reasons of fear of intimidation or coercion.

iv. Careful preparation

Intake processes should build in adequate time for preparation of the parties to the dispute and for the possibility of discerning fear and a history of violence.

v. Opportunities for face-to-face dialogue

Face-to-face dialogue should be offered as one of a range of strategies that parties may use to resolve conflicts. Under circumstances in which face-to-face dialogue is inappropriate or is rejected by one or more of the parties, there must be sufficient flexibility to enable a dialogue to take place—through shuttle diplomacy, conference call or video-conferencing—if the parties believe this to be constructive.

vi. Advocacy and support

Participatory processes should welcome friends, family and supporters (whether or not they are legal representatives), who may serve an important function offering emotional and intellectual support to participants. It is important that participatory processes remain within the ultimate control of the disputants and that this clarification be made to disputants and their representatives.

vii. Confidentiality

The assurance of confidentiality usually provided for processes working toward agreed outcomes is critical to their efficacy. However, there are many cases when the outcome of the process ought to be made public.

The issue of confidentiality must be discussed. It may be helpful to include discussing and signing a written statement at the beginning of a participatory process, explaining the importance of treating disclosures as confidential among participants.

In addition, it is important that the legal profession and tribunals recognize the importance of confidentiality in these processes. Courts should continue to demonstrate respect for the confidentiality of such processes and resist pressure to reopen agreements other than in exceptional circumstances.

In addition, emphasis should be placed on the need to ensure that the private discussions that take place within these processes do not spread throughout the wider community, introducing embarrassment and possibly mistrust into the process and undermining the continuation of such processes.

viii. Fairness

The principles of participatory processes require that the parties themselves ultimately make the decisions regarding what they can accept as "fair." However, this does not remove the need to monitor both the genuine voluntariness of a decision to accept a particular outcome and the quality of the outcomes of participatory processes. Where there are standards, they ought to be discussed with the parties. Monitoring may be facilitated by some (limited, anonymous) publication of outcomes in cases. Dissemination of outcomes should be a matter for negotiation between the parties. As noted above, there are instances in which the public interest requires that outcomes should be made public in some form.

ix. Relevant and realistic outcomes

Agreements reached in participatory processes must reflect the available resources of the communities or be within the means of the individual disputants. Compliance and durability are important indicators of both the efficacy and the credibility of participatory processes. Where possible, compliance and durability should be monitored.

x. Efficiency

Programs should ensure that participants clearly understand what is expected of them in advance and that meeting time is used effectively.

xi. Systemic impact

Participatory projects have the potential to contribute to the development of capacity within the community to deal with problems collectively and consensually. This capacity-building can be further enhanced by incorporating training for volunteers and others into program design and equipping these individuals with conflict resolution skills that they can use in the future in their workplaces and communities.

xii. Flexibility and responsiveness

Participatory processes should foster a spirit of responsiveness and respect for the unique circumstances of each conflict. The assumption of self-determination that lies at the heart of participatory processes for individuals and communities alike means that affected persons can and must be trusted to make decisions over the design details of their own conflict resolution process—such as who should be present, how long the meeting should last, what will be discussed, and what types of solution or outcomes should be considered.

8.2   A PROACTIVE ROLE FOR GOVERNMENT

The Law Commission believes that although many participatory justice projects do well without governmental aid, the latter is often needed to flourish. The Commission believes that the role of government in this sector is one of careful balancing between supporting community autonomy and providing necessary help and guidance.

The Law Commission of Canada recommends that:

6.   Governments adopt a proactive role to facilitate the development of participatory conflict resolution initiatives.

Governments must continue to demonstrate leadership in developing a culture of participatory justice. Governments can demonstrate such commitment by implementing international agreements that promote the use of participatory processes such as, the *UNCITRAL Model Law on International Commercial Conciliation.*

7.   Governments continue to actively provide participatory processes to resolve conflicts within their institutions, in their disputes with citizens and when they provide conflict resolution services, such as in the court system or in administrative tribunals.

Governments must support participatory initiatives in a way that recognizes and celebrates the diversity of the field and values local knowledge while protecting the public interest in fair, non-coercive dispute resolution processes. The Law Commission proposes an oversight approach to regulation, using partnerships with existing centres of research. Regulation as oversight should take the form of broad threshold standards, leaving the projects themselves to determine their specific operating practices, according to local conditions.

8.   Governments develop partnerships with existing centres of research in participatory justice and local communities that have an interest in participatory justice to stimulate the sharing of information and best practices and to educate the public on initiatives of participatory justice.

There is a range of actors and institutions currently promoting the development of participatory justice practices. Various governments have also expressed a desire to implement innovative methods of conflict resolution. A number of centres of research focus on promoting participatory justice. In addition, the private and the voluntary sectors also use and develop programs of participatory justice. There is a need for coordination to facilitate the exchange of information between these agencies and to encourage the development of best practices. Governments can accomplish this by:

- Establishing a network that connects existing research centres, centres of excellence, community groups and government departments engaged in participatory justice; and

- Providing funding to centres of research in participatory justice;

- Hosting conferences and workshops on participatory justice to bring together academics and practitioners working in criminal and non-criminal forms of participatory justice, to exchange information, research and best practices.

The coordinating function for governments should also involve informing the public about participatory justice and giving support in the form of advice (for example, training or assistance with program design) and funding. Governments can accomplish this by :

- Educating the public about participatory justice processes;

- Training community members and conflict resolution professionals in consensus-building processes and techniques;

- Providing opportunities for the media to better understand participatory justice processes;

- Assisting programs with evaluation and monitoring;

- Identifying and sponsoring ongoing research on program development, delivery and impact.

9.   Governments encourage centres of research and excellence to work in partnership with communities to develop best practices in participatory justice, including evaluation frameworks.

Governance of participatory justice ought to support communities, whose programming needs should be determined in light of local conditions and challenges. To encourage the development of best practices, governments should work with centres of research and excellence to undertake the following:

•   The development of evaluation criteria and processes that reflect the values and principles of participatory processes that could help maintain the quality of the programs;

•   The development of strategies to ensure that programs function adequately and with transparency and integrity.

10.   As governments develop new social or economic programs, they seek to incorporate participatory justice processes in them to resolve disputes between citizens or between governments and citizens, with the appropriate safeguards noted above.

8.3   STRENGTHENING A PARTICIPATORY CULTURE

The wholehearted acceptance and use of participatory processes will take time. A proactive government role is an important step and sends an important message. In addition, further steps can be taken by many other actors in the justice system and in civil society to promote the use of participatory justice. They include minimizing the existing disincentives to the use of participatory processes as well as promoting its use. The list below is by no mean exhaustive. It is provided as indicative of the type of initiatives that should be undertaken by different actors within the justice system.

The Law Commission of Canada recommends that:

11.   The Legal Aid Plans should review their tariffs to include compensation for counsel preparation for, and participation in, participatory processes (such as mediation, circles, group conferences) at the same rate as conventional litigation or trial work.

12. The Canadian Institute for the Administration of Justice and the National Justice Institute should continue to create opportunities for judges to attend training in alternative conflict resolution processes and to develop appropriate skills in this area as well as to ensure that such training is available to all new judges.

13. Provincial law societies continue to ensure that the continuing education programs provide training for lawyers in participatory justice and should encourage all their members to undertake such training. Being able to advise clients on the suitability of selecting a participatory process, preparing clients for such a process, and representing them in such a process should be considered essential professional skills.

14. Provincial law societies review their codes of professional conduct to ensure that the role of the lawyer as an advocate in restorative or consensus-based justice processes is adequately anticipated. They should ensure that lawyers are charged with a duty to discuss alternatives to adversarial justice with their clients; that lawyers are alert to the vulnerability of some clients in such processes and take steps accordingly; and that counsel understands the basis of effective participation in such processes, including the duty to respect confidentiality.

15. Canadian colleges and universities, in particular law schools, continue to increase and encourage the teaching of participatory processes to law students.

16. Businesses and voluntary organizations consider reviewing their policies to ensure that employees' participation in participatory processes is considered in the same light as court attendance.

17. Businesses and voluntary organizations continue to develop participatory justice projects to resolve conflicts within their organizations.

Conclusion

The capacity of citizens to participate meaningfully in the democratic process poses challenges for the design of public institutions. Increasingly, Canadians are disengaging from these institutions, and in the process, becoming more sceptical about the government's capacity to respond to legitimate expectations. The Law Commission of Canada believes that the growth of participatory justice models is consistent with citizen-centred models of governance.

Participatory justice processes allow citizens to be part of decision-making that affects their lives. In this sense, they contribute to a healthy democracy. This report was designed to contribute to the development of participatory justice culture rooted in democratic principles. The report first reviews the context in which restorative justice and consensus-based justice projects developed, and describes the principles that support their on-going work. It identifies the special challenges that face participatory justice processes. It also aims at supporting a culture of participatory justice, where different actors, governmental and others, have a role to play. Finally, it serves as a basis for further dialogue and reflection on the way in which we resolve our conflicts and strengthen our social relationships.

Over the past three years, the Commission has consulted with Canadians about the provision of meaningful methods of conflict resolution. The Commission's consultations revealed that Canadians want choices for resolving their conflicts. In addition, many Canadians want to actively participate in the conflict resolution process. They view this as an aspect of citizenship and of their ability to regulate their own lives. Participatory justice processes respond to this need.

Participatory justice processes are not a panacea. They will not solve all the ills that affect our society. As is the case for any human conduct, there will be mistakes. In particular, the participation of weaker parties, financially, emotionally or intellectually to participatory processes requires special attention. There are concerns that participatory processes may serve to reinforce existing vulnerabilities. This is the challenge of processes operating in an unequal society. Participatory justice processes impose a special responsibility to mediators and facilitators to respond to power imbalance, just as judges should. But it is the essence of participatory justice processes that the responsibility to addressing inequality be shared among the participants. All actors in participatory justice processes must respond to the challenge of conflict resolution processes that embody our democratic values of justice and equality.

The challenge for governments is finding a way to support participatory justice processes without limiting their innovative potential. As discussed in this report, there are some tensions in this role for governments. On the one hand, there are pressures to create coherence and uniformity to prevent risks of malfunctioning of participatory processes. On the other hand, there is an even better case to be made for preserving the creative and innovative power of many participatory processes. We would not want to lose the ability to continue to respond creatively to the new problems that will confront our society. As citizens, it is incumbent upon us to recognize the delicate role that governments must play in the development and support of participatory processes. The solution to better conflict resolution will not come from governments but from the respectful and honourable participation of citizens in the resolution of their conflicts, through the many processes described in this Report.

In its consultation and research on this issue, and in this report, the Commission has attempted to strike a balance and respond to challenges similar to the ones facing governments. In a way, it wanted to lead by example. Therefore, this report does not propose a single orthodoxy to participatory justice. It presents and respects the different perspectives and fears toward participatory processes, supports and celebrates the committed work of many volunteers in participatory justice, and aims to create an occasion for self-reflection, dialogue and action.

It is in that context that we have partnered with the National Film Board for the production of the DVD, *Community Mediation: Two Real-Life Experiences* Experiences that forms part of this Report. This cinematographic work presents one of the many projects that exist in Canada. It is designed to stimulate reflection for mediators and participants alike. We hope that it will be a tool to strengthen our culture of participatory justice.

Bibliography

Contents

1. **Discussion Papers and Reports Published by the Law Commission of Canada**

Law Commission of Canada, *Communities and the Challenge of Conflict: Perspectives on Restorative Justice* (video). Available in French: *Le défi des conflits pour les collectivités: Points de vues sur la justice réparatrice.* Available in hard copy from the Law Commission of Canada.

Law Commission of Canada, *From Restorative Justice to Transformative Justice* (Ottawa: Law Commission of Canada, July 1999). Available in French: *De la justice réparatrice à la justice transformatrice.* Available in hard copy from the Law Commission of Canada and online: <http://www.lcc.gc.ca>.

Law Commission of Canada, *Restoring Dignity: Responding to Institutional Child Abuse in Canadian Institutions,* (Ottawa: Law Commission of Canada, March 2000). Available in French: *La dignité retrouvée : La réparation des sévices infligés aux enfants dans les établissements canadiens.* Available in hard copy from the Law Commission of Canada and online: <http://www.lcc.gc.ca>.

Law Commission of Canada, *What is a Crime? Challenges and Alternatives,* (Ottawa: Law Commission of Canada, 2003). Available in French: *Qu'est-ce qu'un crime? Des défis et des choix.* Available in hard copy from the Law Commission of Canada and online: <http://www.lcc.gc.ca>.

2. **Background Research Papers Prepared for the Law Commission of Canada**

Alter, S., *Apologizing for Serious Wrongdoing: Social, Psychological and Legal Considerations* (Ottawa: Law Commission of Canada, May 1999). Available in French: *La présentation d'excuses relatives à une faute grave: considérations sociales, psychologiques et juridiques.* Available in hard copy from the Law Commission of Canada and online: <http://www.lcc.gc.ca>.

Cooley, D., *Restorative Justice in Canada: Lessons Learned* by (Ottawa: Law Commission of Canada, 2002). Available in hard copy from the Law Commission of Canada and online: <http://www.lcc.gc.ca>.

Evans, H. and Advokaat, E., *The Language of Community in Canada Social Relationships: Communities Paper* (Ottawa: Law Commission of Canada, July 2001). Available in French: *Le langage de la collectivité au Canada.* Available in hard copy from the Law Commission of Canada.

Ferguson, G., *Community Participation in Criminal Jury Trials and Restorative Justice Programs* (Ottawa: Law Commission of Canada, 2001). Available in hard copy from the Law Commission of Canada.

Llewellyn, J.J. and Howse, R., *Restorative Justice: A Conceptual Framework* by (Ottawa: Law Commission of Canada, 1999). Available in French: *La justice réparatrice: Cadre de réflexion.* Available in hard copy from the Law Commission of Canada and online: <http://www.lcc.gc.ca>.

Poirier, D. and Poirier, N., *Why Is It So Difficult to Combat Elder Abuse and, in Particular, Financial Exploitation of the Elderly?* (Ottawa: Law Commission of Canada, July 1999). Available in French: *Pourquoi est-il si difficile de lutter contre la violence envers les aînés et en particulier contre l'exploitation économique dont ils sont victimes?* Available in hard copy from the Law Commission of Canada and online: <http://www.lcc.gc.ca>.

Ryan, J. and Calliou, B., *Aboriginal Restorative Justice Alternatives: Two Case Studies* (Ottawa: Law Commission of Canada, 2002) [unpublished research report archived at the Law Commission of Canada].

Schulte-Tenckhoff, I., *The Concept of Community in the Social Sciences and Its Juridical Relevance* (Ottawa: Law Commission of Canada, September 2001). Available in French: *Le concept de communauté dans les sciences sociales et sa pertinence juridique.* Available in hard copy from the Law Commission of Canada.

Stewart, W., Huntley, A. and Blaney, F., *The Implications of Restorative Justice for Aboriginal Women and Children Survivors of Violence: A Comparative Overview of Five Communities in British Columbia* (Ottawa: Law Commission of Canada, July 2001). Available in French: *Les conséquences de la justice réparatrice pour les femmes et les enfants autochtones qui ont survécu à des actes de violence: un aperçu comparatif de cinq collectivités de Colombie-Britannique.* Available in hard copy from the Law Commission of Canada and online: <http://www.lcc.gc.ca>.

Wellman, B., *The Persistence and Transformation of Community: From Neighborhood Groups to Social Networks* (Ottawa: Law Commission of Canada, 2001) [unpublished research report archived at the Law Commission of Canada].

3. Reports

Aboriginal Peoples Collection of Canada, *The Four Circles of Hollow Water* (Ottawa: Public Works and Government Services Canada, 1997).

Alberta Task Force on the Criminal Justice System and Its Impact on the Indian and Métis People of Alberta, *Justice On Trial: The Report of the Task Force on the Criminal Justice System and Its Impact on the Indian and Métis People of Alberta* (Edmonton: Government of Alberta, 1990).

Benoit, J., Kopachevsky, J., Macdonald, S. and MacDonald, G., *Evaluating the Effects and Methods of Mediation: A Summary Report* (Halifax: Institute of Public Affairs, Dalhousie University, 1986).

Bonta, J., Wallace-Capretta, S. and Rooney, J. *Restorative Justice: An Evaluation of the Restorative Resolutions Project* (Ottawa: Solicitor General of Canada, 1998).

British Home Secretary, *Restorative Justice: The Government's Strategy* (London: Office of the Home Secretary, 2003).

Canada, Royal Commission on Aboriginal Peoples, *Bridging the Cultural Divide: A Report on Aboriginal People and Criminal Justice in Canada* (Ottawa: Supply and Services Canada, 1996).

Canadian Sentencing Commission, *Sentencing Reform—A Canadian Approach: Report of the Canadian Sentencing Commission* (Ottawa: Canadian Sentencing Commission, 1987).

Canadian Welfare Council, *Indians and the Law: A Survey Prepared for the Hon. A. Laing* (Ottawa: Canadian Welfare Council, August 1967).

Collaborative Justice Project, *Final Report on the Collaborative Justice Project for Fiscal Year 1999/2000* (Ottawa: Collaborative Justice Project, 2001). Available online: <http://www.ccjc.ca>.

Douglas, K. and Goetz, D., "Bill C-7: The Youth Criminal Justice Act" Legislative Summary 356E, (Ottawa: Library of Parliament, Legislative Research Division, 2000).

Ellis, D., *Evaluation of the Hamilton Family Court Pilot Mediation Project* (Hamilton: Ellis and Associates, 1994).

Evaluation, Audit and Review Group, *Regulatory Reform Through Regulatory Impact Analysis: The Canadian Experience* (Ottawa: Treasury Board, 2002).

Goundry, S., *Restorative Justice and Criminal Justice Reform in B.C.: Identifying Some Preliminary Questions and Issues* (Victoria: B.C. Association of Specialized Victim Assistance & Counselling Programs, 1997).

Gustafson, D. and Bergin, S., *Promising Models in Restorative Justice: A Report for the Ministry of the Attorney-General of British Columbia* (Victoria: Ministry of the Attorney-General, 1998).

Hann, R., Barr, C. and Associates, *Evaluation of the Ontario Mandatory Mediation Program: Final Report—The First 23 Months* (Toronto: Ontario Queen's Printer, 2001).

Indian Justice Review Committee (Canada), *Report of the Saskatchewan Indian Justice Review Committee* (Regina: The Committee, 1992).

Lajeunesse, T., *Evaluation of Community Holistic Circle Healing: Hollow Water First Nation. Volume 1: Final Report* (Ottawa: Solicitor General of Canada, 1996).

LaPrairie, C., *Defining the Objectives and Roles of Saskatchewan Justice in Aboriginal and Restorative Justice* (Ottawa: Ministry of the Solicitor General, 1996).

LaPrairie, C., *Examining Aboriginal Corrections in Canada* (Ottawa: Ministry of the Solicitor General, 1996).

Latimer, J., Dowden, C. and Muise, D., *The Effectiveness of Restorative Justice Practices: A Meta-analysis* (Ottawa: Department of Justice, 2001).

Macfarlane, J. and Zweibel, E., *Systemic Change and Private Closure in Human Rights Mediation: An Evaluation of the Mediation Program at the Canadian Human Rights Tribunal* (Ottawa: Canadian Human Rights Tribunal, 2001).

Macfarlane, J., *Building on "What Works": An Evaluation of the Saskatchewan Queen's Bench Mediation Program* (Regina: Saskatchewan Justice, 2003).

Macfarlane, J., *Court-based Mediation in Civil Cases: An Evaluation of the Toronto General Division ADR Centre* (Toronto: Ontario Ministry of the Attorney General, 1995).

Macfarlane, J., Manwaring, J. and E. Zweibel, *Negotiating Solutions to Workplace Conflicts: An Evaluation of the Public Service Staff Relations Board Grievance Mediation Pilot* (Ottawa: Public Service Staff Relations Board, 2001).

Macleod, L.H. and Associates, *Assessing Efficiency, Effectiveness and Quality: An Evaluation of the ADR Program of the Immigration Appeal Division of the Immigration and Refugee Board* (Ottawa: Immigration and Refugee Board, 2002).

Manitoba, *Report of the Aboriginal Justice Inquiry of Manitoba, Volume 1: The Justice System and Aboriginal People* (Winnipeg: Queen's Printer, 1991).

Marshall, T.F., *Restorative Justice: An Overview* (London: Home Office, 1998).

Ministry of the Attorney-General, *A Restorative Justice Framework* (Victoria: Ministry of the Attorney-General, 1999).

New Zealand Ministry of Justice, *Restorative Justice: A Discussion Paper* (Wellington: Ministry of Justice, 1995).

Office of Juvenile Justice and Delinquency Prevention and the Balanced and Restorative Justice Project, *Engaging the Community in Restorative Justice* (Minneapolis: U.S. Department of Justice, 1998).

Ontario Civil Justice Review, *Civil Justice Review: Supplemental and Final Report* (Toronto: Ministry of the Attorney General, 1996).

Rockhill, N., *Building the Caseload: Report from the Conflict Resolution Service* (Toronto: Fund for Dispute Resolution, 1993).

Royal Canadian Mounted Police, *A Report on the Evaluation of RCMP Restorative Justice Initiative: Community Justice Forums as Seen by Participants.* Available online: <http://www.rcmp-learning.org/restjust/docs/ccap0004.htm> (date accessed: 17 September 2003).

Solicitor General of Canada and the Aboriginal Healing Foundation, *Mapping the Healing Journey: The Final Report of a First Nation Research Project on Healing in Canadian Aboriginal Communities* (Ottawa: Solicitor General of Canada, 2002).

Transition House Association of Nova Scotia (THANS). Abused Women in Family Mediation: A Nova Scotia Snapshot. A Report Prepared by the Transition House Association of Nova Scotia (Halifax: THANS, 2000).

4.   Books and Chapters

Abel, R., *The Politics of Informal Justice: The American Experience* (New York: Academic Press, 1982).

Achilles, M. and Zehr, H., "Restorative Justice for Crime Victims: The Promise and the Challenge" in G. Bazemore and M. Schiff, eds., *Restorative Community Justice: Repairing Harm and Transforming Communities* (Cincinnati: Anderson Publishing Co., 2001).

Asch, M. ed., *Aboriginal and Treaty Rights in Canada: Essays on Law, Equity and Respect for Difference* (Vancouver: University of British Columbia Press, 1997).

Ayres, I. and Braithwaite, J., *Responsive Regulation: Transcending the Deregulation Debate* (New York: Oxford University Press, 1992).

Backhouse, C., *Colour-Coded: A Legal History of Racism in Canada, 1900-1950* (Toronto: The Osgoode Society and University of Toronto Press, 1999).

Bazemore, G. and Schiff, M., eds., *Restorative Community Justice: Repairing Harm and Restoring Communities* (Cincinnati: Anderson Publishing, 2001).

Bazemore, G., Pranis, K. and Umbreit, M.S., *Balanced and Restorative Justice for Juveniles: A Framework for Juvenile Justice in the 21st Century* (St. Paul: Center for Restorative Justice and Peacemaking, University of Minnesota, 1997).

Bell, D., *Faces at the Bottom of the Well: The Permanence of Racism* (New York: Basic Books, 1993).

Bodine, R.J. and Crawford, D.K., *The Handbook of Conflict Resolution: A Guide to Building Quality Programs in Schools* (San Francisco: Jossey-Bass, 1998).

Bovens, M., *The Quest for Responsibility* (New York: Cambridge University Press, 1998).

Braithwaite, J. and Roche, D. "Responsibility and Restorative Justice" in G. Bazemore and M. Schiff, eds., *Restorative Community Justice: Repairing Harm and Transforming Communities* (Cincinnati: Anderson Publishing Co., 2001).

Braithwaite, J., "Restorative Justice" in M.H. Tonry, ed., *The Handbook of Crime and Punishment* (New York: Oxford University Press, 1998).

Braithwaite, J., *Crime, Shame and Reintegration* (New York: Cambridge University Press, 1989).

Bush, R.A. and Folger, J.P., *The Promise of Mediation: Responding to Conflict Through Empowerment and Recognition* (San Francisco: Jossey-Bass, 1994).

Cayley, D., "Security and Justice for All" in H. Strang and J. Braithwaite, eds., *Restorative Justice and Civil Society* (New York: Cambridge University Press, 2001).

Cayley, D., Expanding Prison, *The Crisis in Crime and Punishment and the Search for Alternatives* (Toronto: Pilgram Press, 1999).

Chornenki, G., "Mediating Commercial Disputes: Exchanging 'Power Over' for 'Power With'" in J. Macfarlane, ed., *Rethinking Disputes: The Mediation Alternative* (Toronto: Emond Montgomery, 1997).

Church, C. and Shouldice, J., *The Evaluation of Conflict Resolution Interventions: Framing the State of Play* (Ulster: International Conflict Research, 2002).

Church, C. and Shouldice, J., *The Evaluation of Conflict Resolution Interventions, Part II: Emerging Practice and Theory* (Ulster: International Conflict Research, 2003).

Clarke, S., Ellen, E. and McCormick, K., *Court-ordered Civil Case Mediation in North Carolina: Court Efficiency and Litigant Satisfaction* (Chapel Hill: Institute of Government, University of North Carolina, 1995).

Cohen, S., *Visions of Social Control* (Cambridge: Polity Press, 1985).

Costantino, C. and Merchant, C., *Designing Conflict Management Systems* (San Francisco: Jossey-Bass, 1996).

Daly, K., "Revisiting the Relationship Between Retributive and Restorative Justice" in H. Strang, and J. Braithwaite, eds., *Restorative Justice: Philosophy to Practice* (Aldershot: Ashgate, 2000).

Derksen, W., *Confronting the Horror: The Aftermath of Violence* (Winnipeg: Amity Publishers, 2002).

Eglash, A., "Beyond Restitution: Creative Restitution" in J. Hudson and B. Galaway, eds., *Restitution in Criminal Justice* (Lexington: Lexington Books, 1975).

Enright, R. and the Human Development Study Group, "The Moral Development of Forgiveness" in W. Kurtines and J. Gewirtz, eds., *Handbook of Moral Behaviour and Development*, (Hillsdale, Erlbaum, 1991).

Galaway, B. and Hudson J., eds., *Criminal Justice, Restitution, and Reconciliation* (Monsey, N.Y.: Criminal Justice Press, 1990).

Ganlin, H., "Mediating Sexual Harassment" in B. Sandler and R. Shoop, eds., *Sexual Harassment on Campus* (Toronto: Simon and Schuster, 1997).

Garland, D., *The Culture of Control: Crime and Social Order in Contemporary Society* (Chicago: University of Chicago Press, 2001).

Hadley, M.L., ed., *The Spiritual Roots of Restorative Justice. SUNY Series in Religious Studies* (Albany: State University of New York Press, 2001).

Hill, The Honourable Justice C., "Expanding Victims' Rights" in A.D. Gold, ed., *Alan D. Gold's Collection of Criminal Law Articles*, online: <http://www.quicklaw.com> (Quicklaw: GOLA [database], 1999).

Hudson, J., Morris, A., Maxwell, G. and Galaway, B., eds., *Family Group Conferences: Perspectives on Policy and Practice* (Australia: Federation Press, 1996).

Husk, G., "Making Community Mediation Work" in J. Macfarlane, ed., *Rethinking Disputes: The Mediation Alternative* (Toronto: Emond Montgomery, 1997).

Kakalik, J., Dunworth, T., Hill, L., McCaffrey, D., Oshiro, M., Pace, N. and Vaiana, M., *Just, Speedy and Inexpensive?* (Arlington: Rand Institute for Civil Justice, 1997).

Karp, D.R. and Walther, L., "Community Reparative Boards in Vermont: Theory and Practice" in G. Bazemore and M. Schiff, eds., *Restorative Community Justice: Repairing Harm and Transforming Communities* (Cincinnati: Anderson Publishing Co., 2001).

Kolb, D.M. and Associates, *When Talk Works: Profiles of Mediators* (San Francisco: Jossey-Bass, 1994).

Kurki, L., "Evaluating Restorative Justice Practices" in A. Von Hirsch, J. Roberts, A. E. Bottoms, K. Roach and M. Schiff, eds., *Restorative Justice and Criminal Justice: Competing or Reconcilable Paradigms* (Oxford: Hart Publishing, 2003).

Lane, P., Bopp, J. and Bopp, M., *The Sacred Tree* (Lethbridge: Four Worlds Development Press, 1986).

LaRocque, E. "Re-examining Culturally Appropriate Models in Criminal Justice Applications" in M. Asch, ed., *Aboriginal and Treaty Rights in Canada: Essays on Law, Equity and Respect for Difference* (Vancouver: University of British Columbia Press, 1997).

Lax, D. and Sebenius J., *The Manager as Negotiator: Bargaining for Competitive Gain* (New York: Free Press, 1986).

Lind, E.A. and Tyler, T., *The Social Psychology of Procedural Justice* (London: Plenum Press, 1992).

Macfarlane, J., ed., *Dispute Resolution: Readings and Case Studies*, 2nd ed. (Toronto: Emond Montgomery, 2003).

Macfarlane, J., ed., *Rethinking Disputes: The Mediation Alternative* (Toronto: Emond Montgomery, 1997).

Marshall, T. and Merry, S., *Crime and Accountability: Victim/Offender Mediation in Practice* (London: Home Office HMSO, 1990).

Maxwell, G.M. and Morris, A., "The New Zealand Model of Family Group Conferences" in C. Alder, and C. Wundersitz, eds., *Family Conferencing and Juvenile Justice: The Way Forward or Misplaced Optimism?* (Canberra: Australian Institute of Criminology, 1994).

Mayer, B., *The Dynamics of Conflict Resolution* (San Francisco: Jossey-Bass, 2000).

McAdoo, B., *The Impact of Rule 114 on Civil Litigation Practice in Minnesota* (Minneapolis: Minnesota Supreme Court Office of Continuing Education, 1997).

McDonald, J. and Moore, D., "Community Conferencing as a Special Case of Conflict Transformation" in H. Strang and J. Braithwaite, eds., *Restorative Justice and Civil Society* (New York: Cambridge University Press, 2001).

McGillis, D., *Community Dispute Resolution Programs and Public Policy* (Washington, DC: National Institute of Justice, 1988).

Merry, S., "Defining 'Success' in the Neighborhood Justice Movement" in R. Tomasic and M. Feeley, eds., *Neighborhood Justice: Assessment of an Emerging Idea* (New York: Longman, 1982).

Morris, A. and Maxwell, G., "Restorative Conferencing" in G. Bazemore and M. Schiff, eds., *Restorative Community Justice: Repairing Harm and Transforming Communities* (Cincinnati: Anderson Publishing Co., 2001).

Osborne, D. and Gaebler, T., *Reinventing Government: How the Entrepreneurial Spirit Is Transforming the Public Sector* (Reading: Addison-Wesley Publishing Company, 1992).

Pargament, K. and Rye, M., "Forgiveness as a Method of Religious Coping" in E. Worthington, ed., *Dimensions of Forgiveness: Psychological Research and Theological Perspectives* (Philadelphia: Templeton Foundation Press, 1998).

Pargament, K., *The Psychology of Religion and Coping: Theory, Research, Practice* (New York: Guilford Publications, 1997).

Peachey, D., "The Kitchener Experiment" in M. Wright and B. Galaway, eds., *Mediation and Criminal Justice* (Newbury Park, CA: Sage, 1989).

Pearce, B. and Littlejohn, S., *Moral Conflict: When Social Worlds Collide* (Newbury Park, CA: Sage, 1997).

Pepinsky, H. and Quinney, R., eds., *Criminology as Peacemaking* (Bloomington: Indiana University Press, 1991).

Pepinsky, H., "Peacemaking in Criminology and Criminal Justice" in H. Pepinsky and R. Quinney, eds., *Criminology as Peacemaking* (Bloomington: Indiana University Press, 1991).

Picard, C.A., *Mediating Interpersonal and Small Group Conflict* (Ottawa: The Golden Dog Press, 1998).

Postman, N., *Amusing Ourselves to Death: Public Discourse in the Age of Show Business* (New York: Viking, 1985).

Pranis, K., "Restorative Justice, Social Justice and the Empowerment of Marginalized Communities" in G. Bazemore and M. Schiff, eds., *Restorative Community Justice: Repairing Harm and Transforming Communities* (Cincinnati: Anderson Publishing Co., 2001).

Quinney, R., "The Way of Peace: On Crime, Suffering and Service" in H. Pepinsky and R. Quinney, eds., *Criminology as Peacemaking* (Bloomington: Indiana University Press, 1991).

Retzinger, S. and Scheff, T., "Strategy for Community Conferences: Emotions and Social Bonds" in B. Galaway and J. Hudson, eds., *Restorative Justice: International Perspectives* (New York: Criminal Justice Press, 1996).

Roach, K., *Due Process and Victims' Rights: The New Law and Politics of Criminal Justice* (Toronto: University of Toronto Press, 1999).

Ross, R., *Returning to the Teachings* (Toronto: Penguin, 1996).

Ruth, M., *Stories of Negotiated Justice* (Toronto: Canadian Scholar's Press Inc., 2000).

Shearing, C., "Transforming Security: A South African Experience" in H. Strang and J. Braithwaite, eds., *Restorative Justice and Civil Society* (New York: Cambridge University Press, 2001).

Silbey, S. and Ewick, P., *The Common Place of the Law: Stories from Everyday Life* (Chicago: University of Chicago Press, 1998).

Strang, H., "The Crime Victim Movement" in H. Strang and J. Braithwaite, eds., *Restorative Justice and Civil Society* (New York: Cambridge University Press, 2001).

Stuart, B., "Sentencing Circles: Making Real Differences" in J. Macfarlane, ed., *Rethinking Disputes: The Mediation Alternative* (Toronto: Emond Montgomery, 1997).

Tesler, P., *Collaborative Law: Achieving Effective Resolution in Divorce Without Litigation* (Chicago: American Bar Association Family Law Section, 2001).

Thibaut, J. and Walker, L., *Procedural Justice: A Psychological Analysis* (New York: Erlbaum, 1975).

Tonry, M., ed., *The Handbook of Crime and Punishment* (New York: Oxford University Press, 1998).

Tyler T. and Lind E.A., "A Relational Model of Authority in Groups" in M. Zanna, ed., *Advances in Experimental Social Psychology*, vol. 25 (New York: Academic Press 1992).

Umbreit, M.S., *Victim Meets Offender: The Impact of Restorative Justice and Mediation* (Monsey, NY: Criminal Justice Press, 1994).

Ury, W., Brett, J. and Goldberg, S., *Getting Disputes Resolved* (Boston: Program on Negotiation, Harvard University, 1993).

Van Ness, D. and Strong, H., *Restoring Justice* (Cincinnati: Anderson Publishing, 1997).

Von Hirsch, A., *Doing Justice: The Choice of Punishments: Report of The Committee for the Study of Incarceration* (New York: Hill and Wang, 1976).

Von Hirsch, A., "Penal Theories" in M. Tonry, ed., *The Handbook of Crime and Punishment* (New York: Oxford University Press, 1998).

Von Hirsh, A., *Past or Future Crimes: Deservedness and Dangerousness in the Sentencing of Criminals* (New Brunswick, NJ: Rutgers University Press, 1985).

Von Hirsch, A., Roberts, J.V., Bottoms, A., Roach, K. and Chiff, M., eds., *Restorative Justice and Criminal Justice: Competing or Reconcilable Paradigms* (Oxford: Hart Publishing, 2003).

Wachtel, T. and Gold, P., "Restorative Justice in Everyday Life" in H. Strang and J. Braithwaite, eds., *Restorative Justice and Civil Society* (New York: Cambridge University Press, 2001).

Waters, W., *Mediation in the Campus Community* (San Francisco: Jossey-Bass, 2000).

Wikstrom, P., "Communities and Crime" in M. Tonry, ed., *The Handbook of Crime and Punishment* (Oxford University Press, 1998).

Zehr, H., *Changing Lenses: A New Focus for Crime and Justice* (Waterloo: Harold Press, 1990).

Zweibel, E., "Hybrid Processes: Using Evaluation to Build Consensus" in J. Macfarlane, ed., *Dispute Resolution: Readings and Case Studies*, 2nd ed. (Toronto: Emond Montgomery, 2003).

5.   Journals and Articles

Abel, R., "Contested Communities" (1995) 22:1 *Journal of Law and Society* 113.

Albert, R. and Howard, D., "Informal Dispute Resolution Through Mediation" (1985) 10 *Mediation Quarterly* 99.

Alfini, J., "Trashing, Bashing and Hashing It Out: Is This the End of 'Good Mediation'?" (1991) 19 *Florida State University Law Review* 47.

Archibald, B., *A Comprehensive Canadian Approach to Restorative Justice: The Prospects for Structuring Fair Alternative Measures in Response to Crime* (prepared for delivery at the 1998 Conference on Making Criminal Law Clear and Just, Queen's University, Kingston, Ontario, November 1998).

Ashworth, A., "Victim Impact Statements and Sentencing" [1993] *Criminal Law Review* 498.

Aubert, V., "Competition and Dissensus: Two Types of Conflict and Conflict Resolution" (1963) 7 *Journal of Conflict Resolution* 26.

Bailey, M., "Unpacking the 'Rational Alternative': A Critical Review of Family Mediation Movement Claims" (1989) 8 *Canadian Journal of Family Law* 61.

Bargen, C., *Safe Schools: Strategies for a Changing Culture* (prepared for delivery at the 6th International Conference on Restorative Justice, Simon Fraser University, Vancouver, B.C., June 2003).

Bendersky, C., "Culture: The Missing Link in Systems Design" (1998) 14:4 *Negotiation Journal* 307.

Berzins, L., *"Restorative" Justice on the Eve of a New Century: The need for Social Context and a New Imagination* (prepared for delivery at the Dawn or Dusk in Sentencing Conference, Canadian Institute for the Administration of Justice, Montreal, 25 April 1997).

Blagg, H., "A Just Measure of Shame? Aboriginal Youth and Conferencing in Australia" (1997) 37:4 *British Journal of Criminology* 481.

Bluehouse, P. and Zion, J. W., "Hozhooji Naat'aanii: The Navajo Justice and Harmony Ceremony" (1993) 10:4 *Mediation Quarterly* 327.

Braid, K., "Arbitrate or Litigate: A Canadian Corporate Perspective" (1991) 17 *Canada–US Law Journal* 465.

Braithwaite, J., "Conferencing and Plurality: Reply to Blagg" (1997) 37:4 *British Journal of Criminology* 502.

Braithwaite, J., "Restorative Justice: Assessing Optimistic and Pessimistic Accounts" (1999) 25 *Crime and Justice* 1.

Braithwaite, J., "The New Regulatory State and the Transformation of Criminology" (2000) 40:2 *British Journal of Criminology* 222.

Braithwaite, J. and Makkai, T., "Trust and Compliance" (1994) 4 *Policing and Society* 1.

Brazil, W., "Hosting Settlement Conferences: Effectiveness in the Judicial Role" (1987) 3 *Ohio State Journal on Dispute Resolution* 1.

Bryan, P., "Killing Us Softly: Divorce Mediation and the Politics of Power" (1992) 40 *Buffalo Law Review* 441.

Bush, R.A., "Defining Quality in Dispute Resolution: Taxonomies and Anti-taxonomies of Quality Arguments" (1989) 66 *University of Denver Law Review* 381.

Christie, N., "Conflicts as Property" (1977) 17:1 *British Journal of Criminology* 1.

Clairmont, D., *Penetrating the Walls: Implementing a System-Wide Restorative Justice Approach in the Criminal Justice System* (prepared for delivery at the 6th International Conference on Restorative Justice, Simon Fraser University, Vancouver, B.C., June 2003).

Clairmont, D., "Restorative Justice in Nova Scotia" 2000 1:1 *Isuma: Canadian Journal of Policy Research* 145.

Conbere, J.P., "Theory Building for Conflict Management System Design" (2001) 19:2 *Conflict Resolution Quarterly* 215.

Cormier, R.B., "Restorative Justice: Directions and Principles—Developments in Canada" (prepared for delivery at the Technical Assistance Workshop of the Programme Network of Institutes, 11th Session of the Commission on Crime Prevention and Criminal Justice, Vienna, April 2002).

Costantino, C., "Using Interest-based Techniques to Design Conflict Management Systems" (1996) 12 *Negotiation Journal* 207.

Daly, K., *Restorative Justice and Punishment: The Views of Young People* (prepared for delivery at the American Society of Criminology Annual General Meeting, Toronto, November 1999).

Daly, K., "Restorative Justice in Diverse and Unequal Societies" (1999) 17:1 *Law in Context* 113.

Daly, K. *Restorative Justice: The Real Story* (prepared for delivery at the Scottish Criminology Conference, Edinburgh, September 2000).

Davis, G., "The Theft of Conciliation" (1985) 32 *Probation Journal* 7.

Delgado, R., "Conflict as Pathology: An Essay for Trina Grillo" (1997) 81 *Minnesota Law Review* 1391.

Delgado, R., Dunn, C., Brown, P., Lee, H. and Hubbert, D., "Fairness and Formality: Minimizing the Risk of Prejudice in Alternative Dispute Resolution" (1985) 6 *Wisconsin Law Review* 1359.

Dhami, M. and Joy, P., *Challenges to Establishing Community-based Restorative Justice Programs: The Victoria Experience* (prepared for delivery at the 6th International Conference on Restorative Justice, Simon Fraser University, Vancouver, B.C., June 2003).

Druckman, D., Broome, B. and Korper, S., "Value Differences and Conflict Resolution" (1988) 32 *Journal of Conflict Resolution* 489.

Edwards, A. and Haslett, J., *Domestic Violence and Restorative Justice: Advancing the Dialogue* (prepared for delivery at the 6th International Conference on Restorative Justice, Simon Fraser University, Vancouver, B.C., June 2003).

Eisenberg, H.B., "Combating Elder Abuse Through the Legal Process" (1991) 3:1 *Journal of Elder Abuse and Neglect* 65.

Fisher, C., "Towards a Sub-culture of Urbanism" (1975) 80 *American Journal of Sociology* 1319.

Fogarassy, T., "An Administrative Law Critique of the British Columbia Mediation and Arbitration Board of the *Petroleum and Natural Gas Act*" (1992) 5 *Canadian Journal of Administrative Law and Practice* 245.

Galanter, M. and Cahill, M., "Most Cases Settle" (1993–94) 46 *Stanford Law Review* 1339.

Galligan, P., *The Intersection and Confluence of the Existing System of Litigation and Alternative Dispute Resolution* (prepared for delivery at the Justice to Order meeting of the Canadian Institute for the Administration of Justice, Saskatoon, October 1998).

Gilson, R.J. and Mnookin, R.H., "Disputing Through Agents: Cooperation and Conflict Between Lawyers in Litigation" (1994) 94:2 *Columbia Law Review* 509.

Gordon, M.L., "'What Me, Biased?' Women and Gender Bias in Family Law" (2001) 19:1 *Family Law Quarterly* 53.

Green, R., "Aboriginal Community Sentencing: Within and Without the Circle" (1997) 25 *Manitoba Law Journal* 77.

Griffiths, C.T., "The Victims of Crime and Restorative Justice: The Canadian Experience" (1999) 6:4 *International Review of Victimology* 279.

Grillo, T., "The Mediation Alternative: Process Dangers for Women" (1991) 100:6 *Yale Law Journal* 1545.

Ireland, P., "Reflection on a Rampage through the Barriers of Shame: Law, Community and the New Conservatism" (1995) 22:2 *Journal of Law and Society* 189.

Jackson, M., "In Search of the Pathways to Justice: Alternative Dispute Resolution in Aboriginal Communities" (1992) 26:1 *University of British Columbia Law Review* 147.

Jackson, M., "Locking Up Natives in Canada" (1988-89) 23:1 *University of British Columbia Law Review* 216.

Kobly, P., "Rape Shield Legislation: Relevance, Preference and Judicial Discretion" (1992) 30 *Alberta Law Review* 988.

Kochan, T.A., Lautsch, B.A. and Bendersky, C., "Massachusetts Commission Against Discrimination Alternative Dispute Resolution Program Evaluation" (2000) 5 *Harvard Negotiation Law Review* 233.

Kruk, E., "Power Imbalance and Spouse Abuse in Divorce Disputes: Deconstructing Mediation Practice via the 'Simulated Client' Technique" (1998) 12:1 *International Journal of Law, Policy and Family* 1.

Kurki, L., "Restorative and Community Justice in the United States" (2000) 27 *Crime and Justice* 235.

Lacey, N. and Zedner, L., "Discourses of Community in Criminal Justice" (1995) 22:3 *Journal of Law and Society* 301.

Lande, J., "Failing Faith in Litigation? A Survey of Business Lawyers and Executives' Opinions" (1998) 3 *Harvard Negotiation Law Review* 1.

Lande, J., "Getting the Faith: Why Business Lawyers and Executives Believe in Mediation" (2000) 5 *Harvard Negotiation Law Review* 137.

Lande, J., "How Will Lawyering and Mediation Practices Transform Each Other?" (1997) 24 *Florida State University Law Review* 839.

Lande, J., "Using Dispute Systems Design Methods to Promote Good Faith in Court-connected Mediation Programs" (2002) 50:1 *UCLA Law Review* 69.

Lande, J., "Possibilities of Collaborative Law" [forthcoming].

LaPrairie, C., "The 'New' Justice: Some Implications for Aboriginal Communities" (1998) 40:1 *Canadian Journal of Criminology* 61.

Lawrence, J., "Collaborative Lawyering: A New Development in Conflict Resolution" (2002) 17 *Ohio State Journal on Dispute Resolution* 431.

Lerman, L., "Mediation of Wife Abuse Cases: The Disadvantageous Impact of Informal Dispute Resolution on Women" (1984) 7 *Harvard Women's Law Journal* 57.

Leung, K. and Lind, E.A., "Procedural Justice and Culture: Effects of Culture, Gender and Investigator Status on Procedural Preferences" (1986) 50 *Journal of Personality and Social Psychology* 1134.

Lind, E.A., Huo, Y.J. and Tyler, T., "... And Justice for All: Ethnicity, Gender and Preferences for Dispute Resolution Procedures" (1994) 18 *Law and Human Behaviour* 269.

Macfarlane, J., "Collaborating with the Collaborators: Preliminary Results from a Three-year Research Study" (prepared for delivery at the American Association of Law Schools, Washington, D.C., 2003).

Macfarlane, J., "Culture Change? A Tale of Two Cities and Mandatory Court-connected Mediation" (2002) 2002:2 *Journal of Dispute Resolution* 241.

Macfarlane, J., "Mediating Ethically: the Limits of Codes of Conduct and the Potential of a Reflective Practice Model" (2002) 39:4 *Osgoode Hall Law Journal* 78.

Macfarlane, J., "What Does the Changing Culture of Legal Practice Mean for Legal Education?" (2001) 20 *Windsor Yearbook of Access to Justice* 191.

Macfarlane, J., "Why Do People Settle?" (2001) 45 *McGill Law Journal* 663.

Maloney, L. and Reddoch, G., *Restorative Justice and Family Violence: A Community-based Effort to Move from Theory to Practice* (prepared for delivery at the 6th International Conference on Restorative Justice, Simon Fraser University, Vancouver, B.C., June 2003).

Martin, D. and Mosher, J., "Unkept Promises: Experiences of Immigrant Women with the Neo-criminalisation of Wife Abuse" (1995) 8 *Canadian Journal of Women and the Law* 3.

Maxwell, G., *Achieving Effective Outcomes in Youth Justice: Implications for New Research for Principles, Policy and Practice* (prepared for delivery at the 6th International Conference on Restorative Justice, Simon Fraser University, Vancouver, B.C., June 2003).

McEwen, C. and Maiman, R., "Mediation in Small Claims Court: Achieving Compliance Through Consent" (1984) 18 *Law and Society Review* 11.

McEwen, C., "Toward a Program-based ADR Research Agenda" (1999) 15:4 *Negotiation Journal* 325.

McEwen, C. and Mainman, R., "Small Claims Mediation in Maine: An Empirical Assessment" (1984) 33 *Maine Law Review* 244.

Medley, M. and Schellenberg, J., "Attitudes of Attorneys Towards Mediation" (1994) 12 *Mediation Quarterly* 185.

Menkel-Meadow, C. "The Many Ways of Mediation: The Transformation of Traditions, Ideologies, Paradigms, and Practices" (1995) 11:3 *Negotiation Journal* 217.

Menkel-Meadow, C., "The Transformation of Disputes by Lawyers: What the Dispute Paradigm Does and Does Not Tell Us" (1985) 25 *Missouri Journal of Dispute Resolution* 3.

Menkel-Meadow, C., "Towards Another View of Legal Negotiations: The Structure of Problem-solving" (1984) 31 UCLA *Law Review* 754.

Merry, S. and Silbey, S., "What do Plaintiffs Want? Reexamining the Concept of Dispute" (1984) 9:2 *The Justice System Journal* 151.

Miller, R. and Sarat, A., "Grievances, Claims and Disputes: Assessing the Adversary Culture" (1980-81) 15 *Law and Society Review* 525.

Moore, D., "Shame Forgiveness and Juvenile Justice" (1993) 12:1 *Criminal Justice Ethics* 3.

Nader, L., "Controlling Processes in the Practice of Law: Hierarchy and Pacification in the Movement to Re-form Dispute Ideology" (1993) 9:1 *Ohio State Journal on Dispute Resolution* 1.

Nergard, T.B., "Solving Conflicts Outside the Court System: Experience with Conflict Resolution Boards in Norway" (1993) 33:1 *British Journal of Criminology* 81.

Otis, The Honourable Justice L., "The Conciliation Service Program of the Quebec Court of Appeal" (2000) 11:3 *World Arbitration and Mediation Report,* online: <http://www.tribunaux.qc.ca/mjq_en/c-appel/about/conciliation.html> (date accessed: 17 September 2003).

Pavlich, G., *Deconstructing Restoration: The Promise of Restorative Justice* (prepared for delivery at the International Conference on Restorative Justice, Tubingen, Germany, October 2000).

Pavlich, G., "The Power of Community: Government and the Formation of Self-identity" (1996) 30:4 *Law and Society Review* 707.

Pearson, J., "Mediating When Domestic Violence Is a Factor: Policies and Practices in Court-based Divorce Mediation Programs" (1997) 14:4 *Mediation Quarterly* 319.

Peterson, M., "Developing a Restorative Justice Program: Part One" (2000) 5:3 *Justice as Healing* 1.

Putnam, R., *The Decline of Civil Society: How Come? So What?* (prepared for delivery as the John L. Manion Lecture, Canadian Centre for Management Development, Ottawa, February 1996).

Resnick, J., "Managerial Judges" (1982) 96 *Harvard Law Review* 374.

Richardson, G., Galaway, B. and Joubert, M., "Restorative Resolutions Project: An Alternative to Incarceration" (1996) 20:2 *International Journal of Comparative and Applied Criminal Justice* 209.

Rifkin, J., "Mediation from a Feminist Perspective: Promise and Problems" (1994) 2 *Law and Inequality* 21.

Riskin, L., "Mediator Orientations, Strategies and Techniques" (1994) 12 *Alternatives* 111.

Roach, K., "Changing Punishment at the Turn of the Century: Restorative Justice on the Rise" (2000) 42:3 *Canadian Journal of Criminology* 249.

Roberts, J. V. and Laprairie C., "Sentencing Circles: Some Unanswered Questions" (1996) 39:1 *Criminal Law Quarterly* 69.

Rowe, M., "The Post-Tailhook Navy Designs an Integrated Dispute Resolution System" (1993) 9:3 *Negotiation Journal* 203.

Rudin, J., *Pushing Back: A Response to the Drive for the Standardization of Restorative Justice Programs in Canada* (prepared for delivery at the 6th International Conference on Restorative Justice, Simon Fraser University, Vancouver, B.C., June 2003).

Rugge, T.A. and Cormier, R., *Department of the Solicitor General of Canada, Restorative Justice in Cases of Serious Crimes: An Evaluation* (prepared for delivery at the 6th International Conference on Restorative Justice, Simon Fraser University, Vancouver, B.C., June 2003).

Sander, F., "The Future of ADR" (2000) 1 *Journal of Dispute Resolution* 3.

Savarase, J., "'Gladue' Was a Woman: Should Sentencing from a Restorative Perspective Also Be Feminist?" (prepared for delivery at the 6th International Conference on Restorative Justice, Simon Fraser University, Vancouver, B.C., June 2003).

Schneider, C., "A Commentary on the Activity of Writing Codes of Ethics" (1985) 8 *Mediation Quarterly* 83.

Schulz, J.L., "Mediator Liability in Canada: An Examination of Emerging American and Canadian Jurisprudence", 32 *Ottawa Law Review* (newly italicized)(2001) 269.

Sholar, T., "Collaborative Law—A Method for the Madness" (1993) 23 *Memphis State University Law Review* 667.

Shonholtz, R., "Neighborhood Justice Systems" (1984) 5 *Mediation Quarterly* 3.

Silbey, S. and Merry, S., "Mediator Settlement Strategies" (1986) 8 *Law and Society Policy Review* 7.

Sullivan, D. and Tifft, L., "The Negotiated and Economic Dimensions of Restorative Justice" (1998) 22:1 *Humanity and Society* 38.

Sullivan, D. and Tifft, L., "The Transformative and Economic Dimensions of Restorative Justice" (1998) 22:1 *Humanity and Society* 38.

Thibaut, J., Walker, L., LaTour, S. and Houlden, S., "Procedural Justice as Fairness" (1974) 26 *Stanford Law Review* 1271.

Thomson, A., *Formal Restorative Justice in Nova Scotia: A Pre-implementation Overview* (prepared for delivery at the Annual Conference of the Atlantic Association of Sociologists and Anthropologists, Fredericton, N.B., October 1999).

Titley, F. and Dunn, T., "Mediating Sexual Abuse Cases" (1998) 10:1 *Interaction* 6.

Trubek, D.M., Sarat, A., Felstiner, W., Kritzer, H.M. and Grossman, J.B., "The Costs of Ordinary Litigation" (1983) 31 UCLA *Law Review* 72.

Turpel, The Honourable Justice M.E., "Sentencing within a Restorative Paradigm: Procedural Implications of R. v. Gladue" (1999) 4:3 *Justice as Healing* 2.

Tyler, T., "Conditions Leading to Value Expressive Effects in Judgments of Procedural Justice: A Test of Four Models" (1987) 52 *Journal of Personality and Social Psychology* 333.

Tyler, T., "The Role of Perceived Injustice in Defendants' Evaluations of Their Courtroom Experience" (1984) 18 *Law and Society Review* 51.

Tyler, T., Rasinki, K. and Spodick, N., "The Influence of Voice on Satisfaction with Leaders: Exploring the Meaning of Process Control" (1985) 48 *Journal of Personality and Social Psychology* 72.

Tyler, T., Rasinski, K. and McGraw, K., "The Influence of Perceived Injustices on the Endorsement of Political Leaders" (1985) 15 *Journal of Applied Social Psychology* 700.

Umbreit, M., "Mediation of Victim–Offender Conflict" (1988) 31 *Journal of Dispute Resolution* 84.

Umbreit, M.S., Coates, R.B. and Roberts, A.W., "The Impact of Victim–Offender Mediation: A Cross-National Perspective" (2000) 17:3 *Mediation Quarterly* 215.

Waldman, E., "Identifying the Role of Social Norms in Mediation: A Multiple Model Approach" (1997) 48 *Hastings Law Journal* 703.

Walklate, S. "Reparation: A Merseyside View" (1986) 26:7 *British Journal of Criminology* 287.

Welsh, N., "Making Deals in Court-connected Mediation: What's Justice Got to Do with It?" (2001) 79:3 *Washington University Law Quarterly* 787.

Welsh, N., "The Thinning Vision of Self-Determination in Court-Connected Mediation: The Inevitable Price of Institutionalization?" (2001) 6 *Harvard Negotiation Law Review* 1.

Wissler, R.L., "The Effects of Mandatory Mediation: Empirical Research on the Experience of Small Claims and Common Pleas Courts" (1997) 33 *Willamette Law Review* 565.

Zariski, A., "Disputing Culture: Lawyers and ADR" (2000) 7:2 *Murdoch University Electronic Journal of Law.*

6.   Research Studies

Canadian Centre for Justice Statistics, *Adult Correctional Services in Canada, 2000/01* (Ottawa: Statistics Canada, 2002).

Canadian Centre for Justice Statistics, *Canadian Crime Statistics* (Ottawa: Statistics Canada, 2001).

Coates, M.L., Furlong, G.T. and Downie, B.M., *Conflict Management and Dispute Resolution Systems in Canadian Non-unionized Organizations* (Kingston: Industrial Relations Centre, Queen's University, 1997).

Cormick, G.W., Dale, N., Emond, P., Sigurdson, S.G. and Stuart, B.D., *Building Consensus for a Sustainable Future* (Ottawa: National Round Table on the Environment and the Economy, 1996).

Correction Service of Canada, *A Framework Paper on Restorative Justice and the Correctional Service of Canada* (Ottawa: Correction Service of Canada, 1998).

Mackay, R.E. and Brown, A.J., *Community Mediation In Scotland: A Study of Implementation* (Dundee, Scotland: University of Dundee, Department of Social Work, 1998).

Nadeau, J., *Critical Analysis of the UN Declaration of Basic Principles on the Use of Restorative Justice Programmes in Criminal Matters* (Leuven, Belgium: University of Leuven, Centre for Advanced Legal Studies, 2001).

Provincial Association Against Family Violence, *Making It Safe: Women, Restorative Justice and Alternative Dispute Resolution* (St John's: Provincial Association Against Family Violence, 2000).

Sherman, L.W., Strang, H. and Woods, D.J., *Recidivism Patterns in the Canberra Reintegrate Shaming Experiments (RISE)* (Canberra: Centre for Restorative Justice (AUS) and the Criminal Research Council, 2000).

Spencer, C., *Diminishing Returns: An Examination of Financial Responsibility, Decision Making and Financial Abuse Among Older Adults in British Columbia* (Vancouver: Gerontology Research Centre, Simon Fraser University, 1996).

The Church Council on Justice and Corrections, *Satisfying Justice: Safe Community Options That Attempt to Repair Harm from Crime and Reduce the Use or Length of Imprisonment.* (Ottawa: The Church Council on Justice and Corrections, 1996).

Umbreit, M.S., *Mediation of Criminal Conflict: An Assessment of Programs in Four Canadian Provinces* (St. Paul, MN: Center for Restorative Justice and Mediation, School of Social Work, University of Minnesota, 1995).

Umbreit, M., Coates, R.B. and Voss, B., *Restorative Justice Dialogue: Annotated Bibliography of Empirical Studies on Mediation, Conferencing and Circles,* (St. Paul, MN: Center for Restorative Justice and Peacemaking, School of Social Work, University of Minnesota, 2003).

Wemmers, J. and Canuto, M., *Victims' Experiences with, Expectations and Perceptions of Restorative Justice: A Critical Review of the Literature.* (Ottawa: Policy Centre for Victims Issues, Department of Justice Canada, 2001).

7. Legislation and Regulations

Bankruptcy and Insolvency Act, R.S.C. 1985, c. B-3.

Bankruptcy and Insolvency General Rules, C.R.C., c. 368.

B.C. Reg. 127/98.

Canada Labour Code, R.S.C. 1985, c. L-2.

Canadian Charter of Rights and Freedoms, Part I of the *Constitution Act, 1982,* being Schedule B to the *Canada Act 1982,* (U.K.), 1982, c. 11.

Canadian Environmental Assessment Act, S.C. 1992, c. 37.

Canadian Human Rights Act, R.S.C. 1985, c. H-6.

Code of Civil Procedure, R.S.Q. 2001, c. C-25.

Criminal Code, R.S.C. 1985, c. C-46.

Commercial Arbitration Act, R.S.B.C. 1996, c. 55.

Condominium Property Act, R.S.A. 2000, c. C-22.

Divorce Act, R.S.C. 1985, c. 3 (2nd Supp.).

Family Law Act, R.S.O. 1990, c. F-3.

Family Law Act, S.N.W.T. 1997, c. 18, s. 58(1).

Farm Debt Mediation Act, S.C. 1997, c. 21.

Insurance (Motor Vehicle) Act, R.S.B.C. 1996, c. 231.

International Commercial Arbitration Act, R.S.B.C. 1996, c. 233.

Justice for Victims of Crime Act, S.M. 1986-7 c. 28. This was repealed by *The Victim's Rights and Consequential Amendments Act,* S.M. 1998, c. 44.

Law Society Act, R.S.O. 1990, c. L-8.

Local Government Act, R.S.B.C. 1996, c. 323.

Alta. Reg. 971/97 (Mediation Rules of the Provincial Court, Civil Division for Alberta).

Mass. Ann. Laws c. 233, § 23D.

Mineral Tenure Act, R.S.B.C. 1996, c. 292.

Mining Right of Way Act, R.S.B.C. 1996, c. 294.

Municipal Government Act, R.S.A. 2000, c. M-26.

Nisga'a Final Agreement Act, S.B.C. 1999, c. 2.

O. Reg. 194/90 (Ontario Rules of Civil Procedure).

Petroleum and Natural Gas Act, R.S.B.C. 1996, c. 361.

Residential Tenancies Act, R.S.N.W.T. 1988, c. R-5.

Queen's Bench Act, S.S. 1994, c. Q-1.01.

Status of the Artist Act, S.C. 1992, c. 33.

Strata Property Act, S.B.C. 1998, c. 43.

Queen's Bench (Mediation) Amendment Act, S.S. 1994, c. 20.

Victims of Crime Act, R.S.B.C. 1996, c. 478.

Victims' Bill of Rights, S.O. 1995, c. 6.

Victims' Bill of Rights, C.C.S.M. 1998 c. V-55.

West's Ann. Cal. Evid. Code § 1160.

8.   Cases

M. v. H., [1999] 2 S.C.R. 3.

G.O. v. C.D. H., (2000) 50 O.R. (3ᵈ) 82.

R. v. Clough, 2001 BCCA 613.

R. v. Gabriel, [1999] O.J. No. 2579 (S.C.J.), online: QL.

R. v. Gladue, [1999] 1 S.C.R. 688.

R. v. J.F., 2001 NBCA 81.

R. v. Latimer, [2001] 1 S.C.R. 3.

R. v. Longaphy, 2000 NSCA 136.

R. v. Marchment, [2000] O.J. No. 3559 (S.C.J.), online: QL.

R. v. Moses, 1992, 3 C.N.L.R. 116.

R. v. Proulx, [2000] S.C.R. 6.

R. v. Trottier, 2001 ABPC 35.

R. v. Wells, [2000] 1 S.C.R. 207.

9.   Online Resources

Indian and Northern Affairs Canada, Funding Agreements, online: <http://www.ainc-inac.gc.ca/ps/ov/agre_e.html> (date accessed: 17 September 2003).

Justice Quebec's Victims of Crime Resources, online: <http://www.justice.gouv.qc.ca/english/publications/generale/rec-ress-a.htm#rights> (date accessed: 17 September 2003).

Morris, C., "Conflict Resolution and Peacebuilding: A Selected Bibliography", online: <http://www.peacemakers.ca/bibliography/bib25evaluation.html> (date accessed: 17 September 2003).

Nadeau, J., *Critical Analysis of the UN Declaration of Basic Principles on the Use of Restorative Justice Programmes in Criminal Matters* (Leuven, Belgium: University of Leuven, Centre for Advanced Legal Studies, 2001) at 36. Online: <http://www.restorativejustice.org/asp>.

New Brunswick Victim Services Program, online: <http://www.gnb.ca/0276/corrections/vicser_e.asp> (date accessed: 17 September 2003]).

Okalik, P. [Premier], Speaking notes, National Aboriginal Policing Conference, October 2000, online: <http://www.gov.nu.ca/nunavut/english/premier/press/apc.shtml> (date accessed: 17 September 2003).

Royal Canadian Mounted Police, *Restorative Justice: A Fresh Approach*, online: <http://www.rcmp-grc.gc.ca/ccaps/restjust_e.htm> (date accessed: 17 September 2003).

Rural Development Canada online: <http://www.rural.gc.ca>.

United Nations Economic and Social Council, "Basic Principles on the Use of Restorative Justice Programs in Criminal Matters" (Vienna: UN Commission on Crime Prevention and Criminal Justice, 2002), online: <http://www.restorativejustice.org/rj3/Undocuments/UNDecBasic PrinciplesofRJ.html> (date accessed: 17 September 2003).

"What Is a Conditional Sentence?" Conditional Sentencing Series Fact Sheet 1 (Research and Statistics Division, Department of Justice Canada), online: <http://canada.justice.gc.ca/en/ps/rs/rep/fs_cs_001e.pdf> (date accessed: 17 September 2003).

Youth Canada Association online: <http://www.youcan.ca/>.

10. Other Reports, Materials and Model Legislation

Correctional Service of Canada, *Canadian Resource Guide to Restorative Justice and Conflict Resolution Education Programs* (Ottawa: Correctional Service of Canada), online: <http://www.csc-scc.gc.ca/text/prgrm/rjust_e.shtml> (date accessed: 17 September 2003).

Florida Rules for Court-appointed and Certified Mediators, Rule 10.035. (Florida Supreme Court Dispute Resolution Center, 1998).

Hart, C. and Macfarlane, J., "Court-annexed Mediation: Rights Instincts, Wrong Priorities?" *Law Times,* April 28–May 4, 1997.

Umbreit, M.S., *Fact Sheet: The Impact of Restorative Justice "What We are Learning from Research?"* (St. Paul, MN: Center for Restorative Justice and Peacemaking, School of Social Work, University of Minnesota, 1997).

United Nations, "Basic Principles for the Use of Restorative Justice Programmes in Criminal Matters", online: <http://www.restorativejustice.ca/National Consultation/BasicPrinciples.htm at III(3)> (date accessed: 17 September 2003).

United Nations Commission on International Trade Law, *UNCITRAL Model Law on International Commercial Arbitration,* 1985.

United Nations Commission on International Trade Law, *UNCITRAL Model Law on International Commercial Conciliation,* 2002.